ISRAEL, ELIHU AND CADWALLADER WASHBURN

A CHAPTER IN AMERICAN BIOGRAPHY

A Da Capo Press Reprint Series

THE AMERICAN SCENE
Comments and Commentators

GENERAL EDITOR: WALLACE D. FARNHAM
University of Illinois

ISRAEL, ELIHU

AND

CADWALLADER WASHBURN

A CHAPTER IN AMERICAN BIOGRAPHY

COMPILED BY

GAILLARD HUNT

DA CAPO PRESS • NEW YORK • 1969

A Da Capo Press Reprint Edition

This Da Capo Press edition of
Israel, Elihu and Cadwallader Washburn
is an unabridged republication of the
first edition published in New York in
1925.

Library of Congress Catalog Card Number 71-87440

Published by Da Capo Press
A Division of Plenum Publishing Corporation
227 West 17th Street
New York, N. Y. 10011

Manufactured in the United States of America

ISRAEL, ELIHU AND CADWALLADER WASHBURN

A CHAPTER IN AMERICAN BIOGRAPHY

THE MACMILLAN COMPANY
NEW YORK · BOSTON · CHICAGO · DALLAS
ATLANTA · SAN FRANCISCO

MACMILLAN & CO., LIMITED
LONDON · BOMBAY · CALCUTTA
MELBOURNE

THE MACMILLAN CO. OF CANADA, LTD.
TORONTO

The Norlands

ISRAEL, ELIHU

AND

CADWALLADER WASHBURN

A CHAPTER IN AMERICAN BIOGRAPHY

COMPILED BY

GAILLARD HUNT

New York
THE MACMILLAN COMPANY
1925

TABLE OF CONTENTS

v

vi *Table of Contents*

ISRAEL, ELIHU AND CADWALLADER WASHBURN

A CHAPTER IN AMERICAN BIOGRAPHY

THE HOME

One cold day early in the winter of 1868 Charles Ames Washburn stood in the front porch of his father's house, and as the winds swept through the surrounding woodland the words of Tennyson's *Oriana* formed into sound from his lips:

"When the long dun wolds are ribbed with snow,
And loud the Norland whirlwinds blow."

From that time the Washburn place became "The Norlands."

But however severe the winters may be, the summer climate is benignant and delightful, and there is nothing to suggest bleakness in the meadows when they are green, or in the forests when they are in leaf.

About forty miles from its mouth where it flows into the Kennebec, the Androscoggin River passes over a long stretch of rough rocks projecting from its bed and forming rapids which used to be known as Livermore Falls and where are now the mills and the village of Livermore Falls. Rising on either side of the river at this point is a succession of hills so high that in a flatter region they might be called mountains, and about five miles to the westward of the Falls, after several of the hills have been passed, lies the place where the Washburns have lived for more than a hundred years, and where all of the elder Israel Washburn's children were born. It marks the very center of the town of Livermore which is in the extreme north of the county of Androscoggin and is some forty miles from the sea. Looking from the porch of the homestead, in front and to the right stretch the Oxford Hills; to the left lie the lesser Androscoggin Hills. Behind the Oxford Hills rises, in the distance, the dim, blue outline of the White Mountains forty miles away. Between the hills glisten small lakes of clear water. Scattered at random are long stretches of green valleys surrounded with deep woods. It is doubtful if there is any spot in all of Maine more beautiful than The Norlands.

Where the homestead now stands Dr. Cyrus Hamlin, the father of Hannibal Hamlin, built a large, square, two-story house about one hundred and fifty years ago. He sold it to Artemas Leonard in 1805, from whom Israel Washburn bought it in 1809. In 1843 it was pulled down, and a pleasant white cottage took its place. In 1867 an addition to this house was in progress of building when the whole was burned; and immediately afterwards the large, roomy house, with broad verandahs, wide hall, and many windows, which now stands, was erected. Around it are the elm trees which Israel Washburn planted with his own hands, and maples planted by Charles Ames Washburn.

About fifty yards from the house is The Norlands church, a white, old-fashioned structure with a spire one sees from a distance when approaching, where the Washburns have always worshipped. It was built with Israel Washburn's aid in 1829.

The long avenue of elms leading to the house is bordered to the west by a great hedge of arbor vitæ—above which stretches the beautiful panorama of hill and valley, lake and forest, and on clear days is visible the distant peak of Mt. Washington. Under the shadow of the elms is a small, grey stone gothic building erected by the sons to the memory of their mother and given as a library to the country-side. Beyond this again is a quaint, single-storied house with cupola, used seventy years ago as the district school. Surrounding the original property are the summer homes of a later generation of Washburns, covering together some hundreds of acres.

The great natural beauty of this site was undoubtedly a factor in the lives of the men who grew up there. The old home retained a vital place in their thought and constantly they returned to the silence of the hills for rest and inspiration. A still greater factor was their mother, a woman of indomitable will and ambition, eager for her sons' advancement, forcing and directing their talents,— and winning for herself their imperishable love and admiration. She lived to see them grow into manhood and to be repaid for her unselfish devotion to them.

After the father's death the brothers jointly owned and kept up The Norlands, the last owner being William Drew of Minnesota, the youngest, who died July 29, 1912.

It is related that once when the sons of Israel Washburn were gathered together at The Norlands, being then mature men who had established themselves in their generation, a dispute arose over the question of who among them had most distinguished himself, and it was agreed to submit the question to a secret ballot. The votes were deposited, and when they were counted it was found that each brother had received one vote. Each one had, in fact, voted for himself. A second ballot was then taken and Cadwallader Colden Washburn received all the votes except his own.

His brothers looked upon him with esteem. He was a representative in Congress, but so were three of them. He was governor of his state, but so was one of them. He never represented his country in a foreign state, as two of his brothers did; never was in the Senate as one was; nor in the Cabinet as another was. One of his brothers was in the navy during the Civil War and acquitted himself creditably, but Cadwallader was the only one who attained high military rank. He was the fighting man. When he died at the age of sixty-four he had carried the title of general for twenty years. He had achieved distinction in that walk of life in which ambitious men most crave distinction.

When the brothers voted him the greatest of them they did not have in mind that he was the richest. They were all thrifty and shrewd money-makers. In their view, to accumulate a competency and have his family secure from want was the duty of a man. They ordered their lives so as to accomplish this end; but they took this duty as a matter of course and measured a man's importance in the community without reference to the measure of his wealth.

While Israel, the eldest son, was taking root in the parent state, his brothers yielded to a feeling of restlessness and impatience to try their fortunes in other communities, where life was freer, opportunities of success were more abundant, and advancement was more rapid. Of his six brothers, five went to the West. Israel was in some sort the mentor and guardian of the younger boys, and as soon as he became a man helped them in their educational projects.

The father's straitened circumstances, after the failure of the store, fell most heavily on him, Sidney, Elihu, and Cadwallader. The brothers who grew up after these fared more easily, being helped by those older. None, however, knew the comfort of opulence until he had acquired it for himself.

Prosperity and power came to them all, won by their own strength and ability. Israel, Elihu and Cadwallader served in Congress at the same time, a circumstance which excited much comment and is without parallel. Two of them, Israel and Cadwallader, were governors of their states. Elihu, Charles, and Israel published works of value. A family to show a Secretary of State, two ministers abroad, a senator, a major general, three authors, two governors and four representatives in Congress distributed among five brothers, gives proof of a power of success above other families.

The men were devotedly attached to each other. While circumstances threw them apart geographically they corresponded often. When one could help another he considered it his first duty to do so. They bandied rough jokes among themselves as brothers do, but they were intensely proud of each other and intensely loyal to each other. They had much influence upon one another. The central objects of their devotion were the old father and mother on the farm at Livermore. As they made money they supported the establishment. They improved the house and added more acres to the estate. Each of them returned to the old place when he could and renewed his allegiance to the head of the house.

When the mother died May 6, 1861, the father continued to live at the place and the same life went on. When he died September 1, 1876, the brothers kept the place and kept up the old life. Some one of them was there much of the time; the others came when they could, to renew the memories and associations of their childhood and early manhood. What may be termed family public opinion flourished and was a recognized force with them.

Israel Washburn's foremost friends and those for whom

he felt the strongest affection were those whom he had known when he was a young lawyer winning his way at Orono; but, although he spent so much time in Washington and lived for thirty years in Portland, the spot for which he had the fondest devotion was the home of his childhood, The Norlands.

ISRAEL WASHBURN, JR.

ISRAEL WASHBURN, THE ELDEST SON

INHERITANCE AND EARLY TRAINING

Israel Washburn was born at Livermore on June 6, 1813. From infancy he was small. His father was a short man and his mother not tall. When he reached manhood he stood not more than five feet six inches in height. As a child his hair was tow-colored, and it was light and straight when he was a man. He wore it parted far on the side and brushed across his broad forehead. His eyes were light blue; his complexion pale; the mouth large, the upper lip straight; the nose large and broad; the chin large; the neck short, and the chest deep enough for a man of greater stature. His hands were well shaped, the fingers rounded. From this it is evident he was not a symmetrically proportioned person, the body being too large for the legs, and his features irregular; but his whole make-up denoted physical and mental strength and sound health. He had no personal vanity, but was exquisitely neat in his apparel. His clothes were made for him for many years by the same tailor in Portland and he was particular about the fit and material. He read well and was fond of reading aloud. When he spoke to an audience,—and he began public speaking almost as soon as he was admitted to the bar,—his voice was clear and musical and of great power— a chest voice which could carry as far as he chose to send it.

Israel Washburn was a New Englander of unmixed English stock and traditions. The first record of the family is found in Worcester County, England, the surname being derived from Little Washbourne in Overbury.

7

There Sir Roger Washbourne flourished during the latter half of the Thirteenth Century, the name being spelled variously Washbourne, Wasseburn, Washburne, but by the time a member of the family came to America it had become Washburn. A descendant of Sir Roger Washbourne, John Washbourne, moved from Little Washbourne to Evesham, a few miles distant, and from this branch came another John, who went to Plymouth Colony about 1631, and was joined by Marjorie, his wife, and their sons in 1635, she being the daughter of Robert Moore. One of John Washburn's sons married Elizabeth Mitchell and had eleven children, one of whom, Samuel, married Deborah Packard, also of English descent, and they had a son named Israel born in 1684, this being the first American-born Israel Washburn. He married Waitstill Sumner in 1708 and their fourth son, born in 1718, was also called Israel. The family had been living in Bridgewater, Massachusetts, up to this time, but Israel moved to Raynham; and on March 4, 1776, he was elected a member of the Committee of Correspondence, Inspection and Safety of that town, served in the militia, and, for a brief period in 1778, was a sergeant in Captain John Shaw's company in the Revolutionary War. One of the sons of Israel Washburn and Waitstill Sumner, also named Israel, born in Raynham in 1755, was also in the Revolution as a private in James Williams, Jr's., company at the battle of Lexington.

This Israel's son, also called Israel, was the father of the Israel of this work. He was born at Raynham in 1784, and came to the District of Maine in 1806, where he taught school in the town of Woolwich and engaged in ship building at Whites' Landing, now Richmond, on the Kennebec River. In 1809 he moved to Livermore, bought the farm and a store from Artemus Leonard, and farmed and traded, until in 1829 the store failed, and thereafter he supported his family by the farm with the aid of a small legacy which had come to his wife. In 1859 he became blind; an operation for cataract of the eyes was unsuccessful, and for seventeen years, until his death (within two months of ninety-two), he lived in darkness. During this time his sons were his main support. When his business failed, his brother, Reuel Washburn, assumed his debts, and many years later Israel Washburn's sons paid with interest the full amount thus advanced.

In his prime, Israel Washburn had been active in political life and public affairs remained his greatest interest up to the end. He was a member of the general court of Massachusetts for four years, from 1815 to 1819.

In 1812, at Livermore, he had married Martha or "Patty" Benjamin. She was twenty years old, the daughter of Lieutenant Samuel Benjamin, the descendant of John Benjamin who arrived in America in 1632 in the *Lion* and was a proprietor of Cambridge and Watertown, Massachusetts. Samuel Benjamin was in the Revolution, serving in Captain Daniel Whitney's company at Lexington, Bunker Hill, Monmouth, and finally Yorktown; in all more than seven years. His wife was Tabitha Livermore, descended from the early settlers, a relative of Deacon Elijah Livermore, after whom the town was named. The eldest child of Israel Washburn and Martha Benjamin was born when his father was twenty-nine years old and his mother twenty-one. They called him Israel, being the fifth Washburn of that name in Massachusetts. He was the eldest of a family of eleven children, eight boys and three girls, only one of whom, a boy, William Allen Drew, died in infancy, November 28, 1822.

After the rudiments of his education had been acquired from the schools in the vicinity, his father's failure cast him on his own resources at the age of sixteen, and he helped his father with the work on the farm, but in the course of two years went to live in North Livermore with his uncle, Reuel Washburn, with a view to studying law; and his uncle instructed him also in Latin and Greek.

Reuel Washburn was a graduate of Brown University, Providence, Rhode Island, a lawyer of large practice, and, like all of his family, fond of public life, being a member of the state senate in 1827 and 1828 and in the latter year the Whig candidate for Congress. He claimed that he had been elected, but the House after investigation decided that his Democratic competitor, James W. Ripley, had won by five votes. Probably no lawyer in his section of Maine had a sounder reputation at the bar than Reuel Washburn, and Israel Washburn was fortunate in having him for preceptor.

He studied law with his uncle until he was admitted to the bar in October, 1834, when he was twenty-one years old. He was married on October 24, 1841, to Mary Maud Webster, of Orono, Maine. This young lady was the daughter of Colonel Ebenezer Webster, a lumber merchant in that village, a man of substance, who assisted his son-in-law in his progress. This Mrs. Washburn was the mother of his four children, all born at Orono. His wife died in Minneapolis, June 30, 1873, and in January, 1876, he married Miss Rebina Napier Brown of Boston, Massachusetts, who still survives and lives in California.

For ten winters, when he was a member of the House of Representatives (having taken his seat at the age of twenty-nine) he was in Washington. He was fond of travelling for brief periods in the summer; and made two or more trips to Europe; but never lived anywhere other than in Maine. In 1820, when he was seven years old, Maine had separated from Massachusetts and been admitted to statehood.

When he went to Washington he was forty-five years old and he then saw the border of the South for the first time and slavery on slave territory. The heart of the South he never saw until twenty years after slavery had been driven from it. Among his friends and correspondents there were no Southerners, and it is doubtful if he ever knew a slaveholder intimately. He had, however, a knowledge of the West which was inevitable with four younger brothers there.

He was an assiduous collector of facts concerning the history of Maine and of that part of it in which he was born and lived. His *Historical Notes of Livermore* was the longest product of his pen; his address on the occasion of the dedication of a town hall at Orono in 1874 showed how effective he had made his interest in the history of that village. The most carefully prepared and elaborate essay he ever wrote was that on the north-eastern boundary question, wherein he demonstrated the injustice which had been done to Maine by the treaty of Washington with Great Britain in 1842, which surrendered to Canada a strip of territory which Maine had claimed. It was read before the Maine Historical Society of which he was a member for nineteen years, being its president some of that time. He was deeply rooted in the soil of Maine and he looked at public questions from her point of view. This is not to say that his point of view was narrow, for the strong convictions which came from familiarity with a certain aspect were tempered by a broad mental vision, a sympathetic nature, a cultivated mind and a warm imagination.

The great work of his life was his contest against the extension of the slave power in America; then against slavery itself in America. The part he took in the struggle and the practical and effective direction he gave to the opposition to slavery entitle him to rank with the historical characters of the most important period of American history after the Revolution.

His industry and talent and attractiveness as a speaker called attention to him in Orono soon after he opened his law office.

He had been admitted to the bar at Bangor, which was an enterprising place and afforded good opportunities for a young lawyer; but Washburn chose, as offering better chances, the town of Orono, ten miles farther up Penobscot River. When he went there it had a population of about 1500 people, and when he left it, thirty years later to settle in Portland, it had not more than 2000. The chief industry was lumbering until 1834 when a great land "boom" was promoted. However, this soon collapsed and a temporary slump in affairs resulted.

When he started in Orono he knew one man of influence, Benjamin Brown of Vassalboro. There were half a dozen lawyers and in 1836 he formed a partnership with Henry E. Prentiss, which lasted for two years when Prentiss moved to Bangor. Thereafter Washburn had no partner.

In 1843, nearly ten years after his arrival, a Universalist church [1] was formed and he became an active member. He had always belonged to that denomination, as his father

---

[1] See Washburn's historical address delivered at Orono in 1874 in Centennial Celebration and Dedication of Town Hall, Orono, Maine, March 3, 1874, Portland, 1874.

had before him. The church at Livermore was Universalist.

Politics in the town were Democratic in 1834; but in 1837 there was a notable Whig victory, and in 1840, a division of the town having been made, it became a Whig community. Washburn's public service began almost immediately after his settlement and he was made a justice of the peace and quorum. Two years after his arrival, in 1836, he served on the School Committee and often at later periods.

In 1839 he was town moderator and again in 1842, 1843, and 1848. There his experience was interesting and valuable. The governor was John Fairfield, who had led the state in the famous "Aroostook War" in 1839, when she prepared to invade Canada. He was a Democrat, and went from the governorship to the United States Senate, where he took high rank. A man of accomplishments and great personal charm, of strict integrity and honor, he was a model governor and kept the whole state government up to high level. Washburn served as a member of the Committee on Elections, and, being one of the minority, often prepared minority reports. During his service the governor laid before the legislature correspondence with Daniel Webster, the Secretary of State, on the subject of the treaty with England settling the northeastern boundary question.

The service in the state legislature was the last public service of Israel Washburn, until he was elected a representative in Congress in 1851.

ENTRY INTO POLITICAL LIFE

The elevation of Israel Washburn to the national House of Representatives came as a natural promotion. He had obtained a prominent position in his party while it was the minority, and was nominated for representative in 1851 when it was still doubtful whether the tide had turned. The incumbent was Charles Stetson of Bangor, a Democrat, lately judge of the municipal court of Bangor, a graduate of Yale and a man of standing in his community. In the contest for the office there was much excitement but no acrimony. The five nominations which he afterwards obtained came without opposition, and his majorities increased steadily.

The affairs of the nation were approaching a critical stage when he took his seat in Congress, and the part Maine was to play in the approaching struggle was uncertain.

In spite of some opposition the state had separated from Massachusetts in 1819, the people of the Maine District voting in favor of the separation by a majority of 10,000. There was not much political sympathy between Maine and the original state, the "Down Easters" being Republicans (as Democrats were then called), when Massachusetts was the home of Federalism. The constitution of Maine went much farther on the road to democratic government than Massachusetts had gone up to that time. There was less restriction on the right of suffrage; property qualifications for holding office were abolished, and there was no compulsory support of religion, all of these things then being features of the fundamental law of Massachusetts.

The separation having been accomplished Maine sought admission as a state of the Union. Her eligibility was not disputed, and the bill admitting her was passed by the House January 3, 1820; but in the Senate it emerged from committee joined to another bill admitting Missouri with a constitution providing for the extension of slavery. Then took place the first great struggle, after the constitution had been adopted,—over the extension of the slave power. It was settled by the First Missouri Compromise, by which Missouri became a slave state and a line was drawn below that state north of which freedom was to exist and south of which slavery might be adopted by states as they came into the Union at their option. John Holmes, who represented the Maine District in the House, was a member of the committee which framed the Compromise, and reported it to the House. It was passed March 2, 1820, and the next day Maine took her place as one of the states of the Union. Missouri was admitted a year later, and thereafter slavery was not the great question in Congress for a generation. During the years in which Israel Washburn was growing into manhood and forming his views the men with whom he associated regarded slavery as a settled question which it was dishonorable to bring forward as a national issue.

Maine cast its first electoral vote in 1824 for John Quincy Adams, who was a Republican; in 1828 and 1832 it voted for Andrew Jackson; for Van Buren in 1836; for Harrison in 1840; for Polk in 1844; Taylor in 1848; Pierce in 1852; and Buchanan in 1856. The first senators, John Chandler and John Holmes, were Republicans.

In 1841, twenty years after the Missouri Compromise

settlement, in spite of the disapproval of both Whigs and Democrats, the slavery question was brought into the politics of the state by the Liberty or Abolition party, which proposed to accomplish the emancipation of the blacks and was simply opposed to slavery anywhere in America under any conditions whatever. The orthodox parties were surprised when it polled 12,000 votes. At about the same time the Free-Soil party appeared, pledged to opposition to extension of slavery and soon it formed a coalition with the Liberty party. With neither of these parties had Washburn sympathy or affiliation. He was still a Whig, a Clay man, a Missouri Compromise man. The state was even more opposed to slavery agitation than he was, for it was still Democratic when he was elected to Congress in 1851. Dr. John Hubbard, of Hallowell, a Democrat, was governor, and, while Dr. Hubbard's successor, William G. Crosby, was a Whig, he was elected chiefly on the issue of the sale of intoxicating liquors which had now become an active and confusing factor in state politics. The law prohibiting the sale was passed in 1851, and since then it had been difficult to determine the true temper of the Maine electorate on national political questions, so much attention was given to this local social question.

Israel Washburn never sympathized with the agitation for prohibiting the sale of intoxicating liquors. He was fully alive to the evils produced by strong drink. They were manifest in a notable degree in Maine and especially in river communities like Orono; but he never believed they could be cured by law and he never approved of making the question a part of the program of his party.

Before Crosby's election, Edward Kent, a Whig, had been elected governor in 1838 and again in 1841, and he had been the only Whig governor. When Washburn took his seat in Congress, he and Robert Goodenow were the only Whigs in the Maine delegation of seven members. Both senators, James W. Bradbury and Hannibal Hamlin, were Democrats. After the new Republican party had been formed, a Democrat, Samuel Wells of Portland, was elected governor in 1855; but the next year the Republicans having combined with the "Free-Soilers," Hannibal Hamlin, who had become a Republican, was elected governor, and from that time the fluctuations were frequent between the parties, the preponderance of victories being with the Republicans.

In 1850 the application of California to be admitted into the Union as a free state had started the smoldering fires of the slave question into flame. If it came in as a free state the equilibrium between the free states and the slave states would be destroyed, and national power would be with the free states, where abolition sentiments were spreading at a rate alarming to the South. Again Henry Clay came forward with a series of compromises which it was hoped would quiet the contending sections. The two chief compromises were that California should be admitted to the Union as a free state, but that slavery might go in, or stay out of any territory, as the people wished; and its status as a slave state or a free state should be settled when the territory should apply for admission as a state. This provision in reality only postponed and aggravated the difficulty; but, as it did not restrain the introduction of slavery into a territory, it encouraged its introduction. Another provision of the compromise was a fugitive slave law of great severity and very offensive in its provisions to the people of the free states.

The compromise was accepted by Washburn and his

party. Their first thought was to quiet the public mind
and prevent danger to the Union. They soon found,
however, that the public mind would not be quieted, and
that they must surrender to the slave interest or fight it.
The Congress of 1851 had few men of national reputation in the House. Georgia sent Alexander H. Stevens;
Indiana, Thomas A. Hendricks; Kentucky, John C.
Breckinridge; Massachusetts, Horace Mann; Ohio, Joshua
R. Giddings; Pennsylvania, Thaddeus Stevens; there
were hardly any others who had achieved extensive reputation or were to do so. The Senate was stronger. It
included Isaac Toucey of Connecticut, James A. Bayard
of Delaware, S. A. Douglas of Illinois, Henry Clay of
Kentucky, serving his last term, Pierre Soulé of Louisiana,
Hannibal Hamlin of Maine, Charles Sumner of Massachusetts, Lewis Cass of Michigan, Jefferson Davis of Mississippi, John P. Hale of New Hampshire, Hamilton Fish and
William H. Seward of New York, Salmon P. Chase and
Benjamin F. Wade of Ohio, R. Barnwell Rhett of South
Carolina, John Bell of Tennessee, Sam Houston of Texas,
and R. M. T. Hunter and James M. Mason of Virginia, all
men of power who made their mark in their generation.
    The Whigs were hopelessly in the minority in both
houses and in the lower house numbered only 91 to 142
Democrats. When the ballot for Speaker was taken the
Democrats put forward Linn Boyd, of Kentucky, an old
member; but the opposition did not unite on a candidate,
casting complimentary votes for half a dozen different
ones. Mr. Washburn with nineteen other members, voted
for Joseph R. Chandler of Pennsylvania. Up to 1847
this latter had been the editor of an advanced Whig
paper. He had an interest in literature, having written
an English grammar, and was active in prison reform and

kindred subjects. Doubtless Washburn's preference for him was due to a sympathy with his tastes. He indulged a similar predilection when the election of a chaplain took place. Some ten clergymen were candidates and on the first ballot Washburn and five others voted for Orville Dewey, the Unitarian. On a later ballot he voted for Littleton F. Morgan, the Episcopal candidate, who was elected.

Israel came to Washington with the evident expectation of staying in the House and set himself to learn the House business. He became a good parliamentarian and was put on the Committee on Rules. His range of interests was wide,—embracing contested elections, affairs of the District of Columbia, deaf mute education, Revolutionary pensions, the mileage of members and all railway questions. He was industrious in attending to the interests of his constituents, presented bills for their personal relief, and never missed an opportunity of urging a measure if it promised to inure to the advantage of Maine. He was not a frequent debater, but made many short speeches and a few carefully prepared long ones. He is represented as having been naturally a quick-tempered man; but although the passions of the members raged tempestuously during the whole time of his service in the House and personal insults and conflicts were frequent, and although he became recognized as a leader among the radical anti-slavery members and expressed his opinions fearlessly and strongly, he never had a personal altercation with any member on the floor of the House, never was called to order, never bothered the House with personal explanations. The reason for this is that he never dealt in personalities in his speeches; but always bent his attention upon the measures he was opposing or advocating. His life in Washington broadened his horizon. He met men from all sections of the country and he formed friendships which endured. The membership of the House improved in character after 1852. In 1853 his brother Elihu came from Galena, Illinois, William H. English from Indiana, Nathaniel P. Banks and Thomas D. Elliot from Massachusetts. The next congress saw Howell Cobb from Georgia, Humphrey Marshall from Kentucky, Henry Winter Davis from Maryland, John A. Bingham and John Sherman from Ohio, Quentin S. Morrill Justin from Vermont, and Israel's brother Cadwallader from Wisconsin. In 1857 Owen Lovejoy came from Illinois, Eli Thayer from Massachusetts, L. Q. C. Lamar from Mississippi, Francis P. Blair, Jr., from Missouri, Edwin B. Morgan from New York, Zebulon B. Vance from North Carolina, Samuel S. Cox, George H. Pendleton, and Clement L. Vallandigham from Ohio, and Horace Maynard from Tennessee. In 1859 he met John A. Logan of Illinois, William S. Holman of Indiana, Henry L. Dawes of Massachusetts and Roscoe Conkling of New York.

His surroundings in Washington were pleasant. He attended the session of 1851 with his wife, who usually spent a large part of the winter with him in Washington. The first winter they lived at Mrs. Carter's boarding house on Capitol Hill and formed a mess with six other Whig members, John Allison of Pennsylvania, who maintained his personal friendship with Washburn even after he left Congress in 1857 and who served in the Treasury Department as register in 1869, when Washburn was collector of the port of Portland; Thomas M. Howe, also of Pennsylvania, a Free-Soiler as well as a Whig; James H. Duncan and Zeno Scudder of Massachusetts, George G. King of Rhode Island, and James Meacham of Vermont. These messes, it should be remarked, often had political significance and were the center of political activity. There could be no doubt of the attitude of the one which Washburn joined on this first service. The year 1851 was the only one which he spent in a mess, however. Willard's Hotel had been recently completed—one of the largest hotels in the country at the time—and there he spent the following winters except for the sessions of 1856 and 1857 when he and his two brothers, Elihu and Cadwallader, kept house at No. 29 Indiana Avenue, his wife presiding over the establishment.

Among the important friendships which he formed, as the service in Washington progressed, was one for William H. Seward, whose follower he became. How intimate their relationship was is shown by the following letter:

SEWARD TO WASHBURN

Auburn, May 21st, 1860.
My dear Washburn: Will you do me the favor to go to my home in F. Street, and send home to me here my servants, John the waiter, and Louisa the cook. Pay them such money as they need, for the journey and otherwise. It will give you some trouble to get them through Baltimore since they are colored though free.

Pray supply Nicholas the coachman and Charlotte the chambermaid with funds, for their need. All the servants can be trusted to fix the sums they want. The two latter will remain at Washington. My family need the two former here. Please tell Nicholas and Charlotte that I shall return to Washington about the first of June, for the residue of the session.

I am very sorry to impose this care upon you, but you are generous and affectionate. You may draw on me at sight here, or wait my return to Washington for the money you advance. I have instructed my Colleague, King, to pair me off, and telegraph me for any special vote.
Always faithfully yours.

Soon after he came to Washington he formed the acquaintance of Gamaliel Bailey. He told how he made the acquaintance of the intrepid editor in December, 1851, when Fillmore was President, when no Northern Whig who was unwilling to submit to Southern opinion and dictation on the subject of slavery was regarded as of good standing in the party. He was impressed with Bailey's convictions that a truly national organization based on dislike of slavery and opposition to its extension, must be built up. "Other journalists and politicians were fighting slavery. Dr. Bailey fought it, too, but he did more—he told men how, and how only, they could fight it successfully." The first issue of his paper, *The Daily National Era*, appeared January 1, 1854. It was dedicated simply to freedom and resistance to the slave power. It was a high-toned paper of good literary quality. John G. Whittier was associate editor and occasionally printed a poem in it. On March 28, 1854, Bailey announced that the Whig party was no more, and from that time on urged the formation of a new party, which should be simply the Party of Freedom. Washburn liked the tone and temper of the paper, and it is probable that he himself contributed in its columns.

Another editor with whom he formed intimate relations was Horace Greeley. A bond of sympathy was that both were Universalists. They were in political accord, but did not always agree on the question of the best methods to employ to accomplish their ends.

FINDING HIS PLACE IN CONGRESS

Israel Washburn's first speech in Congress was made on January 2, 1852, the question being the manner of receiving Louis Kossuth, the Hungarian patriot. That interesting character had come to the United States on the invitation of the government in an American man-of-war, and hoped to obtain moral and material aid for his country's struggle for independence. His picturesque appearance and fervid eloquence had caught the popular fancy, and he was received with enthusiasm wherever he went. In those days the young country of freedom conceived itself to be charged with the mission of distributing the blessings of liberty and free government among less fortunate peoples of the earth. It had given moral aid to the South Americans in their revolt against Spain, to the Greeks in their struggle with Turkey, and now was ready to do a like service for Hungary, although not many of those who flocked to hear and applaud Kossuth had more than a vague idea of the facts of Hungary's recent history. In the idea that it was our duty to concern ourselves with the liberties of mankind, Washburn participated. Of a revolutionary race, associated at home with old people who told anecdotes of the Revolution from personal knowledge, living in a community where foreigners rarely came and whence few of themselves travelled far, he and his neighbors never doubted that this country was a great and shining beacon of hope to the benighted masses of other lands. He was in favor, therefore, of giving Kossuth extraordinary honors. When, however, the proposition that Congress should receive him in its halls came up for action, a debate

23

arose which showed that one half of the country had developed a fear of liberty speeches unless qualified, and the other half was concentrated on seeking aid from any source to carry on the struggle for liberty at home. In the course of his tour Kossuth had been honored by a convention of Abolitionists in Pennsylvania, with an address which expressed the hope that freedom might soon prevail in the United States. It was proposed to amend the motion which was made in the House to receive him by adding an expression of disapproval of the Abolitionists' sentiments, and saying that the House did not believe Kossuth had given sympathy to the Abolitionists, who had, while extending him a welcome, "expressed the hope that his herculean labors in this (freedom's) behalf would conduce to the overthrow of oppression not in Hungary alone, *but in the United States* and throughout the world." This amendment was defeated.

Mr. Washburn moved to add this to the invitation to Kossuth:—

"Provided, that nothing in this resolution shall be construed as impairing the effect, or questioning the policy of the measures passed by the last Congress, known as the compromise measures."

The proviso was far-fetched, but no more so than the motion it sought to displace, and if Democrats could seize the occasion to record their views, so might Whigs. Washburn's motion having been ruled out as irrelevant he made a *pro forma* amendment in order to speak, and urged that all extraneous questions be dropped from the pending proposition, and that Kossuth be received with the hospitality and distinction becoming the occasion.

A month later he had another chance to demonstrate his abounding optimism and faith in his country, when, on

March 2, 1852, he spoke for the project of government aid to the proposed European and North American Railway. It was his bill; the idea appealed to him in many ways and he never abandoned it. The project was to run a railway from New York to Halifax, or White Haven, Nova Scotia, where it would meet a steamship line for Galway, Ireland. Most of the road was already built, all except fifty miles from Waterville to Bangor, and eighty-five to one hundred miles to connect it with the New Brunswick road. New Brunswick would carry on the enterprise to the coast. Maine would build the connection between Waterville and Bangor, but $3,000,000 was wanted from the national government to run the tracks to New Brunswick. Washburn calculated that the new route would shorten the time of the voyage to Europe from seven days and fifteen hours to five days and five hours.

Beside the great benefit which this country would derive from being brought into closer proximity to the old world he pictured the advantage to Ireland from the introduction of the American spirit of industry and improvement and the benefit to all nations of more intimate knowledge of American institutions. This was the only important bill he introduced at that session.

As a new member and one of the minority he was obliged to content himself with such committee assignments as the Speaker chose to give him. He was put on the Committee of Revised and Unfinished Business, but in the next Congress he went on the Select Committee on the Pacific Railway (probably because of his interest in railway projects, demonstrated in his advocacy of the European and North American Railway). He was still serving on this committee when he left Congress in 1861. In 1853 he served on the important Committee on Revolutionary

Pensions; and in the next Congress, being now one of the majority, he received the chairmanship of the Committee on Elections. He had served in a similar capacity in the House of Representatives of Maine. He was on the Committee on Ways and Means in 1857 (and later chairman), up to the last year of his service. These details are evidence of the fact that, as his congressional service went on, he became one of the leaders of the House.

But railways and contested elections were the unimportant business of the House. The question of slavery extension soon arose to overshadow every other issue.

On May 24, 1852, Washburn delivered his first long set speech. It took one hour in delivery. The subject in everybody's mind at the time was the approaching presidential nominating conventions soon to be held in Baltimore. The chief Democratic candidates were Cass, Buchanan, Douglas, and Marcy; but Franklin Pierce, whom nobody thought of for the nomination when Washburn spoke, was nominated. The chief Whigs in the public eye were Fillmore, the President, Scott, and Webster, and Scott was chosen.

The subject of Washburn's speech was "The Compromise as a National Party Test." He said that a question of vital interest to the Whig party was now claiming its decision. It was simply whether or not the principles of the party were to be abandoned and all questions subordinated to a new test which should make the reclamation of fugitive slaves in a particular manner and by a particular law the leading idea of the party. He himself came from an extreme Northern state but he held no extreme views. Nevertheless, he utterly repudiated the demand made by certain men that a national party should declare the recognition of the fugitive slave law as a perpetuity to be the great purpose of its existence. The idea of finality in regard to the details of any law was ridiculous. Resolutions could not make public sentiment nor stop its progress. The people of the North recognized that neither the general government nor the free states had anything to do with slavery in the states, and that they were bound, under the Constitution, to return fugitive slaves; but the present law was ugly and harsh in its provisions and Northern men did not like it. A law less obnoxious and equally effective and constitutional might be prepared by men who had a right to object to being cast out of the Whig party and gibbeted as enemies to the Constitution and the Union. He objected to the introduction of the compromise articles into the Whig creed, because one law would then be made more sacred than other laws; because the proposition violated the theory of the right of presidential veto, by requiring that the candidate for the presidency should be pledged in advance to veto any law inconsistent with the compromise; because the proposition bound only the North and not the South, the latter being privileged to change the compromise and the former pledged not to change it; because it would increase agitation and tend to form sectional parties. As for the Union, that must be maintained at all hazards.

By this speech Washburn's attitude was made clear. He wanted a national party. He was willing to give the South the rights it had under the Constitution; but he was not willing to pledge himself to make no change in an obnoxious fugitive slave law, nor to promise that the compromise measures of 1850 should bind him forever. We see clearly that the more radical anti-slavery sentiments had already affected Whigs of his school, and that they were taking a more advanced position than they had taken before. In the course of the speech he had a short colloquy with Alexander H. Stevens of Georgia in which he showed alertness in repartee. He quoted a remark of Stevens made in 1845 that he was no defender of slavery in the abstract, and Stevens objected to the quotation as being partial. He had said, he insisted, "that the subjection of the African to the white man, or African slavery, bore the impress of the Creator himself, and that wherever the African and the white races were found in the same proportions as they are in the South, the dependence of the inferior upon the superior race, or slavery, must exist."

Washburn replied: "I would like to have the Gentleman make the discrimination. If he is opposed to all slavery in the abstract, how can he be in favor of African slavery in the concrete?"

The platform actually adopted by the Whig convention at Baltimore reflected Washburn's contentions. It acquiesced in the compromise measures and deprecated further agitation of the questions, but required enforcement of the fugitive slave acts only "until time and experience shall demonstrate the necessity of further legislation." It was half-hearted; the party was not united; General Scott went down in merited defeat, and Franklin Pierce was elected by a large majority.

FOUNDING A PARTY

Again there was a Northern man with Southern principles for President, and again the Northern Whigs found themselves in the power of the slave-holders of the South. In January, 1854, Stephen A. Douglas introduced in the Senate his bill for erecting the two territories of Kansas and Nebraska, allowing each to say whether it should or should not have slavery, thus destroying the old compromise of 1821 for both were above the line marked for freedom. From this time on, the position of the Whigs of Washburn's school was clear and well-defined. They were to fight, at every turn, the increasing demands of the slave power. It was useless to fight in Congress, however, without the support of an aroused constituency, and Washburn and his friends set themselves to the task of wakening the people to the danger that confronted them. Thomas M. Brewer, the Naturalist, editor of the *Boston Atlas*, wrote from Boston, February 7, 1854:

> You see I took the liberty to borrow some of your last letter to impress our readers with the general indignation at Washington. . . . I am greatly troubled at the apathy which prevails at the North, and at no place more than in this city. I am at times inclined to doubt whether Boston could be aroused even if the question involved the introduction of slavery here in Massachusetts.

From New Hampshire, however, he heard a more encouraging recital. Amos Tuck wrote from Exeter, March 18, 1854:

> Now let Frank Pierce consummate his treason, if he dare. There is a North, thank God! We have found out

29

where, even the people of N. Hampshire had a heart and
soul, stored away in a secret place under their waist-
coats. . . . We have effected our object—rebuked treason,
condemned the Nebraska Bill, and discarded the President. Any amount of money asked for, was provided in all
places in the state, and the extent of corruption was beyond
all precedent—never before equaled in any part of the
country, unless in some city hot hole of infection. The
democratic loss was, by the desertion from their standard
of their best men. I think they (the leaders) can never
recover from the consequences of having *tried* to betray
their country. . . . The Whigs and Free-Soilers are welded
together in this state, and cannot again be separated. We
feel that the way is open for emancipating our state, and
bringing out in future the true characteristics of our people,
so long belied by the most unworthy demagogues that ever
entered a free state.

Pass this to your brother also.

On April 7, 1854, Washburn delivered the most important and poignant speech that he had thus far made and in
the large number of strong speeches made on both sides
of the question, now before Congress, his was one of the
most vital.

He began by stating that the purpose of the Kansas-
Nebraska bill was simply to extend the area of slavery,
and then showed what a change had come over Southern
sentiment, which in earlier days had regarded slavery as an
evil which must ultimately be uprooted. He insisted that
Congress could do what it chose with the territories and
ridiculed the idea that "a tent full of hunters or outlaws
or the first half dozen men who go in the Territory" could
properly control its destiny. The project, too, required
them to control it in favor of slavery. Suppose, he said,
the people should choose to taboo slavery, the slave owner
would deny the validity of the law and the Supreme Court

would decide that it was incompetent under the Constitution for a territorial legislature to pass any law prohibiting slavery. He pleaded for the observance of the Missouri Compromise. Concerning the bill, he said that the excitement which would follow its passage would increase; the North would not acquiesce in it, as in the Compromise of 1850. Up to the present time it had never been deeply and thoroughly stirred. "She had been influenced by abstractions and sentiment, rather than by the power of direct interest." But if the bill passed she would become convinced of the aggressiveness of slavery; that it (slavery) knew no law and would keep no faith. She would then become united and arrayed in fierce and unrelenting opposition to the institution. If the great body of the Southern Whigs were determined to make a sectional issue of the question, then there was no national Whig party to be dissolved and the Northern Whigs must bid their former co-partisans a "long good night." There would be a North, then, insisting upon "restriction in the Territories, non-intervention in the States."

All the efforts of the anti-slavery men were vain, and the Kansas-Nebraska bill, repealing the Missouri Compromise and throwing all the territories open to slave settlement so that the national power would be with the slave holding states, was signed by President Pierce, May 31, 1854.

It had passed the House on May 8, and the day after Israel Washburn took the step which was probably the most important in his career as a public man.

As we have seen he had formed a friendship with Gamaliel Bailey, who was persistently urging through the *National Era* that the advance of the slave interests could not be effectively checked by the Whig party. It was apparent that that party was really dead, although it knew it not; that many of the Whigs were lukewarm on the subject of slave extension; that many leaders of the party, desirous of having a Southern followihg, were willing to permit the South to have its own way; that in fact the party was not an anti-slavery party, and that actually such was the great need of the hour. Washburn's speech of May 24, 1852, showed that he was even then willing to fall away from the Whig party if he could find another effective party organization to take its place. His speech of April 7, 1854, showed ah increased readiness. All political action with him meant party action. An idea was useless to him unless the means were provided for giving it effect.

Two others of his friends in Washington were Thomas D. Eliot and Edward Dickinson, representatives from Massachusetts, who boarded together at Mrs. Crutchett's on the northwest corner of sixth and D streets. They, too, had discussed with Washburn and Bailey (and there must have been a number of others consulted) the project of forming a new party, having as its great central idea resistance to the slave power. A few hours after the Kansas-Nebraska bill passed the House, Washburn called a meeting of Anti-slavery members of the House, about thirty, Whigs, Democrats, and Free-Soilers, at the rooms of Thomas D. Eliot, who represented the New Bedford district of Massachusetts, and Dickinson, to concert action to resist the advance of slavery. There were a few Democrats asked and several Free-Soilers, but most of those concerned in the movement were Whigs. They met on the morning of May 9. Bailey, it would appear, was the only outsider present. Washburn made an address and urged the formation of a new party to be dedicated to freedom—to the resistance of the slave power and the restriction of slave territory—and suggested that it be called the Republican party, "In which *all men who thought alike* on the vital question of the time,—that of slavery extension,—should act together." Some of the Whigs present were reluctant to abandon the name and party affiliations to which they had become attached by long association and many political campaigns; but conditions had changed and a new issue of overwhelming importance confronted them, so they cast in their fortunes with the new organization.

There has been dispute over the question of the time and place of the formation of the Republican party. Unquestionably Washburn's meeting was not the first one at which the matter was discussed; but it is equally unquestionable that it was the first meeting attended by national leaders whose determination was weighted with authority. Each man who attended it represented an important constituency and any recommendation he might make would influence many voters.

Soon after the meeting was held Washburn went home and made a speech to his constituents at Bangor in which he described the necessity for a new alignment of parties in resisting the encroachments of the slave power and suggesting that the new party be called Republican, this being the first public suggestion of that name.

Dr. Bailey, who had been so important a factor in founding the party, died in 1867, and in the *Universalist Quarterly* for July, 1868, Washburn described the calling of the meeting and Bailey's part in the movement.

"No name," he said, "connected with the anti-slavery movement in this country, will be permanently associated with that movement unless it shall be that of one who was a leader in some necessary work of preparation, or an exponent of some special truth or idea, or the organizer of some timely and practical method, relating thereto, and indispensable to its success.

"John Quincy Adams and Joshua R. Giddings did special and necessary pioneer work as champions of free discussion and the right of petition. Garrison, Sumner and Mrs. Stowe illustrated the essential barbarism of slavery. Fessenden and Chase demonstrated the power and duty of Congress to forbid its extension. Seward and Greeley (divided, as they have been, during these later years, in opinion and action) were apostles 'of the equal and indestructible rights of man. But ably and successfully as these men (and others who acted with them) labored in their respective fields, a work more difficult, if not more important, than theirs, remained to be accomplished,—the practical work, the work of organization. It was necessary that the people who had been convinced of the wrong and danger of slavery, acting as they were in different political parties to which they were strongly wedded, should be taken out of these organizations and brought together in a new one founded upon opposition to slavery.

"The man who was to do this work, who was to combine and organize the scattered forces of anti-slavery opinion; in other words, *the immediate founder of the Republican party*, was Dr. Bailey."

Dr. Bailey was a philanthropist and doctrinaire and also a sagacious statesman, and he saw earlier than most anti-slavery men the necessity of being practical. "Both parties aimed to be what was called *national;* and if Northern men endeavored to make the party to which they belonged to any extent anti-slavery, they were charged with attempting to make it anti-national,—it might be

Anti-Northern and yet national, but it could not be national and Anti-Southern! In fine, the slave-holders furnished the principles and controlled the policy of both parties."

Later Dr. Bailey matured the plan and arranged the preliminaries for organizing the national Republican party. He drafted the call for the convention which met at Pittsburgh, February 22, 1856, when the party was formally organized. "Under the former methods of opposing slavery within the old parties, controlled as they were by the slavery influences, no advance had been made. On the contrary, freedom had been losing ground, from year to year, until at last it became a question whether she had any ground to stand on,—even in the States of the North. It was to Dr. Bailey more than to any other man that the country was indebted for the simple but invaluable instruction, how Slavery could be checked and Freedom saved. The memory of this wise and good man should be enshrined in the hearts of all Republicans. Congress should erect his monument in the Capitol."

Washburn's generosity in according the chief credit to Dr. Bailey does not alter the fact that Bailey acted with him; that the fateful meeting was called by him; that it was his position in the House which enabled him to give form and substance to Bailey's project; that it was he who suggested the name for the new party. In a speech on January 10, 1859, he disclosed why the name Republican had been chosen. It was because the earliest party of the people, which Thomas Jefferson had founded, had borne that designation. Thus it was identified with the Declaration of Independence, with freedom and the equality of man.

PROGRESS OF THE NEW PARTY

Washburn and Bailey began a coöperation which bore fruit. Having undertaken a great work Washburn threw himself into it with energy. The following letter of Edward Kent reflects fairly well his own sentiments at this time.

Bangor June 21 1854.

My dear Sir: Our State Convention is, as you know on the 29th. What course will then be taken is somewhat doubtful—The strong and nearly unanimous opinion of the Whigs of this section, is in favor of, at once, openly declaring that whilst we hold fast to our opinions and intend to maintain them, when the actual situation of the country shall call for their defence or enforcement, we are satisfied the present crisis demands the united zealous and honest efforts of all opposed to the recent outrages involved in the Nebraska bill, and to the manifest schemes of the Southern leaders to extend the area of Slavery, indefinitely—by conquest, or purchase, or robbery . . .— to bend and prostitute all the power of the East and all the interests of the country, to advance . . . this single interest and institution, and to use the free States as convenient auxiliaries in the work and to keep with us or cut us adrift hereafter, as their policy, their passions or their presumed strength may dictate and that in view of the momentous issue and the necessity of *instant* and united action to strike a blow that shall be felt, instead of beating the air, and making mere outcries—and knowing that a large and respectable portion of the former Democratic party in this State have with great independence . . . avowed their determined opposition to these schemes, and their purpose to labor for the repeal and for the restoration of the ancient landmarks and have in public meeting, placed themselves on the broad platform on which we stand, and avowed their willingness to act with all who agree with them in feeling and sentiment, and have placed in nomination a citizen who has openly declared his sentiments in a clear and satisfactory manner, that we will make no nomination, but advise all Whigs to unite upon the true man already nominated and standing as a candidate before the people.—And also advising to a similar *union* (not coalition) in elections for Congress and State and County officers.

Our present plan is to go up to see the Whigs, the day before the Convention and have a free talk. We have sundry men who wish to be Candidates, and a portion of the sea board and Kennebeck etc., I suppose will be unwilling to agree to the omission of a nomination. But I think the feeling is growing stronger in favor of a fusion. Some of our people say we must wait for the great States to move. But our election is first and Maine, as in 1840 and in 1848 did great service in moving early and decidedly. I am opposed to any half way measures. Either go in boldly or not at all. As for the Old Whig party, as an efficient actor in the future, the idea to me is simply childishly absurd—

Clayton, Badger and Jones did the business for it—as Charles Lamb said about the oyster pie.—That secret caucus was the funeral of the National Whig party—or rather the choking and stabbing—preparatory to the funeral, on the last night of the Nebraska bill—when Judge Wade pronounced the funeral sermon a capital one. We may not and I think had better not be in a hurry to discard the name or to a certain extent the old organization—These will "subside" like Judge Weston's cases, naturally and by degrees, to be revived if occasion offers.

The question is what shall we do—The question is often asked what do our friends at Washington say? What says Gov. Seward, who by the way seems fast coming into favor with the old conservatives. His calm, quiet and yet faithful and earnest remonstrance in his last speech,—so free from clap trap and furious tirades and personal denunciations,—has given him a high position in the regard of

cool, national and reflecting men of all parties. What says
Pitt, (sometimes called Fessenden for shortness)?—What
Farley and Benson?—I think if the course indicated is
taken Morrill can be elected over all others.—I see that the
Whigs have called a convention in the Oxford District for
the 30th of June.—It seems to me that this district must be
yielded to the Democrats and especially if Cumberland is
to have a Whig.—Ask Fessenden about this.—Write me.

How strongly they felt is shown by a letter from J. Z.
Goodrich, Stockbridge, July 15, 1854.

There is an indescribable anxiety on the part of multi-
tudes in the country lest the Tombs' and Douglas' *pacifica-
tion*—(another term for *permanently establishing* slavery
in Kansas)—bill shall be passed by the House. Perhaps
I feel this anxiety more than many others, knowing as I do
the means which have hitherto been so successfully re-
sorted to, to pass measures of a kindred character through
a closely divided House. But the anxiety is general. . . .
Let me assure you that the Free States expect the true men
of the House to prevent that bill by some means, and if
necessary by *every means* within their reach under the rules
of the House, from becoming a law. The great heart of the
North will hold you justified, more than justified, in re-
sorting to every measure known to the rules, and wear out
the session and indeed the remainder of this Congress in
keeping Frank Pierce's fingers from that bill. As sure as
that bill becomes a law at this session, Kansas will be in
the Union before the 4th of March as a slave state. The
next House will be more strongly fortified against the slave
power, and knowing this the purpose is to use the present
House. I do not ask it irreverently, and yet I ask, 'Can
any good come out of Nazareth?' The fact that Douglas
urges this bill is the best, the *very best* evidence you can have
that it was conceived in mischief, and will bring forth, if
adhered to, iniquity and *nothing else*. The fact that he
says it is fair, is the very best evidence you can have that it

is not fair, but on the contrary a cheat, an abominable cheat and fraud. Stop it! Stop it! Stop it!!!

Before quoting the following letter from Edward Kent the reader may be reminded that a "doughface" was a weak Whig who was willing to be used by the Southern party, being as plastic as dough in their hands, and a "hunker" a conservative Whig disposed to ignore the changed issues which confronted him. At the time the letter was written a notable contest for the Speakership, which will be mentioned again, was in progress.

Boston, Decr. 15th. (*1855*)

Dear Washburn: We hope you will stick to Banks, until a final decision. I would not yield to the "doughfaces." Better have Richardson, than show at the outset that the Anti-Nebraska and Anti Slavery extension party is defeated by being compelled to take an unsound or uncertain man. If you hold on you must elect Banks, or one "of the same sort." You cannot too soon learn and act upon the certain fact, that nothing but the union of the elements of opposition, based upon the *Slavery extension* issue, can prevent the success of the Democracy. And if this Congress falters,—we can do nothing.—But do not try to conciliate doughfaces with frightened fawns. Take strong ground— but not too *extended* in particulars.—The nationality of Freedom and the sectionalism of Slavery—the doctrine in the Kane and Lemon cases—and the Nebraska bill are the true grounds—I think—. Above all stick to the Union and deny that we are dissolutionists.

I go to Maine in a day or two—Again I say as well as I can in this dark room where I cannot see my lines—yield nothing to a desire to organize—or to conciliate old hunkerdom—"Work and wait" even until the 4th of March if necessary.

The relations of the writer of the next letter to Mr. Washburn require a word of explanation. James G.

Blaine was only twenty years old and still living in Pennsylvania when Washburn was elected to Congress, and he
did not move to Maine until 1854, after Washburn's
reëlection. Washburn was, therefore, of a political generation before him and never accepted his leadership; but
Blaine was hardly settled in Maine before he began to use
Washburn. The men were too unlike to be sympathetic;
Washburn was a solid, hard-working man of sound knowledge and of rigid integrity, and Blaine was a man of
feverish activity, of brilliancy, of knowledge gained
hastily, and of easy political morals. As half owner
and editor of the *Kennebec Journal* at Augusta he was
a politician almost from the day of his arrival in Maine;
and within, two years we find him offering advice
to Washburn although he was only twenty-six years old
at the time.

Augusta Jany, 17/56.
    Dear Sir: Have you *one hundred* men "good and true"
voting for Banks? If so, and an organization is not effected
in a few days, would it not be well for you to unite in an
address to your constituents showing how the Richardson
and Fuller men factiously prevent an organization by
voting against the *plurality* rule? You are better prepared
than I, to judge of the practicability and propriety of such
a step but in the present temper of the public mind here,
I think it would have a good effect—
    By our legislative proceedings you will have seen that
Kansas has been on the carpet once.—We intend to give
the subject "wholesome agitation" at the proper time.—
Both wings of the Coalition are afraid of the question and
will do all they can to prevent a direct vote. Morse bears
himself very well and has no peer in the House—
    What do you think will be done with the application of
Kansas? The Coalition here are absolutely building all
their hopes on her admission as a State this winter. That

out of the way, they think they can rush Buchanan over the course without difficulty. . . .

The following letter relates to plans for nominating a Republican candidate for the Presidency; but the spurious letter of Frémont to which Mr. Blaine alludes has not been found. It does not appear to have been printed.

Augusta Feb. 12/56.

My Dear Sir: Is the movement for Frémont well thought of at Washington?

We have discussed it here for the past three or four weeks. I have never seen anything take so well. Unless something very unforeseen should occur, you may rest assured there is no man of all those who have been named for the nomination, who would make such a run in Maine. It is perfectly idle (in my opinion) to think of taking Seward or Chase.—We should be run under so far that we would never rise to the surface again.—The popular mind is just prepared for such a man as Frémont and I think if no mistakes be made between this time and his formal "trotting out," he would be formidable against the pro-slaveryites—especially if the Anti-Nebraska Know Nothing element could be well pleased with one of their men associated on the ticket for V. Presd. How would Pollock of Penna. do?[1]

I enclose a copy of a letter written by Frémont during the past autumn. You will please exhibit it only to those who are admitted to the "third degree" of Republicanism, as I obtained it under that confidence, tho you may have already seen a copy from the same source.

The letter as a whole would not do for publication, but you will observe that he avows sentiments which could be judiciously re-wrought into a popular and telling letter at the *right* time. The part on 3rd and 4th pages which I have included between . . . would answer capitally well for

[1] James Pollock, then governor of Pennsylvania, having been elected as a Union-Republican.

publication at any time, though the allusion to the "abolitionists" (*underscored*) had as well be left out in the New England edition—I hope however that nothing will be published from him for some time yet—

I don't know how many of our delegates will go to Pittsburgh though I understand that there will perhaps be four or five, Morrill probably among them. Urge Weston to go and if you can, go with him yourself and keep things straight—I have some fear that too many *radicals* will find their way in and press some resolution upon the convention which would be illtimed and prove permanently injurious.—Weston's cool discriminating head would do good service and you *must* go along if you can.—You could then sound the delegates on the Frémont question and let us know whether to pin our faith on him or not.—

Our State politics are dull—giving no signs to reckon by.—So far as we can judge however Republican stock is on the rise—assuredly it is not falling—the election of Banks did us immense good and helped all you Representatives amazingly—The enemy have appeared crestfallen ever since the result was known.

I should be glad to hear from you at your earliest leisure—particularly with regard to Frémont, for many of our leading men in this State are disposed to push his name forward with energy—

Will Buchanan win at Cincinnati? or will not Pierce and he mutually kill each other and give way to Cobb or Hunter or Rusk or some one still less prominent—We figure that way just now.

In haste

Very truly yours.

Judge McLean's name has been mentioned I see for the Presidency—It·wont take well here—his fugitive slave law decisions would kill him.—

The Morrill to whom allusion is made in this letter was Anson Peaslee Morrill, a Free-Soiler and Prohibitionist, the first Republican governor of Maine, a brother of Lot Myrick Morrill, afterwards Secretary of the Treasury and senator from Maine. He was not a delegate to the first Republican convention at Pittsburg, but George M. Weston was. Both Morrill and Weston were delegates to the second convention at Philadelphia, June 17, 1856, when Frémont and Dayton were nominated, but Washburn was not a delegate to either convention.

BLAINE TO WASHBURN

Augusta Me. Feb. 21/56

I have this moment learned that the Frémont letter of which I forwarded you a copy some days since is a *sham*— The game was played on the folks of the *Portland Advertiser* who transmitted me a copy in perfect good faith— thinking it genuine—Unless I am much mistaken from information derived through another channel I take Frémont to be even more thoroughly a Republican than the tone of that *bogus* letter would indicate.—

You *Reps* in Washington who have so large an influence in controlling Presidential nominations must not strand us by attempting to run Seward or Chase—It would run us under I am sure, especially in the event of the Dem's putting forward a man of the Buchanan conservative stripe—*Straight whigs* in this State such as Getchell and Rowell of Somerset would I feel confident, go with us on Frémont—on Seward they would not, and are quite bold to say so in public and private.—We must link that element with us and destroy the cry of sectionalism else we are beaten to death even in Maine.—With good nominations and judicious working we can carry the State though in my judgment not with that ease which some of our over sanguine friends boast of.—I will write you my views of this at length when I have leisure and give them to you for what they are worth.

I hope the proceedings at Pittsburg may be guided with wisdom and I shall be much pleased to hear that you are there—

Please destroy the Frémont letter—

In haste.

Blaine to Washburn

Augusta Feb. 22, 56.

You will have learned that the Frémont *hoax* is known to us. We were of course glad to know the letter was spurious, setting no high estimate upon it, and plainly seeing as I expressed to you the damage its publication would create.

I have no doubt it was concocted by those who are desirous of killing off Frémont. I think the same with regard to the *Catholic* story to which you allude. Frémont's name evidently shows that he is of French descent and as the Carolinas had large colonies of French Huguenots among their early settlers I doubt not he springs from them. If so he would be far enough from "Catholicism," to satisfy the most cordial hater of the Pope. Can you not find this matter out and write me in regard to it definitely and satisfactorily? I do not wish to give Frémont up.

Banks would run better out of New England than at home—I do not think he stands high in this state nor in Mass.—Such papers as the Boston Chronicle, Worcester and Providence (R.I.) Journals and others of decided character and ability would oppose him bitterly, while for Frémont they would go it with a rush. Banks has the character of an "artful dodger" in politics and I do not think he would prove available as a Presdt. candidate—

What effect is the "dodge" at Phila. going to have on our prospects? I am afraid they will cheat a large number of honest Anti-Neb'ska men with their *say-nothing* platform.—If we find it impossible to concentrate on the Presidency with a hope of success, we must take such a course as will save our state and our districts. We must not prove worse than heathen by neglecting to provide for our own households. . . .

I think the Radicals however are a *little ahead* just now.

On March 24 the *New York Tribune* printed an editorial on Maine politics entitled, "The Straight Whigs." It explained that they were a faction which talked of Whig principles but voted in such a way as to subserve the purposes of the Nebraska Democracy. In Maine the Straight Whigs were led by George Evans, the attorney general, and William George Crosby, for two years governor of the state. Then followed a letter dated Belfast, December 18, 1852, from Crosby to Stephen Stark at Waterville, proposing a covert coöperation in the legislature between the Straight Whigs and the Democrats. The origin of the letter is explained by the following:

BLAINE TO WASHBURN

Augusta March 18, '56.

I send herewith a communication for the N. Y. Tribune which I wish you to hand to Mr. Greeley for insertion at the *earliest practicable* moment. It contains the famous Crosby letter which you have perhaps seen and a consultation of our best advisers yesterday P. M. resulted in the conclusion that it was best to bring the letter out in the Tribune in the first place—*One* weighty reason for this is the fact that all our papers here feel a reluctance to take the lead in the matter and lay themselves liable to all kinds of cross questioning as to how they came in possession of a confidential letter. Nobody however would ever think of questioning the Tribune, for it is more than a newspaper—it is a distinct Northern *institution*—Another reason is that we wish to avail ourselves of the 8000 circulation which the Tribune has in Maine to give the letter wide distribution at this time. After it is once out all our papers here will ring the changes on it throughout the campaign. As I was only allowed a part of last evening to write the communication I had not time to *make it short* and had to run over it as rapidly as possible. It contains however the material explanations and is satisfactory to our friends here. If Greeley objects to the length, tell him he *must* favor us this time—Its publication *just now* is of the greatest consequence to us and will do more to break down straight

Whiggery than all the influences we have yet brought to
bear—(I mean the publication of the letter, not my comments.) It is very evident that the Straights are preparing
to reënact their game of last year and this Crosby letter
will open the eyes of many who might otherwise be lead
astray.

This letter will reach you on Monday the 20th,—If you
can see Greeley the same day and have him send it right
back to New York so as to be inserted in Tribune of Monday
next, 24th, it will suit us exactly—Let it be published by the
25th, at all events. We want it here *without fail* before the
Legislature adjourns, and it is quite possible they may adjn.
on the 29th, or 31st. Morse will probably make a sharp
speech with the letter as a basis if it reaches us in time. We
shall most likely have some sport on the Kansas motion
when the final action comes.

You need have no fear about the genuineness of the
Crosby letter. The original is carefully filed by one who has
a deep interest in preserving it. If Noah Smith is in Washington *do not say a word to him* about this article and please
never mention to *any one* that I have any connection with
it. You can vouch to Greeley that it comes from a responsible source.

I have dated the communication W . . . . the
public can guess between Winthrop, Winston, Windsor,
and Waterville. The last will probably be settled on as it
was Stark's residence.—

Should Greeley not be in Washington when this reaches
you please forward to New York. We would not miss having it published by Tuesday next for $500.—

The Mongrels are in a deal of trouble on the Liquor bill
and they cannot move on any question without aiding us—
They have given up the idea of addressing Davis off the
Bench and are now caucusing over the propriety of sub-
mitting questions to the Court. They see that the matter
will inevitably go there and they wish to prevent the case
being *argued* by our best lawyers. Should they submit
questions it would be a pointed rebuke to Wells' whole
course of proceedings. We are anxious for them to do it.

Matters look well everywhere, though we must not relax
an effort.—Their struggle will be a desperate one—Weston's
20,000 majority is "in my eye and Betty Martin's." If we
get 5000 we shall have accomplished a noble work. I have
not time to write you any political news at length but will
soon—
    Meantime and always shall be glad to hear from you.
                                              In grt. haste
Write me if Greeley will publish.

BLAINE TO WASHBURN

Augusta March 26/56

My Dear Sir: The "Tribune" made a miserable "botch"
of my communication as you will have seen. In attempting
to *editorialize* it, they have made so many bungling errors
as to destroy all its effect and really to do harm rather than
good. Had the communication been inserted as I sent, it
would have been copied into every Republican paper in the
State and would have done good. There were many plain
truths set forth in it, that we are reluctant to speak of in
our editorial columns but which we should have been glad
to copy from the *Tribune*.
    This is the *third* effort that I know of being made within
the year to get something inserted in the Tribune which
would benefit our Maine politics but in every instance have
we failed. Considering that the paper is taken by 8000
Republicans of this State, I think it rather hard that we
cannot be favored occasionally by a share of its columns.
I wish if good opportunity presents you would put these
facts to Greeley—
    Judge Davis's hearing will come off on the 4th of April.
There will be immense excitement attending it. Choate,
R. H. Dana and H. W. Paine have all been engaged as
counsel and will positively be present. It is said today,
though I scarcely believe it, that Geo. Evans has signified
his willingness to be joined with them should his services
be desired. He is quite outspoken in his denunciation of the
proceeding—in his own language as it has been reported to
me "it is damnable"—The wonder here is that the coali-

tion ever resolved to venture on so bold and wild a step. However, *"Quem Deus vult perdere prius dementat"*—The Liquor bill is now being discussed—with strong probabilities that by a disagreement between Senate and House the law of '55 will remain unrepealed—The Senate under Farley's lead goes for *free rum*—the House will not consent to it—many of *their* members in that branch being held in righteous awe by Maine Law Constituencies.

We are delighted over your Kansas triumph and I am rejoiced today to see that Campbell [1] has declined to serve on the Com'tee—I am glad that Banks was firm enough not to appoint D——I feel sure he would have betrayed us and I have not much more confidence in L. D. C$_t$—

We shall keep our columns judiciously *non committal* in regard to a Presidential candidate though we squint at Frémont by publishing complimentary allusions to him etc. He seems to take well in Maine though I often doubt if he be *heavy* enough to make the run. He would make an admirable *Vice*, should the ticket be headed by a man of Whig antecedents as it probably may be—Judging from the tone of the Pittsburg Gazette and other Pennsylvania exchanges, Judge McLean seems to be coming up in that quarter.—My own opinion is that he is politically passée—though he might run well.—I am looking with interest for the result of the doings in Penna. State Convention held today—much depends on the spirit manifested there by the conflicting elements of the opposition—

In grt haste
Yours truly.

BLAINE TO WASHBURN

Augusta Maine, April 2d—56.

My dear Sir: Much obliged for your two last favors— The Crosby letter is doing its work very well without the accompanying comments omitted by the Tribune—The Straights wince under it terribly—

---

[1] Lewis D. Campbell, of Ohio, a Whig, afterwards Minister to Mexico under Andrew Johnson.

Davis's hearing will commence on Friday . . . —His counsel will be Choate, Paine and Dana—Evans was unwilling when it came to the "Scratch" to take a part, tho he is quite outspoken I understand, in condemnation of the procedure.—He thought his position of Atty. General rendered it improper that he should assume an attitude of hostility to the Administration of which he is a component part. I have little confidence in him anyway and tho I shld. have been glad to see him *used* for the benefit *of our side*, I do not much regret his (declension)—

I agree with you entirely in regard to the impolicy of running Davis for Gov. I have tried to impress my views upon some of our friends here who seem disposed to have him nominated—It would as you say be transferring the contest from Kansas to Wells and Davis and would be the exact issue which the Coalitionists would desire above all other things—I hope you will all at Washington protest against it and nip the movement in the bud. We have a great many men in our party who go off *half cocked*—fellows that are "gude nough but more hasty than wise"—They must be made to ride in the rear car instead of on the engine or else we are in constant danger of being thrown from the track.

I happened to be in the back room of our P. O. last evng. when the mail was brought in. Among the bags destined for the Eastern part of the State was an enormous canvas holding five or six bushels and completely filled *to the mouth* with documents franked by T. J. D. Fuller [1] for the 6th dist. I think Douglas' report on Kansas was the article but I could not tell. I was dreadfully tempted to *steal* one to find out what it might be. They are throwing a prodigious quantity of documents in to the State and intend to fight us to the death. As soon as the Legislature adjourns we shall arrange for Benson's [2] *flooding* the Kennebec District with the right kind of matter—B. does not send in the Globe—He did last winter but why not this winter I do

[1] A Democrat member from Maine.
[2] Samuel P. Benson, a Republican member from Maine.

not know. I wish he would, but dont tell him I said so. *Dont you do it* for you have enough to do to take care of yr own district—

Leonard Jones—Eaton of Plymouth, Blake and Cutter of Bangor and numerous other Coalitionists from that region with whom I talk, make great boasts of how they are going to beat *you* in September—I cant get them to say who they are going to run against you tho perhaps you can guess yourself—"forewarned is forearmed" remember.

We shall rely upon you Reps to force Hamlin in to the field as Gub. candidate. From conversations I have had this winter with men from every county and Rep. Dist., in the State I am convinced that he will poll *six or eight thousand* votes more than any other man. There are Dems. not in the Legislature who will support him. The worst of it is that if H. declines, we shall have a lot of Richmonds in the field—such as Jno. M. Wood—Belcher, Muzzy, Morse, Franklin Clark, Knowlton, Downs, *Mel. Weston*, Noah Smith, Coburn and God knows how many more. Hamlin must run, it is absolutely essential that he should in order to consolidate the party—He would aid you in yr congressional canvass *immensely.*

AS A LEADER OF THE REPUBLICAN PARTY

The first important national victory won by the Republican party was in the election of Nathaniel P. Banks to Speaker of the House of Representatives in 1855. The contest for the speakership lasted two months. None of the candidates was able to obtain a majority of votes, and Banks' election was finally accomplished on the 133d ballot after an agreement had been reached by which a plurality of the votes were deemed sufficient to elect. Banks had been elected to Congress in 1853 as a Democrat, coöperating with the Free-Soil party; but his next election was by the Know-Nothings. Whatever else he was, he was an anti-slavery man and for that reason the new Republicans rallied to him. His chief opponent was William A. Richardson of Illinois, a Democrat, and, of course, a Nebraska man, whose chief support was from the South, but he had a few votes from Northern Whigs who followed the Southern leaders—the "doughfaces." It was plain that the old Whig party was breaking up. Washburn had been one of the effective supporters of Banks, and being, for the first time in his congressional service, on the winning side it was then he was made chairman of the Committee on Elections.

On March 14, 1856, he made an important speech on the Kansas contested election case. It was strong, partisan, adroit and effective.

"Mr. Speaker," he said, "for the sake of slavery, solemn compacts of long standing, deliberately entered into, and with mutual considerations, have been destroyed; principles of faith and honor have been cast away like

worthless weeds, ... and, as if these things were not
enough, we are now told that the instruments of this
sectional interest, its gangs and invading armies, may enter
and seize upon our infant Territories, our own Territories,
under the immediate and special protection of the General
Government—Subjugate the people rightfully there,
make laws and elect Delegates for them. . . .

"Slavery, in its claims and demands of to-day, is so
much greater and better than anything else, nay, than all
things else, that to protect and strengthen it, is held to
justify the destruction of whatever stands in its way. . . .
Laws are set aside, and compromises violated for its sake,
and nothing is held sacred against its assaults. . . . All
memories and hopes, all possessions and rights, the Constitution, the Union, the living Gospel of peace on earth
and good will to men are but flax and stubble, when ex-
posed to the consuming flame of this insatiate and inexorable system."

This was the main argument. It was a terrific and un-
answerable attack on the slave party.

Two months later, June 21, he spoke again on the same
subject, the speech being one of the most important and
powerful compositions that ever fell from his pen.

"In this year, 1856, a great moral and political battle is
to be fought. It is the old quarrel—the strife of centuries
and continents—but one of its decisive conflicts is here and
now impending. As it shall be decided, so will run the
history of America and mankind for ages." Taking up the
recently announced doctrine that slavery was "founded in
truth and justice" he denounced it with withering indignation. The ultimate purpose of the slave power was to
make slavery national; its avowed purpose was to dis-
solve the Union if slavery was restricted to the old limits

prescribed for by the Missouri Compromise. The advocates of freedom must rally against Pierce and Buchanan and elect John C. Frémont, recently nominated for the Presidency by the Republican party.

Washburn himself had accepted Frémont willingly, but his preference had been for Judge John McLean, whose dissenting opinion in the Dred Scott case had been such an able denunciation of slavery that it had given him a high position with the new party. Greeley wrote to Washburn from New York, June 13, 1856:

> I shall go for Judge McLean with great heartiness should he be the nominee. At the same time, I prefer a Democrat and a young man to run against old Buck. I admit that Pennsylvania makes a strong appeal for the Judge. But Wilmot is not for him, and all our *old* earnest anti-slavery men dislike him. Come over to Phila. and answer us.

However, the nomination having been made, Greeley accepted it and worked valiantly for Frémont's election. He thought Washburn could help him:

GREELEY TO WASHBURN

New York September 15, '56

Friend W.: I presume you don't speak to common folks now a days but consider:

Gov. Hamlin could help us in New Jersey and Pennsylvania just now. Both states are—in spite of all you hear—doubtful; New Jersey even hard to carry, though I think we shall do it. Now can't you and the Governor come down and stump a few weeks in these two states? You will do great good if you will, even allowing that you make no better speeches than the rest of us. It also happens that the simple word *Maine* goes a great way towards exciting enthusiasm just at present.

I do hope you may come.

A Democrat was elected President again.

When the last Congress before the Civil War came together, Washburn's prestige had been greatly enhanced by the success of his party in Maine. He was still coöperating in a general way with Mr. Blaine; but if he did not form a high opinion of the rising young editor he had reason. The session had hardly begun when he received the following communication:

> *Advertiser Office*
> *Portland, Dec. 16, 1857*

My dear Sir: I have learned recently that the young man from Somerset for whom you procured a cadet's commission at West Point is either about to resign or has already done so—I write you to know if there is any way by which you could give the successorship to a young friend in whom I am interested—a nephew of my wife's?—I am willing to do anything to secure the place for him either in the way of *buying* off all rivals *at any reasonable* price or complying with any conditions that may possibly be linked with success—the young lad spent nearly the whole of the past summer and autumn at the house of Samuel Cole in Greenville, Piscataquis County—pursuing his studies and hunting and fishing at Moosehead. He is therefore a *quasi* if not an entirely *bona fide* resident of your district. With any prospect of procuring the commission he would return to Greenville and remain until June next, when he would proceed to the "Point"—His appointment would therefore be entirely regular *in form* and would be more consonant with the spirit of the law than one half that are made—If you have already promised the place to some other person who would be willing to yield his chance for a matter of *three or four hundred dollars* I would be very glad to pay that sum, provided there would be no appearance of impropriety in the transaction. Of that you would be a better judge, or at least have a better standpoint for judging, than myself. Will you please write me in regard to the matter? I need not express to you the obligation

I will be under to you if you can favor me in the way I desire, nor need I assure you that every opportunity to reciprocate, *personally* and *politically*, will be joyfully and eagerly improved by me.

How beautifully political affairs are working! The crime of 1834 is returning to plague its inventors with fearful force—

Hoping to hear from you soon
I remain in haste
Very truly yours.

This is a remarkable letter which it is difficult to analyze or characterize. His wife's nephew was not really a resident of Washburn's district and consequently not eligible for nomination for West Point by Washburn, but this difficulty was to be overcome by residence after nomination. No unlawful proposition was made, except perhaps that of construction of the nephew's residence. No dishonest suggestion was made, yet one cannot help wondering what manner of boy Blaine supposed was trying to enter the army from Washburn's district that he could be induced to exchange his military aspirations for a few hundred dollars in hand.

He was willing to pay the boy or boys with money if they would retire, and he offered to pay Mr. Washburn for the appointment by personal and political services. It cannot be denied that the letter leaves on the reader's mind an ugly impression of Mr. Blaine. Mrs. Blaine's nephew was not nominated for West Point by Washburn.

The next great speech made by Washburn in the House was that of January 7, 1858, on Kansas and the Lecompton constitution. The act of May 30, 1854, he said, repealing the Missouri Compromise, provided that slavery should not be legislated into, nor excluded from any territory, but the people be left free to form and regulate their domestic institutions in their own way, subject only to the Constitution of the United States. The advocates of slavery would not let Kansas regulate its institutions in its own way, but filled the territory with ruffians from Missouri who were determined to fasten slavery upon the state. The convention, assembled at Lecompton, was composed only of some delegates from the territory; by complicity and fraud half the territory was not represented. The constitution which it put forth was a monster of iniquity, because it provided not only for slavery but that never should any "alteration be made to affect the rights of property in the ownership of slaves." It would be unchangeable except by revolution. There was a seeming but false submission of the slavery question to the people. They might vote for slavery or they might vote that no more slaves be admitted into the state;—that is, that slave-breeding within the state should have the advantage of absolute protection against outside competition. It was not submitted to the people for ratification, but it was proposed in voting for or against it, that every voter must take an oath "to support this Constitution, if adopted, under the penalties of perjury under the Territorial laws."

The speech made a deep impression.

When J. N. Stearns and Co., a firm of publishers in New York, wrote to him on the subject of a publication they were sending him they said:

> *New York—Mar. 13th, 1858.*
> Permit us to add that we have felt our hearts warm within us when we have seen that you in connection with other *true* men from the North have stood up for the principles of Eternal Justice—
> *Votes for the right in Congress and Revolvers* (etc) for Kansas—*and God bless the right.*

An occasional copy of speeches would be acceptable to us as our Congressmen are all on the wrong side—would be acceptable though we do not expect you will neglect your own constituents for us.

Yours truly.

He had a simple plan for dealing with the Kansas question. It was to vote and endeavor to make others vote against the Lecompton constitution and to resist every proposition to make Kansas a slave state. Greeley urged a more complicated course, but Washburn did not approve it.

New York Nov. 'I8, 58

My dear Sir: Thank you for yours. I want to make myself a little clearer.

All great battles are won by the help of some who *have* to help, but are indifferent or hostile to success. So in the present case. Well: what I propose is that you should have an understanding with the South Americans and others who *must* vote for Lecompton, that, while they vote against you on the Main Question, they shall vote *against* the Previous Question and all manner of mob judgments, assuming the post of moderators and insisting on fair play. You know they don't *care* for Lecompton; they only want to stand right on the record. Well, they can vote to give the subject a good ventilation by debate, amendments, etc., and finally vote with Stephens and M. on the Main Question, after having first compelled the Northern supporters of the bill to kill themselves by their votes on amendments; then to kill the bill. It will be easy for Humphrey Marshall to make an amendment that will carry, yet which, being adopted, will leave the bill a doomed wreck. Think of this.

Depend on it, strong efforts and representations will secure half a dozen votes against the Previous Question, etc. which must be given against us in the Main Question.

Yours

On January 10, 1859, Washburn made another important speech in Congress.

He took the floor, he said, for the purpose of presenting some thoughts concerning the Republican party. Two ideas were represented by the parties; one democratic, the other aristocratic. The former rested upon the Declaration of Independence proclaiming the equality of man and that governments derived their just powers from the consent of the governed. The aristocratic principle was expressed in the Lecompton constitution. "The right of property is before and higher than any constitutional sanction; and the right of the owner of a slave to such slave and its increase is the same, and as inviolable, as the right of the owner of any property whatever." The so-called Democratic party was the representative of this constitution; the Republican party drew its inspiration from the Declaration of Independence. The business of the Democratic party was to consolidate an oligarchy in the United States and make it perpetual; of the Republican party, to secure blessings of liberty and to each state a Republican form of government (quoting the Declaration and the Constitution). The vital, central issue of the day was, "Shall this government be a Republic or an Oligarchy?" The Democratic party was the Southern and the slaveholder's party. Its policy was directed by slaveholders. They nominated its candidates for the Presidency. They prescribed the issues. The President had recently said that the Supreme Court had decided that all Americans had an equal right to take their property into the territories under the guardianship of the Constitution. The Constitution of Kansas made at Lecompton had declared that "The right of property is before and higher than any constitutional sanction," and on this constitution the Democratic party stood! Its object was not only to secure another slave state, but a recognition of the doctrine set forth in the Lecompton constitution, thus revolutionizing the government. If that constitution was true then slavery was founded in natural law, and therefore a God-given right. If this dogma was true in Kansas, it was true in Maine.

The Republican party had been called into existence when it became apparent that the Democratic party had been subsidized by the slaveholders. It had been called Republican because it had an odor of genuine nationality, because that was the name which the author of the Declaration of Independence and the father of the Constitution chose to be known by. It had been successful in the elections of eleven of the free states. That it had not been successful in every free state east of the Rocky Mountains was because some of its friends had been unwilling to stand on their own principles and had sought alliances and coalitions with bodies of men whose principles were not the same as their own, but thought to gain something by trading principles for voters and ideas for allies. Such a policy could not and ought not to win. The Republican party had presented issues stronger than had ever been given to the country before. It must have faith in itself. The Whig party had perished because it was too much a party of expedients and circumstances.

Congress had complete power over the territories. It was not true that the Supreme Court in the Dred Scott decision had decided that Congress had no power to prohibit slavery in a territory. The opinions of seven slave-holding judges on this point were mere *obiter dicta* and not binding. Even if they were opinions on subjects before the Court, they would not be binding upon the

Congress or the people. The people were the source of power and the ultimate judges on all political questions. If there existed any man, or number of men who were authorized to decide political questions, and from whose decision there was no appeal, then there was a despotism and it mattered not whether we had one despot or nine, whether we had a king, a directory or a supreme court. He would have Congress on every available occasion assert and exercise the power to legislate for the territories and for the prohibition of slavery in the territories. This should be done so that there would be no presumptions against the right from non-use.

The Republican party did not stop with the assertion that Congress ought to intervene to keep slavery out of the territories. It also maintained that whenever an act of Congress could not do it, the people of the territory should be permitted to do it by legislative authority. It would not leave to the popular sovereignty the power to introduce "an undoubted evil into a territory or commit an acknowledged crime when it can legally prevent it." He would not say to the people of a territory: "Slavery is a great wrong; it will be an everlasting curse to you if you have it; we can keep it from your midst if we will, but we choose not to do so, in order that you may have an opportunity to reject it if that shall be your pleasure." He utterly dissented from those Republicans who thought the policy of intervention to prevent slavery unwise. To leave the question to a few hundred outlaws and runaways when their decision affected all the people of the United States was folly. The question which they were to decide would be whether there were to be more slave states or more free states, whether government was to be Republican or Oligarchical, whether Congress was to be so constituted that it would protect free labor or oppress it. Southern men, who stood where their fathers stood at the close of the second war with Great Britain, would find nothing in the Republican party to object to, but on the contrary find the restoration of peace. But under any circumstances the party must not give up the states in the North in hope of obtaining states in the South. The slavery issues were the all-important ones upon which the party would turn fearless and undiscouraged.

J. D. ANDREWS TO WASHBURN

Private   *Astor House Jany. 13—1859.*
My dear Washburn: I am obliged for your letter which came to me from Boston. I see you have been making a great speech, and from what the papers say, you have put the party, a party which should be upon the threshold of success, upon the right basis.

Send me some copies here, when printed, and can you mail me at an early day, a copy of Cobbs Treasury Report—

Was it not unfortunate that the Naval appropriation bill was not referred to the House.

You cannot form any estimate of the poor opinion universally entertained of this corrupt and weak administration.

It seems plain to me that there is the utmost necessity for a concentration of all our forces in Washington, in Congress, moral, official and political and that there should be a combined attack upon Buchanan and his administration and that henceforward our true policy is the aggressive.

Appropriations should be steadily refused on account of the extravagance of the Executive—and I think the policy will be sustained.

If there are not too many political lame ducks, who have jobs on hand, the plan can be perfected.

Let him, let the canting old scoundrel meet the New House in June.

Remember this, we are strong and they are weak, and do not give up one inch of vantage ground—
Our policy, I say it again, must be aggressive, unyielding—Attack Buchanan and hold the Democracy accountable for all his acts—
I hope our people are about done with in making themselves fools with Douglass— . . .
How is Seward—You should make him brace himself up to an elaborate attack upon the administration—Put the ball in motion—Let Kansas be a secondary matter, apparently, in the debates—
The people are ready, and it will invigorate our party as well as giving them new ideas of new issues, of all the issues, involved in the contest—
I hope you are all well.

The next letter is from Rev. Amory Battles, pastor of the Universalist Church at Orono, an old and devoted friend of Mr. Washburn's.

Bangor, Feb 8, 1859.
Bro. Washburn: I have received a copy of your speech of the 10th, ult. and what is more I have read it too. I thank you for sending it to me and still more for making it. It does honor to your head and heart and shows you are looking towards the Heavenly City instead of Sodom. It has so far as it goes the right ring to it.
It has seemed to me that Republicanism has either been stupid or cowardly or as Dr. Cheever would say, I have thought it had not got its blinkers off. As, I have read in Judge Trumbul's speech the sentiment—quite as low and objectionable to me as the platform of Douglass—that the Republican Party is the White Man's party and is willing to let the black man alone if he will keep out of its way. As I have seen how willing the members of this party in Congress have been to adopt the lowest platform for the sake of some transient and uncertain good so that during the whole of the last session the real antislavery

issue was ignored by them and as the Richmond South declared nothing was said of the wrongs of the Slave! As I have noticed the attempts of the Tribune to sell out to Americans and Silver Greys and form a mere opposition clique bound by no central ideas but flying about like a party of Indians in a guerilla warfare without any fixed system, I have wondered if the scales would ever fall from their eyes to enable them to see the meaning and sublimity of the agitation that is now shaking our country from center to circumference.

With these doubts in my mind you may be assured that it gives me hearty pleasure to learn that some of you are comprehending the great fact that it is for no transient things that the antislavery party is contending but for principles as broad as man and as enduring as God himself. I am glad you and Seward and others are coming to see and avow that the warfare we are engaged in is not one of names and words, but a warfare of ideas eternally antagonistic and the only method to pursue is to follow the straight line of right, not the indirect way of shifting expediencies. As I understand it, we are not contending for the white man or the black man, but for universal man. The question is not, shall slavery spread over new territory simply, but shall it exist at all in our land. It is idle therefore to talk about taking in our colors if slavery will waive its claims to go into Kansas. You might as well say of a fever in your system you will cease attending to it if it will not show itself some particular part of the body, not knowing that if it does not manifest itself there it will somewhere else. If Slavery does not do diabolical things in Kansas it will some-where else.

How utterly futile it is to think of standing on the ticket and rotten platform of Horace Greeley and Co. We might gain a victory thereon but it would not be a victory of ideas but of a party merely without noble principles and with-out heroism. It seems to me that the line which the Tribune would draw between Republicanism and Democracy would represent the fence the farmer made around his field where he kept his hogs—so crooked that when they crawled under it they found themselves in the same field from which they thought they had escaped.

My dear friend I am glad you repudiate such tricks and dicker. Do not I beseech you, suffer the Republican Platform to be lowered. In the name of Freedom and Humanity, is it not low enough already? Rather seek to elevate and broaden it. Remember that nothing but truth and justice can stand permanently—for they alone rest on the solid foundation that God has laid. If one would build a pyramid, does he lay the base stone on the sand or dig down deep to the solid granite? It is no matter whether we succeed in 1860 or not, for the account of God's providence is not to be posted up then, but it is of immense importance for us to plant ourselves on such principles as deserve success. Let us be true to man—to the slave and as you so nobly say "With faith and a good heart" success is certain. I hope you will pardon the length and the seeming advisatory tone of this and believe me, with cordial regards to Mrs. Washburn.

Very Truly your friend.

There was not, however, full confidence in all Republicans. Joshua R. Giddings wrote November 7, 1859, from Jefferson, Ohio:

I may suggest that it (The President's message) be met by a determined effort for the repeal of all enactments by Congress which involve the people of the free states in the support of that institution, which must if the Union be preserved be left entirely with the states in which the constitution left it.

In meeting this question I think you will have less trouble in your own ranks than heretofore. But yet I apprehend there are would-be leaders in the Republican ranks that are quite willing to go farther in the support of slavery than Congress has heretofore gone, but they are not men of sufficient moral courage to say or do much if our friends put on a bold front and speak of those who would lend any support to slavery as men wanting in spirit and in principles.

This letter coincided with Washburn's view. Although the Abolition Society at New York, through William Godell who edited the *Radical Abolitionist*, approached him with energy in a letter of March 19, 1858, it did not gain his membership. His contention was simply that slavery was wrong and must be confined to the states in which it existed.

In the *Universalist Quarterly* for January, 1864, he discussed the question in an able article "The Logic and the End of the Rebellion." He said the slave power had committed suicide by its policy of aggression, which caused loyal men to reach the conclusion that nothing but the utter extermination of slavery would save their own freedom.

"It was not possible for slavery to be removed in any other way. The free States could not destroy it, nor could the General Government. It could be destroyed by the slave owners themselves, and by no other party. Without the assault upon the Government, wantonly and wickedly made by the slave power, no force of public sentiment could have been created, no combination of circumstances could have arisen adequate to the overthrow of this wide-spread and deep-rooted system."

How then could emancipation now be effectively accomplished? The President's proclamation had set all negroes in the states in rebellion free. There were, therefore, no slaves in the Southern states. Under the law no slaves could be imported from abroad. It was competent under the interstate commerce clause of the Constitution to prohibit a slave from going from one state to another.

The states, therefore, might leave their slave codes in full vigor upon the statute books and they be a dead letter. He had no doubt of the President's authority to issue the Proclamation of Emancipation. He did not agree with Charles Sumner's recent article in the *Atlantic Monthly* that the rebel states had ceased to be states of the Union and were now territories which the general government could govern in any way it chose.

Washburn insisted they were still "strictly and legally speaking, states of the American Union, having their boundaries, divisions, subdivisions, and laws, but as having no administration, and no government, except such as may have been provided by the United States, and which must be continued until the time shall come when the loyal people of the states acting under the protection and authority of the United States—but so far as practicable under the forms of their own laws—may properly and safely be permitted to set up governments for themselves—" a policy, it may be remarked, substantially the same as Mr. Lincoln's.

AFTER NINE YEARS IN CONGRESS

It may be doubted whether Israel Washburn's career would not have been more notable if he had stayed in the House instead of leaving that field for the governorship of Maine. His reputation had risen steadily. He felt certain of himself and had demonstrated power as a party leader in the House. The politics of the state had become favorable to him. The legislature of 1854 had elected William Pitt Fessenden to the Senate. He was the rising star in Maine, and he and Washburn had been intimate political and personal friends for many years. As Fessenden's fortunes advanced he might reasonably count on the progress of his own. When Fessenden was elected to the Senate, Washburn sent him the following letter of congratulation:

> *Washington, 1854*
> I sent you three cheers this morning by telegraph, the same that Seward and old Wade and I gave when I communicated to them at Seward's house, three hours ago, the result of yesterday's work at Augusta. Pike (J. S.) is here, and happy. Badger says if Nebraska elected you, it has the merit of doing one good thing. In fine, we are all happy.
> Badger and Seward say the vote cannot be taken on the Nebraska bill, in all probability, before the end of the week. There are many to speak upon it. Seward, Pike, and others say, and I concur with them, that you ought to come on in season to speak against it. They want a speech fresh from the people, a word from the heart of freedom.[1]

[1] From Francis Fessenden's *William Pitt Fessenden* I, 40. The date of the letter is not given.

The state being republican in 1854, Isaac Reed, one of Washburn's friends, wrote from Walsboro, February 10, asking whether he would be willing to accept the post of judge of the supreme judicial court, "and if so would your constituents consent to your vacating your seat in Congress?"

But suggestions of a more exalted position than that of a state judge were made to him soon afterwards, and from this time forward were often repeated. Dr. A. Nourse wrote him from Bath, November 12, 1958.

> My dear Sir: I apprehend that, unless some pains are taken to give a special direction to public sentiment beforehand, we shall have trouble in selecting a candidate for Gov. to succeed Mr. Morrill—The ultra temperance folks, it is said, will insist on our taking a man of their stamp—and how disastrous that would be to the cause of Republicanism in Maine I need not spend time to demonstrate.
>
> Your name has often been mentioned, and always with favor, in connection with the nomination referred to, and if allowed to be used, would give a speedy quietus to the efforts of other aspirants—
>
> I have been pondering this matter ever since I had the pleasure of meeting you in Bath, and my conviction is that a simple acquiescence on your part in what should appear to be the general wish, so far from marring your future political prospects, would tend decidedly to their advancement.
>
> Allow me to hope therefore that you will in no way interfere to counteract the efforts of your friends or prevent the success of a movement which I regard as all important—
>
> Allow me, Sir, to congratulate you on the brilliant light thrown upon our prospects by the late elections, and to hope that I may hear from you at your earliest convenience—
>
> Ever faithfully yours.

To this the following reply was sent:

> *Orono, Nov. 16, 1859.*
> My dear Sir: I think there can be no difficulty in finding and agreeing upon a good candidate for Governor next year outside of the interest you refer to and I trust and believe there will be no occasion to use my name in that connection. You will not doubt me when I say, "I do not want to be the candidate," and there are quite a number of good men and good Republicans whose names have been mentioned as candidates with whom I could not consent to contend for the nomination.
> What I should feel bound to do in a contingency not likely to happen,—I mean in the event that there should be among the Republicans a very certain general, and earnest desire for my nomination, and those to whom I refer should not be in the field and our friends should feel that the cause would be essentially promoted by my being the Candidate, I need not say—for the case cannot arise, I am sure.
> But I thank you, my dear Doctor, for the very high compliment implied in the suggestions and request in your letter—and am
>
> Very truly yours.

So his friends combined and he was brought forward as a candidate for governor. The convention took place at Bangor in Norombega Hall, and two other candidates were brought forward—Abner Coburn of Bloomfield and William Willis of Portland. On the first ballot Washburn had 429 votes, Coburn 242 and Willis 52. Mr. Blaine had supported Coburn, but not aggressively. The importance of the nomination was recognized, for this was a presidential year and the state ticket must help the national ticket. The Democrats nominated Smart: and the Bell and Everitt (or Union) party, Barnes. Washburn's majority in the election was about 20,000, an increase over the majority which Morrill had received the year before of 5000 votes.

No one can doubt that the honor of being governor of Maine was agreeable to Washburn. E. G. Brooks wrote from New York, September 27, 1860, congratulating him on being elected governor and adding: "You ought to have staid in the House till you were elected to the Senate."

Those who urged his election to the governorship thought he would reach the Senate by that route.

He must succeed Hamlin when Hamlin should be Vice President. However, deeply interested as he was in everything pertaining to his state, and so much of a home man, he must have felt a thrill of pride at being called upon to preside over the state. He could remember how twenty years before he had gone to Augusta when John Fairfield was governor and the high respect which all classes and parties paid the governor. The old father and mother were still living, and to give them pride in their eldest son was not the least of the son's incentives. Then there were the brothers forging ahead in the West. There was rivalry and emulation among them and the advancement of one was an honor to them all. It is probable that Israel Washburn's first thought when anything important happened to him was, "What will the people at The Norlands and the younger brothers think?"

Before his own nomination he was intensely concerned about the nomination for the Presidency to be made by the Republican party. He had been a strong Seward man; he was still a Seward man; but the opposition which had followed Seward's conciliatory speeches had caused a falling away from that statesman, and it seemed to Washburn and some others that a compromise candidate might be possible, and that Fessenden could be brought forward. He had no sympathy with the movement to nominate Edward Bates of Missouri, who had attracted attention by his opposition to the slavery movement in Kansas, and had a record of long and honorable public service, for Bates was old and wedded to the old order and the times called for young men who could embrace new ideas.

James S. Pike in a letter of January 29, 1860, cast some light on the current trend of favor.

> *New York.*
> My dear Washburn: I don't like to be held up to answer categorically. But I will say this. Dana had a letter from Fitz Henry a few days ago in which he treats of the folly of going into the "crypt of the catacombs" for a presidential candidate, for which letter I expressed unbounded admiration and tried to get hold of but without success. I have pitched into Horace week after week on his candidate till I had something to do in shutting him up on the subject. I have been disposed to let the Bates' movement go on however, thinking it might work together for good for those that love the Lord, but I am told it is acquiring formidable proportions in the West and elsewhere.
>
> I was at a dinner here the other day given to Frank Blair and he let on a great head in regard to Bates. I do not see where things are coming out.
>
> I have had a very strong belief in Mr. Seward's nomination till Mr. Brown visited Virginia. That little incident has thrown a new cloud over the presidential track and I think obscured Mr. Seward's prospects not a little.
>
> Looking at Mr. Bates as heading the extra liberal wing of the Republicans and Mr. Seward as representing the other extreme, it seems to me as though Mr. Fessenden might be fairly viewed as holding a medium position, and thus turn up strong in the end.
>
> In that hope I at present abide. At any rate I am for Pitt, you are for Pitt, Maine is for Pitt. And in my opinion

Maine will have a good deal to do in settling the question
of the nomination ultimately. She certainly will if she is
well represented at the convention.

Very truly.

A. S. Murray to Washburn

Gorham May 25, 1860.

Dear Washburn: I am in receipt of your letter of the
22nd inst. and beg to refer you to your Brother C. C. W.
who was at Chicago last week, for the information desired.
I could not in an ordinary letter tell you but a small part
of what occurred there and caused the defeat of our friend
Seward.   Greeley and some other men from New York City
were very active, made all sorts of representations and left
no stone unturned to compass his defeat and then all the
Delegates from Penn. (dam their iron and coal) Ohio,
Indiana, Connecticut and little Rhode Island united in
representing that their States could not be carried for
Seward and that defeat with him as our candidate was
certain.

That old sinner F. P. Blair with his two cubs Frank and
Montgomery were very active and bitter against Seward
and did us a good deal of harm with the delegates from Virginia, Kentucky etc. who were inclined to go with us in the
beginning.   I hope no friend of Sewards will vote to give
Frank the seat he is contesting unless he makes a case so
clear that they cannot honestly vote against him and which
I am satisfied he has not made.

We were also embarrassed with the representations that
nearly every Republican U. S. Senator, with a large majority of the members of your House, were against S— and
believed his nomination would end in the defeat of the
party all of which had great weight with many members
of the Convention who were really friends of Seward.   I
regret to learn that so large a portion of the N. Y. members were against him and acting with Greeley and Co. and
believe that all, or nearly all, of them will get (even if they
do not ask it) leave of absence from a seat in the next

Congress. We are down on the *traitors* from our own
State—
I fully agree with you that an error was committed in the
organization of your House last Winter. . . .
There is a rumor circulating that *Senator Hamlin* wrote
to some of the Delegates from Maine advising the nomination of some other man than Seward and that his letter
lost Seward six votes from that State. If this report *is not
reliably contradicted* it will damage the Ticket seriously,
if not fatally, in this State. If the report is untrue the
friends of Hamlin cannot contradict it a moment too
early—The nomination of Lincoln would have been popular
in our State but for the slaughter of Seward. Our Party
for the moment appears paralyzed and if the Democratic
party had any vitality left we should be badly beaten as
so many of our true men say they will not lift a hand to
sustain the ticket, yet I hope and believe we shall carry the
State with a considerable slaughter among our members of
Congress.

Yours truly.

Then came a letter from Mr. Brooks giving concrete
news of the nominations.

180 W. 25th St. New York, June 7, 1860

Bro. Washburn: . . . Do the Senate really mean to
persist in their scoundrelism in respect to Kansas, and to
keep her out?
What, behind the scenes, do they say about the Chicago
nomination? Lincoln is so much better than I feared we
shd. get that I am well satisfied. He is a strong straight
out, *live man*—I heard him here last winter, and liked him
very much. I was afraid we shd. get Bates or some purely
expediency candidate, resurrectionized and galvanized for
the occasion. Seward is terribly cross and sore, isn't he?
I have not been so much of a Seward man since hearing his
speech, as I was before. I especially disliked his with-
holding Greeley's letter, when his friends are so using, and

Greeley is so demanding it. It looks badly. I was disappointed that Cassius Clay was not nominated for V. P.
I think it wd. have strengthened the ticket and was due to
him.

Truly.

E. G. Brooks.

P. S. The Register says there are State Conventions in
Alabama, Georgia, N. Carolina, and S. Carolina. But S. C.
has had no connection with us in the way of Representation
since 1848, and the others have never had any. Moreover
I am informed that these States with Mississippi, organized
what they called "The General Southern Convention of
(Unionists)" in 1858, professedly subordinate to our Gen.
Conv. but that has never paid any attention to us. Do you
think it worth while for us as a Com. to take any notice of
these Convents? My judgment says no. What says
yours? . . .

The nomination of Hannibal Hamlin for the vice
Presidency on the ticket with Lincoln would leave a vacancy in the Senate. Washburn seems to have thought
the time not appropriate for his candidacy, but there was
a formidable movement in his favor. George F. Talbot
wrote him on October 22.

Mathias Me.

My dear Sir: The turn the elections are taking brings up
the Senatorial question in this State with considerable
interest. I have heretofore both by letter and in conversation expressed my preference for you for this place. If I
am not mistaken in our last conversation you doubted if
it would do for you to be a candidate, and expressed the
wish that your friends should do nothing to bring you forward. Will you at an early day and confidentially let
me know your present views and personal wishes in this
matter.

Yourself being withdrawn from the list of candidates, if
you still so desire, what man will be best calculated to defeat the rather too palpable intrigues of Gov. Morrill? I

have had the name of Mr. Morse suggested. What do you think of him, his qualifications and his strength? He is in the same region of the State under the same political antecedents as Mr. Fessenden, the other Senator.

It can be shown that the old Free-Soil party contributed about 25 pr ct of the present Republican party, as large a quota as the Democratic party contributed. And yet the latter faction which has had a lion's share of the party patronage has insisted in alternating with Whig party in all the leading offices of the State and nation. Now that Hamlin is to be promoted in the Senate, not taken out of it, the democratic element will insist that unless Morrill is sent into the Senate too the equilibrium will be disturbed. Might not a successful claim be made now for a sufficiently well known politician of anti-slavery antecedents by way of distributing equitably the representation among the different elements of the party! Please write me briefly your views.

With sincere Respect and highest confidence
Truly yrs.

The rising force in Maine politics, James G. Blaine, had already formed an alliance with Lot M. Morrill and Morrill was sent to the Senate in Hamlin's place. It is hard to ascertain precisely what was Blaine's attitude towards Washburn, but he was assiduous in his efforts to win his friendship. He wrote:

Augusta Dec. 1/60.

My dear Sir: . . . What time will you be in Augusta? There are certain topics of *home concern* which perhaps ought to be touched upon in your Inaugural and concerning which you will have to obtain the minutiae here—

There is considerable feeling in some quarters for the repeal of our "personal Liberty Law"—but I think we shall be able to check it quietly but effectually—I will have an article of some length next week, bearing on the subject—Will send it to you.

> I greatly dislike the idea of our . . . MC's in this State—
> not merely for the loss of dignity but because it will em-
> barrass us politically in several localities and in several
> respects—
> What is the need of tying the number of Reps. down to
> 233? Make the ratio 110,000 (enough in all conscience!)
> and the house wd consist of some 275 or 280—No State
> would lose on its present Representation and it would
> create an unbounded number of Republican members in the
> populous North West—It wd be in every respect a grand
> party movement for us—The only objection that wd be
> used wd be the addtnl expense, but the people dont care a
> fig for that—especially when it is set over against their
> *State Pride*—
>
> In grt haste
Your friend truly.

Washburn attended his last Congress in December,
1860. As soon as the House organized he announced that
he could not serve on the Committee of Ways and Means
as his seat would be vacant on January 1. On December
18 he informed the House that he had sent the resignation of his seat to the governor of Maine. On the day before, December 17, Mr. Adrian offered resolutions reciting that the Constitution was the supreme law of the
land and that the House deprecated the unconstitutional
laws of some states and recommended their repeal, and
Washburn announced that he could not vote for the resolution because he had not sufficient evidence to justify
him in saying the personal liberty laws were unconstitutional. Only thirteen others joined him in voting against
the resolutions. These were the last remarks he made in
Congress. There seemed to be an overweening desire in
Congress to pass resolutions favoring the Union and condemning personal liberty laws.

From this atmosphere he went directly to Augusta to be governor of Maine.

The result of his nine years of congressional service had been to form in his mind a definite political philosophy which is interesting and which fortunately he recorded. In January, 1858, appeared in the *Universalist Quarterly* an article by him on modern civilization. The subject was a large one and he discussed it in a large spirit, with elevation of thought and the stately and eloquent diction which the subject demanded.

"What," he said, "is our modern civilization,—its tendency and destiny, its dangers and hopes? Has it done its best, exhausted its powers, and is it unrobing for a final repose? Must it be with this as it has been with all former civilizations? Shall its history

> Be but the same rehearsal of the past,
> First Freedom and then Glory—when that fails,
> Wealth, vice, corruption—barbarism at last?

We propose to state some of the considerations which have conducted us to the belief that these questions must receive different and more encouraging answers than the tones of impatience and despondency in which they are so often asked, would seem to anticipate."

Was it true that the power of civilization was exhausted? When did it pass its meridian? Not at the beginning of the eighteenth century, nor at the middle of the seventeenth. There were more wars then, than now; the condition of the masses was worse; crimes were more frequent; manners more coarse. Not at the beginning of the nineteenth century. Since then the steamboat and railroad had brought mankind into neighborship. Never was there a time when labor brought in such large rewards as it did now; never were the means of education and improvement so abundant. The spirit of the pulpit was better. There were sermons on toleration, kindness and charity. The laws showed a more enlightened spirit.

The civilization of the ancient world was sure to decay from causes which do not affect our civilization. It was built upon the principles and in the spirit of force. The best cultivated nations of antiquity were engaged in constant wars with other nations, and in subjugation of tribes and peoples. The consequences were luxury and corruption on the side of the few, poverty and slavery with their usual vices on the part of the many. Conquest supplied wealth; wealth begot luxury, wastefulness and corruption. The patrician became effeminate, the plebeian brutal.

"In the fulness of time an Anointed was sent upon the earth to deliver a gospel and illustrate its truth and beauty by a perfect example. This gospel was destined to work a complete revolution in human affairs. It spoke of the brotherhood of man, of the dignity of human nature." A new civilization was formed; the principle upon which it should be founded had been revealed. Civilization had progressed since then slowly, because so much of the old spirit of force remained and was so long in disappearing. Nations still went to war; slavery existed in America, and many now supported it as a good and a right, many whose fathers had pronounced it an evil and a wrong.

"So long as the slaveholders were pleased to make no overt efforts to extend the system of slavery, it was easy and safe for men in either section to talk well and humanely concerning it; but when its inherent necessities required a revelation of its true nature, and compelled the work of aggression upon which it has entered,—when it had succeeded, after the death of General Jackson, in

wresting to its uses the powerful and long-dominant party
of which he was for many years the unrivalled chieftain
if not the acknowledged founder, it became unsafe to speak
of it in terms of condemnation which had been usual in
the North and had been tolerated in the South, and political annihilation awaited any one who did so. Then
shallow and false men, politicians by trade and mere
demagogues, those who make the most noise at the corners
of the streets, in coal-holes and bar-rooms," began to admit
that slavery was not wrong, then to say it was perfectly
right.

But when the final trial should come the North would
be found to be sound. When they should come to perceive
that slavery aggression would, if it was not resisted,
destroy freedom, the masses would rise.

There was danger that the money power would become
centralized and "our eyes must rest occasionally on the
statutes of distribution, as well as those of accumulation."
The perfect state of society was to produce as much as men
need and not to require the time of all to accomplish the
result. Sidney Smith was not wholly wrong when he
defended material aids against mere sentiment. "'What,'
exclaimed the witty parson, 'is the object of all government? The object of all government is roast mutton,
potatoes, claret, a stout constable, an honest justice, a
clean highway, a free chapel.'"

Society had reached the point where the development
of the physical resources of the world was required, and
to aid this development was the appointed business of
mankind. "The press, the steamship, the railway, the
telegraph, all unknown to the old civilization, are the
servants of ours." There were nobler and better things
than material things; but we were fated to depend, in

striving for them, in no slight manner on the friendly services of material things.

> "Here then we rest; rest in confidence upon our Christian civilization—upon the efficiency of the instrumentalities which are founded on the theory that all reform must proceed from the inner life; that it must be of slow growth, extending from the individual to communities, and from communities till it embraces the race; rest in faith that outward things have their uses in this development, and, truly employed, will never prejudice the highest interests of human nature."

WAR GOVERNOR

From his friends and associates in Congress he received genuine congratulations on his election as governor.

JOHN ALLISON TO WASHBURN

New Brighton Penna. December 29th 1860.

Hon. I. Washburn

My Dear Sir: I congratulate you upon your election to the Chief Magistracy of Maine, yet I am sorry that you leave the Halls of Congress. I hope that the Legislature of Maine will serve you as they did Hamlin and send you back to Washington to fill a Seat in the Senate Chamber. I have had various experiences since I saw you, have been much of my time in the West, without being *pecuniarily* benefited. We have gained a great Victory in the election of Lincoln. And our opponents modestly ask us to administer the Government upon their principles, and we have some fools and some knaves in our ranks, who would be willing to do so, could they but get into good comfortable positions. We are fast approaching the time when we will know who are Republicans and who are but Camp followers. What do you think of that old popeyed "pub func" who occupies the Presidential Chair. Is he less a traitor than Cobb. I was right glad the old Genl. Cass left the treasonable camp.

I wish to ask your influence in my behalf and in doing so, bear with me while I write some things which I deem necessary, to a correct understanding of my position.

It is now nearly ten years since we made the acquaintance of each other, in all that time the country has been gradually approaching the political position, which you and I occupied ten years ago. We were far in advance of the old Whig party—shed our tears over its grave—they were

81

but few of them, and not large—inasmuch as it adopted the
Baltimore platform.—And we were in at the birth and
baptism of the Republican party. In my State I was far
in advance of those who now constitute the Republican
party.

I was not a Cameron man, went to Chicago to oppose
him, and did more than any other score of men in the
State to prevent him having *control of our delegation at
Chicago*, and did "fight a good fight" for three days in our
delegation, in opposition to Thad. Stevens. David Wilmot,
G. A. Purveance and others, and afterwards with Stevens
gave the Delegation to *Lincoln* on third choice, *instead* of
Bates, which decided the nomination. I was there as an
Anti Cameron Man. My district preferred Seward and I
would never even consent to compliment such a man as
Cameron, let his wealth and position be what it might. For
this I expected to be marked and proscribed by Cameron
and his followers, and as long as it was supposed that he
would be in the Cabinet, I did not intend to make application for any position, but as Wilmot is to be our Cabinet
officer, I have concluded to ask my old friends who know
me, to "lend me a hand" while I try to make head against
the flunkeys, who now expect to dispense the patronage,
through the influence of Genl. Cameron.

I want a letter from you to Mr. Lincoln, saying to him
what you know of me, as an honest trustworthy man, and
I want you to give me such Credit for consistent fidelity
to the great principles which underlie the Republican Organization—long before the Republican party came into
existence as a party, as you may think I deserve. I do not
know what I will ask for, but I think that few in Pennsylvania have stronger claims upon the party, and surely none
who have stronger claims upon Mr. Lincoln. Your aid in
this matter will be gratefully remembered.

I hope I do not presume too much upon our former
friendship, in making this application. If I do, you will
at least pardon the freedom with which I have written to
you. With many wishes for your health and happiness
I remain Truly Your friend.

When Washburn was elected governor of Maine he and other Republican governors were well aware that a crisis confronted them and that more would be required from them than the regular duties of governor in ordinary times.

Washburn and E. D. Morgan, the governor of New York, had a conference when Washburn passed through New York on his way to Augusta at which it appears other governors were present.

E. D. MORGAN TO WASHBURN

Private   *New York—20th Dec. 1860.*
   My dear Governor: I have your note from Washington. I wish you to come directly to 143—17th. St. where I am staying with a relative.   No persons except Governors will be present.   I wish the meeting a private one so it cannot be at a Hotel, I shall be there at 7 o'clock this evening.
                                        Truly yours.

Governor Washburn's first message was delivered to both houses of the legislature, January 3, 1861.   It was prepared with great care, the English was formal and the views put forth were his matured policy for the welfare of his state.

The state was prosperous, he said.   "It may be doubted that the sun, in his whole course, visits a community whose members are more clear of financial embarrassments, or who are more generally in possession of the means and accessories of comfort and independence than those among whom our lot has been cast."

Maine outstripped all the other states in ship-building, furnishing at least two-fifths of the sailing tonnage of the entire merchant-service.   No state could be better situated for prosecuting the fisheries.   It had exceptionally good water power with the most eligible sites for manufacturing. Large deposits of iron had been found in the counties of Piscataquis and Aroostook and the slate near Bangor was superior to that of Wales. The lumber in the forests seemed inexhaustible. The soil yielded under proper cultivation better returns on account of its proximity to good markets "than the fat acres of the West." The duty of the state government, then, was to take measures "to enlarge our commerce, to place the great business of ship-building on a surer and stronger footing, to extend the employment of our carriers, to increase the number and enhance the profits of our nearby fishermen, to attract the investment of capital in the manifold varieties of manufactures for which the state is preëminently adapted, to work the mines of Katahdin, and open those of Aroostook, to enable Brownville and the neighboring towns to supply the markets of America with slate, to systematize the operations and diversify the employments of those engaged in the lumber trade, and, by all these, to give new incitements and ampler recompense to those who till the soil, by creating an increased demand and nearer markets for the fruits of their industry."

In the Aroostook section was a large area of good land owned by the state and unoccupied. He favored encouragement of Norwegian emigration to it and state assistance to transportation schemes to make it accessible. The best mode was to encourage the European and North American Railway, the great international highway. In this the general government should help. "While I cannot encourage the hope that an application for aid for this work from the Federal Government would meet with sufficient favor at Washington to ensure its success at the present time, and under existing circumstances, its importance to the whole country as well as the government itself, and the sacrifices which Maine so generously made in 1842, of her clear and indisputable rights of property and jurisdiction, for the benefit of the whole country, persuade me that the grant of such aid as might be necessary to effect its accomplishment, would be both wise and just."

He followed with national affairs.

This government, he said, had not been established to advance the interests of slavery. The fathers had, on the contrary, contemplated its restriction and ultimate extinction. The prohibition of the slave trade; recognition of fugitives from labor and service as "persons" and not as property and therefore not reclaimable by any process applicable to property; Jefferson's ordinance of 1784 for the Northwest territory, Dane's of 1787, and the law of 1791 showed this. "Slavery was a weakness, an impolicy, an evil with all; with many, a sin. It was the child of municipal law, local, sectional—not national." But its weakness required for its protection that it should be expanded. Whence the history of its assumptions and claims for the last forty years? It demanded the admission of Missouri as a slave state in 1820; had the Indians removed from Alabama and Georgia in 1830 and from Georgia in 1840; in 1850 obtained an abandonment of the principles of the ordinance of 1787 and had a new and severe fugitive slave law passed. To all of this from the love of peace and the Union, the North had submitted. In 1854 it had thrown the virgin fields of Kansas and Nebraska open to slavery and in 1855 and '56 had begun a reign of violence and terror in Kansas in order that freemen might be driven from it and it brought into the Union as a slave state. The country had been aroused and had elected Abraham

Lincoln and Hannibal Hamlin and a crisis had been precip-
itated. No concessions would be satisfactory to the slave
states which did not secure to them the right of expansion and protection of their peculiar property and the
North could not make such a concession. "But, if not,
we are told that the slave states, or a portion of them, will
withdraw from the Union. No, they will not. They can
not go, and in the end they will not want to go. They
would know that their strength and happiness lay in the
Union. They will learn, as they should know already, that
the people of the free states have no intention of intermed-
dling with their system in the states where it exists by
virtue of the local law, and that they will cheerfully extend
to them all their constitutional and equal rights." It
behooved the North to set itself right without abat-
ing one jot the principles affirmed in the late election.
The personal liberty bills of some of the free states had
been the cause of crimination on the part of most people
in the South and of many in the North. He believed
they had been passed to prevent the kidnapping of free
persons of color and to bring state action into accord
with Supreme Court decrees; but if the laws had in any
state been enacted in violation of the Constitution or
of any constitutional law of Congress, although they
were then mere waste paper, they ought to be repealed.
If Maine had such laws they ought to be repealed. If its
laws were not unconstitutional then "when such action
(as their repeal) is demanded as the condition upon which
you are to be permitted to enjoy your constitutional rights,
your civil and political freedom, you are forbidden to yield
to the requisition by every consideration that can have
weight among men fit to be free." The concessions which
had been demanded of the free states were inadmissible

not only in themselves, but because they were concessions. To grant them would be a dangerous precedent and a transfer of government from the hands of the many to the power of the few. As for secession it had been denied as a right by all the statesmen of the republic up to the present time and all treasonable endeavors against the United States would fail. In such an event all parties would disappear in Maine and all would be patriots and defenders of the Union. He believed that moderation and steadfastness of the free states and the good sense and patriotism of all would save the country from strife.

The message met with general commendation. The Bangor *Whig and Courier* said (January 5, 1861) it was one of the ablest and most patriotic state papers ever presented to the people of Maine. Henry L. Dawes, then a representative from Massachusetts, wrote from Washington, January 6, 1861:

> It was as admirable in tone and temper as in matter—statesmanlike in statement, patriotic in sentiment, and fearless in position. I am glad to perceive that even at your great distance it still appears to you that "they are not going out."

EDWARD KENT TO WASHBURN

Bangor Jany. 6, 1861.

My dear Governor: . . . I have read your message, and this itself is a compliment from an Ex Governor, and I can say to you as, according to your story, Inman or Mc Phetres or some of your up river constituents said to Maj. Tropton when he asked four and sixpence a yard for cotton cloth, "I like your talk."

I have not written a word on the matter, but I have thought it over, and turned it on all sides, and have at times

been a little uncertain in my mind as to what course duty
and patriotism and the Union, required. But I have settled
down in the full assurance that the time has fully come,
when nothing is to be gained, but everything lost, by
temporising or compromising principles and fundamental
doctrines. The fact is, nothing will satisfy unless we yield
all the platform we have announced, fought for and conquered under, and, yet more, cease talking about slavery,
or even thinking it anything short of the perfection of
justice, wisdom and humanity. Now, we may as well meet
the issue. I for one am ready to stand on the doctrine
that slavery is local and cannot exist where there is no law
of the place to create or acknowledge it; and that it cannot
rightfully go or be carried or exist in the territories. I think
also that true policy is to be firm as our granite rocks, but
to say and do nothing unnecessarily to excite feeling. I
am willing to go as far as we can to conciliate, and aid the
friends of the Union in the South and particularly in the
border States. I would yield nothing to fear or threats,
but I would not hesitate to do what public good required
through the unmanly fear of being taunted with cowardice
and retreating. I think our friends owe it to Pres. Lincoln
to strengthen his arm by removing all stumbling blocks
from the Union Cause, and thereby bringing to the support of the new administration the great body of the honest
and patriotic democrats. For one I care but little comparatively for our liberty act, as it is called.—As it stands
it amounts to nothing. A law to be of any use should contain provisions to protect personal liberty and rights. I
think we should not act at all on the subject at this moment,
but wait a time to see if it will do any good to move in the
matter of repeal. I admired your decided declaration that
the South would not go out, and would not want to. I
think there has been a good deal of "method in their
madness," and that the leaders intended to try this as the
last desperate remedy, like quicksilver in a case of stoppage
in the bowels. The great fear is that the mass or the mob
will run beyond the leaders and force them to fight—for a
time. Well—if we must fight, why let us fight. Let us at

all events say that if the Union must be dissolved, so far as the secession dissolves it, unless we yield the point that Slavery is national,—why it must be. At present and until a severance in some way, the laws must be enforced and the supremacy of the Union over State secession and individual rebellion, treason or violation of the laws must be enforced at every hazard—It will be time enough then to talk about a peaceable separation.

Permit me to say that your message is written in an excellent style—clear, forcible, earnest without the spread eagle to *high falute*, or the dull ass to stupify and leaden it.

I almost forgot to thank you for your hints to the Legislature touching our poor salaries. I hope they will find time at least to consider the matter. I know that the people everywhere expect and hope that justice will be done to the hard worked and poorly paid judges.

I trust you find the old quarters comfortable and the chair of State with a soft cushion—

Very truly
Your friend.

SENATOR PRESTON KING OF NEW YORK TO WASHBURN

Washington Jany. 8, 1861.

Dear Sir: I congratulate you on your entrance upon your new duties by the able and patriotic address you have made to your Legislature. I have read that part of it which relates to national affairs with gratification and thank you for sending it to me.

I do not believe there is any real danger to the Union of the States, though if half of what we hear be true, armed force may be required to maintain the supremacy of the constitution and laws in some of the States—If the influence of Traitors had not paralyzed for a time the Executive here it would not have been necessary in my opinion to fire a gun to maintain the authority of the Federal Government—The administration is now straitening up—and if we can escape the commission of any folly by Congress for the next two

months as I have some hope we may, we shall soon find
peace and safety after the 4th of March under a sound and
vigorous administration guided by the principles and
example of the Government under Washington and Jefferson—
With my kind rememberance
Yours truly.

A. Nourse to Washburn

Bath, Jany. 18th, 1861.
My dear Sir: The history and result of the late political
conflict in this city have awakened in my mind a train of
anxious reflections which I hope may prove altogether
groundless but I cannot be at peace with myself if I fail
to disclose them. . . .

Again—Is anybody wise enough to see how civil war
is to be avoided? Attendant upon it, should it come, must
be prostration of business and consequent distress—The
whole roundly and vociferously charged upon the Republican party—unjustly of course. But it was predicted on all
hands that the election of Lincoln would produce this result, and the result did immediately follow. What more
natural than for weak and willing minds to connect them
together as cause and effect? Does not the history of this
country abundantly prove that it is a fearful thing to any
party that a general stagnation of business, from whatever
cause, should happen to occur while they hold the reins of
govt.?

Is there no danger that, even in this state, under the
operation of these two causes, our immense majority will
melt away in a single year? I know well that in the hey
day of prosperity, prophets of evil are but little heeded—
and I have myself ordinarily but little sympathy with their
croakings—But it is sometimes well to snuff a danger in the
distance. I am free to say that if we in all the N. E. States,
take ground as a party against repeal, we shall cripple our
strength prodigiously—and if to this be added civil war,
our danger of defeat this very year would be imminent.

For our avowed principles I would fight to the death—but against being led into false and dangerous issues I solemnly protest—And now Sir, let me conclude by saying that I have the utmost confidence in your political sagacity as well as firmness—and if you have already considered the subject in the light I have endeavored to present it, of course all this goes for nothing—But whatever view you may take of the matter, I have no fear of your charging me with impertinent interference, or of acting from any other than patriotic motives.

I have now discharged my conscience, and have only to add that, come weal or come woe,

I am
Yours ever.

Charles B. Sedgwick of Syracuse, N. Y., was serving his first term in Congress. He wrote to Washburn:

Washington, 25 Jany. 1861.

My dear Israel: . . . . As to standing firm—I find myself leaning the other way and pretty soon I shall become a confirmed secessionist, and if any slave state shows signs of staying in the Union I shall want to apply a little "vis a tergo" and help them out. I don't propose at all events to give any of them anything for staying in the Union.

As for Seward's speech I am frank to say I don't like it—not that it really offers any premium in particular for rascality and treachery, but it seems to, and it furnishes skulking ground for those who wish to dodge and compromise. It is the speech of an adroit politician rather than of a great statesman. If I understand it and "the Court thinks she does," it sets out with most magnificent rhetoric the great value of the Union—it is therefore a great object to preserve it. How?—Not by going on man-fashion to execute and enforce the laws, but by conciliation. To do it—1. I will advise the states to repeal their Personal Liberty laws. 2. I would amend the Constitution. 3. I would with certain conditions vote for a Convention to amend the Constitution. 4. I would make laws against invasion of States.   5. A Southern Pacific R. Road.

When you look at it the offer is certainly not a large one—but to save so precious and valuable a Union I will give a little more. Eliot would make a larger bid, and when you get down to the weaker brethren they would make the States all slave to save the Union. The principle being given up that it is lawful to compromise, it becomes a question of degree. The speech has hurt Seward and shaken the confidence of many of his strongest friends. I cannot but look upon it as demoralizing. Adams proposes to take New Mexico but has executed a flank movement preparatory to a run which old Cherubusco might envy. Sherman will vote for New Mexico. Some of our people will vote all Corwin's propositions and they expect to carry them and very likely will. I don't think W. will be attacked. Scott will rake these old avenues in a way that Washington and his old French engineer never dreamed of when they laid them out. He will be disappointed if his plans fail for want of an Enemy. Mrs. S. Leaves home tomorrow morning for this City. She means to be in at the death. . . .

I hope you are coming on at the head of the Penobscot rangers. I should like to see you in epaulettes and feathers. The speaker (William Pennington of New Jersey) goes on with great *Bonhommy*. He says he has stopped drinking but his nose is a plain denial of his speech. We want you back here. Your successor is a man we should hate to lose but think his health would be better in Maine. Can't you swap offices with him.

Good bye

Truly yours.

After Lincoln's inauguration it became apparent that the governor's prognostications of peace without attempt at disunion were mistaken. The Southern states were, in fact, forming a separate government and the general government was doing nothing to prevent it. Some Republicans seemed to be indifferent on the subject.

GEORGE F. TALBOT TO WASHBURN

Mathias—March 21, 1861.

Dear Governor: . . . Well we are getting along as well as we could expect. Maine was saved from disgracing herself. The President turned up on *our* side. No compromises were adopted. The crisis will continue. The South will stay seceded, and ought to. Success to the New Confederacy at least until they are wholly and irreclaimably gone from us! All the Slave States ought to go with them, and be encouraged to go rather than bribed to stay. At the least a decision to stay in the Union ought to be regarded as a *decision to enter upon a course of gradual emancipation*. Let us not have the shame and peril of *disunion*, and yet retain the element of our danger and weakness. I go for a new Capital on Lake Erie, the acquisition of Canada and the provinces, a Rail Road from Lake Superior to Puget Sound, a great empire on both sides the Great Lakes and Maine, the great commercial point of entering and departure of a gigantic European trade!

Accept my own and Mrs. T's acknowledgment for the honor conferred upon us by Mrs. Washburn's invitation to her levee in the capital which circumstances made it impossible for us to accept.

Truly yours.

The next month brought matters to a crisis and the letters to Governor Washburn show the various aspects it assumed.

MONCURE DANIEL CONWAY TO WASHBURN

Commonwealth Office Boston, April 6.

Hon. Israel Washburn:

My dear Sir: As everything in England just now, as concerns our country, turns upon the Slavery question—which lots of Southerners are trying to smother over there—the friends of our cause (particularly P. A. Taylor,—M. P.

for Leicester; F. W. Newman and S. D. Collett) think they
could make much of their side if they had me over there to
give my lectures on Slavery as it is. This has been responded to by some gentlemen over here who have given
something towards paying my expenses for spending 4 or
5 months over there, speaking at Union and Emancipation
meetings etc. on all occasions. On diligent inquiry we
find that I shall need upwards of a thousand dollars (the
way gold is now selling). It is thought best not to make any
public call on the subject but to solicit subscriptions from a
few persons who, it may be supposed, would be interested
in the matter.

We have already had raised here about $600—Can you
or any friends near you in any way swell the amount? If
so please send what you can give to Wendell Phillips, Esq.,
or to

Yours cordially.

P. S. I shall probably go next Saturday per "City of
Washington" from New York, but whatever is sent will be
sent out to me as I need it. Kind regards and adieus to
Mrs. W.

From J. G. Fellowes

Nashville, Tenn. Apr. 24th 1861.

My dear Sir: When I had the pleasure to rec. a letter
from you a few weeks since, I little thought that we were
upon the eve of events such as are now transpiring. I am
impelled to address you this letter, by the desire that you
should understand the state of public sentiment here. I
greatly fear that the position of Tenn. and of the other
Border States has been misapprehended at the North. But
if this has been the case, that error with reference to the
sentiments of the people of Tenn. at least is about to be
dissipated.

I was in Nashville yesterday. It was a day of more
intense excitement than I have ever before witnessed. But
a few weeks ago we had an exciting canvass for delegates to
the State Convention: I then saw the Candidates of the

Union party stand up before the people and plead the cause of the Union with an energy and a pathos that I have never before witnessed. You are apprised of the result of that election. Out of about 4000 votes in this County but 700 were given for the Secession candidates. But yesterday I saw the same Union candidates stand up before the same people and, with sad countenances and tremulous voices tell them that the last lingering ray of hope had been extinguished. That the events which were upon them, and which had been brought upon them without any agency of theirs, had rendered it indispensable that they should arm in defence of the rights of the South—that her destiny must be our destiny. There are but two classes of men here. All who are not secessionists, proclaim themselves revolutionists. I am satisfied that no man could have carried the flag of the deserted Union through the streets of Nashville yesterday without being in danger of losing his life. I suppose that Andrew Johnson is the most odious man among all parties in Tenn. of any man in America, not excepting Mr. Lincoln himself,—for it is thought here that he has been instrumental in misleading the North with respect to the public sentiment of the State.

We are now on the eve of momentous events. It is impossible to foresee the result. But knowing as I do, the feeling of the Slaveholding States, I feel safe in predicting, that if this contest is to end in the subjugation of the South neither you nor I shall live to see the return of peace. No earthly power can conquer a people, animated with the spirit that now pervades this people. They may be exterminated but they will never be conquered. While the minds of men are in such a state of excitement there are men at the North who take a diabolical satisfaction in adding fuel to the flame. One gentleman in Nashville received a letter yesterday from Philadelphia boasting that they were going to march an army of 25000 negroes upon the South to set the Slaves free. Another gentleman received a document yesterday from the North, on which was written "John Brown is not dead." Are you surprised that the public mind is excited here under such circumstances?

Whatever may be your opinion respecting the originators of this unhappy strife I think you must at least allow the merit of sincerity to the great masses of the Southern people. They do most sincerely and religiously believe, that their all is at stake. With them it appears a life and death struggle. I have lived in Tenn. for sixteen years and never did I hear a disunion sentiment expressed until the last few months.

It has cost the people of Tenn. and Ky. as well as Va. a mighty struggle to come to the conclusion, at which they have now arrived. I see no means by which the dreadful calamity of civil war can be averted. I pray God to raise up some arm sufficiently powerful to quell the rising storm.

I have spent the best part of my life among the people of the South. All my earthly interests are identified with them. I am incapable of becoming disloyal to them in this, the hour of their calamity. I have witnessed the heroic struggle of that gallant band of loyal men who succeeded in driving back the waves of secession from our borders. I had rejoiced greatly in the result of that contest. But alas the events of the last few days have made it a barren victory. I was at church this morning, at a quiet little country church. I heard a lady remark after I returned home that every lady in the church was weeping. Several of the young men, sons of the ladies present had volunteered, and were expecting to be ordered away to the South.

But I have written a longer letter than I intended. I should rejoice to hear something from you, to encourage the hope of a return of more peaceful times.

I have spent the most of my life as a teacher, am still employed in that dignified vocation.

Yours truly.

This letter would have dispelled, finally, the governor's doubts about the South being in earnest, had not the President's proclamation calling for 75,000 volunteers been issued, April 15, and already the state a camp.

The following letters give an expression of its impetus.

J. C. DICKERSON TO WASHBURN

Belfast, April 29/61.

Dear Governor: Sixty four men took the oath today in Capt. Cunningham's company and many more are ready to join.

Capt. Marshal is fast filling up the City Grays who now number 45. Mr. Nickerson, my deputy at Searsport, is doing a fine business—thirty enlisted the first day, and ten have gone over from this place this morning. This company will be full I presume, this week. The solid men of Searsport without distinction of party, are nobly urging on the volunteers.—

A few traitors here have embarrassed enlistment, but they are now spotted, and can do little harm.

Report says that the people surrounded the house of Webster Treat, of Frankfort, and that he fled to escape the halter. This is the same Treat that wrote to Atlanta Ga. last January? assuring the traitors that the "black republicans" had got to walk over the dead bodies of 53,000 democrats before they could reach the south.

I think that another company could be raised here, now that the war spirit is fully aroused.

I am looking after matters in a quiet way.

Truly Yours

P. S.   A. D. Bean of Brooks is laboring hard to get up a company—I learn from a good Union man of that town, that Andrew is really in earnest, enlisted 12 the first day and has a good prospect of filling up his company in a few days—The town of Brooks has called a town meeting to aid in the cause.

J. G. D.

F. H. MORSE TO WASHBURN

London, May 25th, 1861.

My dear Governor: I often think of you and my native State in these striving times.   Unfortunate and sad as the condition of things is in our country, Americans never had occasion to feel more proud of their country than now. The universal and patriotic uprising of a great people for the preservation of their government and free institutions is a most grand exhibition and one that will make a mark in history. It is looked upon in Europe with astonishment, though a great many trading people with the London Times as their organ are continually grumbling at the North, say we want to oppress them and ought to let them go peaceably etc. We have constantly to battle against wrong impressions here. Many merchants here are very ignorant about American affairs, and I can add with justice rather selfish and can see no merit in anything that don't tend to advance their trade. But I believe the heart of the English nation is sound and in sympathy with the North in the great struggle going on there.

I keep a close lookout for all shipments of munitions of war intended for the rebels, ships and suspicious craft of every kind. On landing at Liverpool and finding no consul there and no one taking much interest I employed a man from our State who happened to be there, just the right sort of man to keep on the lookout for all the movements of traders in that port. They do not find ready success here in purchasing goods because their credit is not very good and they have now much trouble or would have if attempted, in shipping anything. No doubt they get off some stuff to Cuba and ports in the Gulf of Mexico, taking their chance in getting them in.

My main object in writing to you now is to say if our State wants any rifles to arm our troops the best English rifle made can now be had here by ordering at once of Mr. Crowningshield the authorized agent for Massachusetts. He came over with me and brought letters of credit for large sums and has fortunately secured *all* the first class rifles that were for sale in London, Birmingham, etc. and all that can be made for some months. There are plenty of guns they call first class but for some defect they have been rejected. Mr. C. has with him a practical gun maker from Springfield, from the Ames factory, and a member of the firm. He has lived in London two or three years setting up machinery from America for manufacturing arms and has great facilities, being known to all the master gun makers. He with his men, inspects all Massachusetts purchases and they are equal to any rifle now in use. These rifles can be delivered in the States for about $16—each, a perfect article, lower than rejected guns can be delivered for by some other parties purchasing here because there is no commission or profit to pay on them. If you want any for our volunteers therefore you can get a cheaper and better article in this way than in any other. They are, Mr. McFarland the practical man from Mass.,—says equal to the best Springfield U. States gun. Ohio has a part of the Massachusetts purchase, but Maine can be supplied if in want. About 2000 are shipped per week, the Whitworth and other rifles. Cannon can be also had; also steamers suitable for any purpose, only we must be a little careful how we reach them.

If I can be of any aid to our good old State please command me. With my best regards to Mrs. Washburn I remain.

Yours truly.

BION BRADBURY TO WASHBURN

Strictly confidential. *Eastport, July 27, 1861.*
My dear Sir: I esteem it as of the highest importance, nay as indispensable to the full success of the Government in suppressing the rebellion, that the free States should remain united in their feelings of loyalty.

It cannot have escaped your observation that in some democratic quarters an attempt is making to alienate the people from the noble cause in which we are engaged. To arouse the Spirit of party, with its prejudices, its pride, its resentments, its animosities, its spirit of revenge, is now the work of a class of men who cannot forget party long enough to save the country.

That the Republican party, (I should speak more correctly perhaps to say individuals in the Republican party) is furnishing the *material* for the organization of an anti-war party by very injudicious language and by some most indiscreet acts, is very apparent.

I am very desirous that the unity of the loyal sentiment in the North should be maintained, for transparent reasons.

Allow me to suggest to you that it would be wise to offer a commission as Colonel to Gen. S. I. Anderson of Portland. I saw him last week. His sympathies are with the South—but he is a high-toned, honorable man. He is the best military man now in the State, and would make the best Colonel of any man in the State. We *need* such men in the service. If he accepts, he will make a true, loyal and noble officer— if he declines, it can do you no harm, nor the cause. Excuse me for making the suggestion to you out of regard to the deep interest I take in the success of our arms and in the maintainence of the Government.

Very truly and respectfully
Yours.

SECOND TERM OF GOVERNORSHIP

On August 7, 1861, at a convention held at Augusta, Mr. Washburn was nominated for a second term as governor without opposition and elected September 9. The vote was light but his majority of the year before well sustained. The Democratic candidate, Mr. Jameson, polled about half as many votes as Mr. Washburn, although a large number of the Republican voters were at the front with the army.

Mr. Blaine did not oppose his nomination. Blaine's power had increased. He was at the head of the party organization and was Speaker of the House of Representatives of Maine. Although he did not enter Congress till 1863 he went to Washington unofficially and looked after the interests of the state with his characteristic restless energy.

BLAINE TO WASHBURN

Washington, 19 Sep, 1861.

My dear Sir: My work here this week has been like fighting "beasts at Ephesus." The Qr. Mr's Dept. were determined to furnish the clothing from New York and the horses, and outfit here—merely giving Maine the privilege of raising the *Men*—My protest against, and denunciation of, such a course was emphatic if not eloquent and I soon drove old Sibley into the instructions which have been already forwarded to you—Tents he was bent on furnishing here—but he at last yielded that point too—So that Maine will be allowed to furnish everything she can and the two Regiments, one of Infantry and Cavalry will disburse some $350,000 of Federal Money in our good State—I feel therefore that I have effected something for the common weal—The great point with Q. M. Dept. was that the Pa. Regt of Cavalry and Young's Ky Cavalry, . . . had their horses furnished here—No other inspection of horses is to be ordered either—Maine, or elsewhere, except such as you direct—the limitation being small as to price—$120 in Washington—

You will observe that all outlays under Q. M's Dept will be paid by Capt. Kensel—Stationed at Boston—Expenses of enlistment, etc. and recruiting—as well as of subsistence before Muster and such other charges as are designated in G. O. No. 70 will be paid by the Mustering Officer— (*Entre nous*) Capt. Hight will be relieved—I have effected the point without any stir or doing anything to wound feelings—Please not put this letter on public files as there is no need of having it known why he is relieved—The funds will be at your command just as rapidly as the bills are audited—so there is nothing to prevent going ahead in the most lively style—Have the Cavalry consist of 12 Companies by all means—Such is the universal advice here—

In addition to the Gen. orders already forwarded, specifically bearing on your official duties, I send you this A. M. all that have been issued touching the Volunteer Service and have procured a promise from the A. A. G. Ruggles that all that may be issued in future shall be regularly forwarded to you—

BLAINE TO WASHBURN

Private and confidential.   *Washington 22 Sept.—1861.*

My dear Sir: Alex. Cummings of the N. Y. World—the most intimate friend perhaps that Cameron has—will be made a Brig. Genl. in the course of a few days—I have the best reason *to know* that Cameron desires that he may have a Brigade raised specially for him consisting of three Infantry Regts.—a Battery of Artillery and a Squadron or possibly Battalion of Cavalry—Not that these precise forces will necessarily or even probably be under his command permanently, but that he may appear to have good reasons at the outset for entering the service and receiving

a commission—He will receive full authority from the War Dept. for raising said forces with ample funds to pay all expenses in the very highest style of outfit and equipment— It will be a good thing I think to reserve one of our future Regts. for this Brigade as Cameron is very anxious to have one from Maine—and of course it will make no odds to the State for whose Brigade the Regt, is nominally raised— Cummings is a man of superior ability—very—I doubt if a single officer, from outside the Regulars, is his equal—He has surprising executive ability—I will more fully explain all the points of the case verbally when I reach home.— Meanwhile all I wish to accomplish is, file the application so that you will make no disposition of the future Regts. inconsistent with furnishing one for this Brigade—It is on the ground principally of obliging Cameron that I wish the arrangement made—It will not hurt our State any, in dealings at the War Dept, to make this little arrangement—
Very hastily yours.

Governor Washburn's second message to the legislature was a war message. He said that slaveholding politicians had discovered that the free states were unwilling that the government should be changed from its original character and administered solely in the interest of slaveholders. The question was simply how to save the Union. "At the present time and under existing circumstances, a conditional Union man is an unconditional traitor." He recounted his efforts to have the coast of Maine fortified. For more than 400 miles the state was separated from British territory by an imaginary line and the population was bitterly hostile. The best means of defense of the state—the territory which had been ceded to Canada by the treaty of Washington—had been taken from the state by the United States, and he was reminded of the memorable declaration of Maine's governor at the time—"Maine has not been treated as she has endeavored to deserve."

Then began the excitement and confusion of mobiliza-
tion. The first regiment of volunteers raised and equipped
by the state had been mustered into service May 3, 1861.
All told the state had furnished 17,124 men, an excess
of 578 of the quota required.

VICE PRESIDENT HANNIBAL HAMLIN TO WASHBURN

Wash. Feb 1, 1862.

Dear Gov: Your letter of the 28th ult is recd. I have
seen the Secy today, the troops at Augusta will have early
orders to move, and in *strict confidence*. I will say that they
will form a part of the expedition against New Orleans—I
so understand it—My relations with the Secy. are close and
intimate, and what I relate *must* be *inter nos*.

It is now confidently believed that Bright will be expelled.

Yours truly.

BLAINE TO WASHBURN

Washington 26 April, 1862.

My dear Sir: Mr. Chase writes you by this mail quite
fully in regard to our proceedings thus far with the accounts.—I think there will be no difficulty whatever in procuring seasonably a formal credit for the payment of our
tax, but in order to insure this with promptness I think it
indispensable that you execute and forward a release of so
much of our claim as will balance the tax—in accordance
with the provisions of the Act of August 5, 1861—The form
of release can best be determined by yourself.

I think there is every prospect of our accts. passing with
trifling qualifications. The auditing officers speak highly
of the manner in which they have been kept—placing them
in this respect equal to if not superior to those of any other
State. I write this fact as Mr. Chase's modesty will hardly
allow him to refer to it specifically. Forward the Release
to Mr. Chase at Willards. Our Cavalry Regt. is all under
Banks command but is divided; 7 companies being near
Warrenton and 5 down the Valley towards Staunton. The

impression is that they will all be united ere long in a grand movement on Richmond. Every one of our Regts. lately on the Potomac is now at Yorktown except the 10th which is with Banks.—I am promised at the Adjt. General's an official statement for you, showing in detail the location of each Regt. and Battery—Tillson, fully armed and equipped, is now near Acquia Creek in McDowell's Corps. All the other Batteries are on Capitol Hill—Leppier I understand will receive his outfit quite speedily—No special promise for the rest.

There is some uneasiness felt here in regard to Mc-Clellan—"Pony" stock with the knowing was never lower—Halleck since reinforced by Pope, is regarded as safe and sure agt. Beauregard—

In haste

Yours truly.

BLAINE TO WASHBURN

Washington; 4th May 1862;

My dear Sir: My wife has been very ill for ten days past at Willard's. Today is the first time she has been able to sit up—This will account to you for my silence on business matters which however I have not neglected and in regard to which I will communicate as promptly as I can—This note is merely explanatory and apologetic——

[1] F. A. P. is in Cincinnati—went about a week since—I saw him several times after I came and talked with him on certain matters—His suggestion was based on the condition of removal and in that event was well based but the impression now is that Gideon will not go out—Your friend Sedgwick's eloquence and logic saved him from a vote of censure—whereat he is greatly rejoiced—and little inclined now to "move his boots"—

But more again on this and other p'ints—

Very truly yours.

[1] Frederick A. Pike, a Republican member from Maine, chairman of the Committee on Naval Affairs, who apparently had aspirations to succeed Gideon Welles as Secretary of the Navy.

The successor of Hamlin in the Senate was as we have seen Lot M. Morrill. He had been Washburn's immediate predecessor as governor, and the unexpired term of Hamlin which he was filling out would terminate in 1863. In spite of all efforts to induce him to serve again as governor, Washburn declined positively. He did not become a candidate for the Senate; but he would have done so had the times been propitious. They were not so, Morrill and Blaine being in league, and Blaine being the chairman of the Republican State Committee. Nevertheless, the Washburn following assumed that he would regularly contest for the seat.

J. W. WAKEFIELD TO WASHBURN

Bath, Me. May 20th, 1862.

Strictly Confidential
Hon. I. Washburn Jr.

Sir: Many and by far the better portion of the Republican Party of our City, prefer your election to the Senatorship, instead of the present incumbent, and presuming you are to be a candidate, we would like to know if you have any preference, as to candidate for Governor, as the Governor no doubt will have, (and undoubtedly will exert) considerable influence in the election of a Senator.

We are soon to hold a caucus for the selection of delegates to the State Convention and no doubt the present office holders who are very strong Morrill men, (for corruption clings to corruption) will exert themselves to secure a Morrill delegation. We are in hopes to fairly and honorably control the caucus.

A very strong effort will be made by them to send one if not two Morrill Representatives to the Legislature from this place. We are very confident that Bath will send two Anti Morrill Rep—as Mr Gilman goes to Portland and therefore is out of the way. Mr. Hayden will be returned without doubt.

We shall have an eye single to our Senatorial Convention, and shall try to have a delegation of the right kind.

Should you have any preference for Governor, and no objection to expressing your choice, should be pleased to know it so we may so work. An early answer will greatly oblige.

Please direct your letter to my address, "Brunswick," Maine and I will go there for it.

> I remain,
> > Very truly Yours.

In September, 1862, there was another and more formal gathering of governors of loyal states. There was a general coöperation among them; but when Governor Randall of Wisconsin had proposed that the general government be asked to pay the governors the same salary as major generals received Washburn responded rather coolly. His own salary from the State of Maine was $1500. The state provided no house for the governor and Mr. Washburn's private fortune was small.

> *Madison, Wis. Dec. 23d, 1861.*

His Excellency
   Gov. Washburn, Maine
   Dear Sir: It seems to me that the large amount of labor and responsibility thrown upon the Executives of the several States during the past season, entitles them to some consideration at the hands of Congress. In all cases where forces enough have been sent from any State to entitle the State to an appointment of Major General, the Governor ought to be paid the compensation of a Major General. In all other cases to be paid the compensation of a Brigadier General, and Congress ought to make an appropriation for the purpose. I propose that we make common cause with our members of Congress to favor such an act. If the idea meets with your approval please correspond with your members on the subject.

> > Very Respectfully.

WASHBURN TO ALEX. W. RANDALL

(Augusta) Jan. 1, 1862.
His Excellency
Gov. Randall,
Dear Sir: I have your letter in reference to the compensation equitably due from the U. S. to the Governors of Loyal States for the large amount of labor and responsibility thrown upon them by the exigencies of the War. I have said nothing to the delegation in Congress from Maine on the subject but have thought I might well leave it to their discretion and sense of propriety.
                    I have the honor to be
                         Very truly yours.

For the next term Abner Corbin of Skowhegan was chosen as the Republican candidate for governor. Probably he would not have been Washburn's choice, as he had been his chief rival for the first nomination when he was supported by the Blaine wing of the party. He had been a member of the legislature, was of respectable parts and popular because of his philanthropy, but he was unknown beyond the borders of his state and commanded no such influence in Maine as Washburn did.

Mr. Blaine, however, continued to look out for the state's interests in Washington and kept Washburn informed of events.

BLAINE TO WASHBURN

Washington 31. Oct. 1862.
My dear Governor: I have not been able to see the Presdt. on the matter of the release of Turner (?) and Hunter though I tried several times—I could not go to Stanton but I went to his shadow, Watson (Assistant Secretary of War) and *exasperated*, well—Watson was very

much mortified—says Draper grossly exceeded his authority
and acted the fool egregiously—Said he would go to
Stanton at once and if you desired it would order the
rearrest of the parties—but this I told him was no way of
mending the matter—I read your wrathful letter to him
and "took on" well myself—Growling and abusing them
is all that is left in this case and I endeavored to do that
well—

Hathaway is doing a good business here as Agent—He
wants assistance'and really needs it—His Bro-in-law S. J.
Tenney would like to come for mere expenses and Hathaway
would like to have him—

You can judge best yourself of the expediency of the
arrangement—

Had a good chat with Fighting Joe Hooker the othei
day—He says "he is tired of winning victories for a Genl.
who is incompetent to take advantage of them"—He is
awfully down on McClellan—so is Halleck— . . . Hooker
warmly applauds Barry—says he is *"practical, intelligent,
enterprising, intrepid and devoted"*—

Hastily Yours.
I leave tomorrow for Pittsburgh.

The following letter from Washburn's friend, C. B.
Sedgwick, illustrates the demoralization in Washington
in the winter of 1862. Others also give evidence of it.

I expect to see you on here every day at the head of the
Maine Militia. Our functionaries were terribly frightened
on Tuesday and proceeded at once to make plain to the
world that they were asses. I confess to great mortification. Washington is in just about as much danger as
Augusta yet twice this winter our Cabinet officers have been
frightened to death. When the Merrimack made her first
appearance in Hampton roads Stanton collected all the
Canal boats together in the channel of the Potomac and now
he has frightened the North out of a years growth because
Stonewall Jackson has driven one of our Generals back a
Sabbath days journey in the Valley. I fear Stanton is a

little light headed and faint hearted and deficient in that genuine "Teutonic pluck" which is the element of success. However, if it brings you down here at the head of the wood-choppers I shall not regret it so much; altho, I don't like the steamer to take out the news—

I suppose you read the papers yet? If so you may have noticed my ferocious speech in favour of recruiting our armies from the loyal men of the South and appointing Robert Small Military Govr. of So. Carolina. I will send you a copy when it is in pamphlet.

"Be you" coming here as Senator soon? It is time and I hope to see you in that position before long.

. . . .

We must try to keep the chain bright. Preserve the consolations of private friendship if we do not save the Country.

Most truly Yours.

On January 5, 1863, Governor Washburn gave a reception to the council and heads of the state departments and addressed them in a short speech thanking them for the loyal support they had given him in his administration and saying its success was due largely to them. The adjutant general replied that the success was due to the governor himself. He then bade them goodbye and soon afterwards left Augusta.

In the extraordinary crisis which had confronted him during his administration he had made no blunders, had shirked no responsibility, had brought his state through with high credit. In the list of great war governors to whom the country owed so much for the success of the Union cause, his name must always be included. How much the administration at Washington appreciated his capacity and accomplishment is shown by the constant demand for him in political circles and the admiration of those seeking him.

Mr. Blaine was after him immediately:

Augusta—19/Feby/63.

Dear Governor: Mr. Young of the Republican State Comtee of N. H. came here yesterday expecting to find you here—as I telegraphed you—

While awaiting your telegram in reply I beg to urge for Mr. Young *for the cause*, the absolute necessity of your going——They want *you* and you *only* and will take no negative answer—

Do let me add an urgent word in their behalf——A speech from you in three or four of their largest towns next week or week after will be of immense value.

BLAINE TO WASHBURN

Augusta, 20 Aug 63.

My Dr Govr: Your first appt for Augusta Monday next—Evening meeting—On your arrival come directly to my house—and stay there so long as you tarry in Augusta— next morning I will take you to Skowhegan in carriage with Gen. Howard—a pleasant ride of five hours—

With kind greeting to Madame

I am as ever

Yours truly.

The saintly Barber speaks with you here—Jewett with you at Skowhegan and Lewiston.

B.

BLAINE TO WASHBURN

Washington; 21 Dec. 1863.

Dear Governor: Kelley can't come at all—Garfield won't agree to consider the case till after his return from Ohio whither he goes to spend the *recess*——

I don't know what kind of a talker Garfield is—His general *cut* and *capacity* disappoint me—He is a big good natured man that doesn't appear to be oppressed with genius——

Hastily and truly.

COLLECTOR OF THE PORT OF PORTLAND

Before the war the similarity between Lincoln's and Washburn's views had made itself manifest. Now as the war progressed this became even more evident. Doubtless Washburn coincided with the resolutions adopted early in 1863 at Augusta—probably he had been consulted and advised what they should be. Benjamin Kingsbury, Jr., advised him March 4, 1863, what they were: "The resolutions do contain a full, square, undiluted endorsement of the Proclamation, of arming the blacks, of compensated emancipation and against *all* compromise with rebels in arms."

Shortly after this Washburn's name was sent to the Senate to be collector of customs for the port of Portland, Maine. Of federal offices this was the most desirable in the state. The salary was $6000 per annum, and there were fees of office, permitted at that time, which made it lucrative. The patronage was considerable and was in the collector's hands. The collector was a political power. The administration was anxious to keep Mr. Washburn actively on its side.

SECRETARY SALMON P. CHASE TO WASHBURN

Unofficial. *Washington Nov. 5, 1863.*
My dear Governor: Yours of 31st is just received. I am glad you accept, though I hold my opinion that it is not what should be tendered to *you*; and I don't wonder that it is not quite to your taste.

What would you say to taking the position of Supervising Special Agent for the other Special Agency comprising

North Carolina? The compensation is not large—$6 per day and 10 cts per mile travel with some percentage which will add perhaps $500 per annum; but the post is important; next indeed to that of the Commanding General. The Regulation enclosed herewith will show the duties. The place is still not *right* for you, but the best I can offer; and you would give great weight and character to the place.

Faithfully your friend.

CHASE TO WASHBURN

Treasury Department, January 29, 1864.

Sir: Accept my thanks for the article you sent me. It is marked by your usual vigor and justice of thought.

I have long been anxious to make a change in the Third Auditorship, but have been utterly unable to find a person who would take it, who was in all respects competent. I have thought a long while of writing to you about taking it, but I felt ashamed just as I did in respect to the Collectorship, to offer you a place so much below your merit. If, however, you can waive considerations personal to yourself in favor of patriotism, as you did in the case of the Collectorship, I shall be very glad to name you to the President as the Third Auditor of the Treasury.

Yours very cordially.

P. S. Fessenden whom I consulted on the question whether you would accept tells me what passed between you and himself in relation to Senatorship and Collectorship. He thinks and I think that your appointment here wd. not interfere with possibilities at home. I shall rejoice in any good that may come to you.

WASHBURN TO CHASE

Unofficial. *Portland, Feby. 2, 1864.*

My dear Governor: You are more than kind to me. I sent you an article, and you offer me an office.

I do not think that I am specially qualified for the labors and duties of an Auditor of the Treas'y, and I am certain that I should not like them. I am sure there are many who can perform them better. So no sense of duty, (I will not say no sense of gratitude), urges me to accept the office to which you have generously proposed to recommend me. If I felt that I possessed any peculiar fitness for the place, I should undoubtedly hesitate to give the answer that I now feel I ought to give. I fully agree with you and Mr. Fessenden as to the effect of accepting this office upon another question—but in all such matters, at least, I am learning to leave the to-morrows to take care of themselves. With perennial thanks for your confidence, I remain

Faithfully yours.

So he continued to serve as collector and in due season events shaped themselves so that the senatorship eluded his grasp again. People outside of Maine depended on him to see that the state should stand firm in support of the war and set an example for other Northern states to follow.

JOHN ALLISON TO WASHBURN

Pittsburgh, Pa. Aug. 25, 1864.

A long time;—some years have intervened and buried its dead and filled its pages of history since I had a letter from you.

Now in this gloomy hour I feel like asking "Watchman what of the night?" How is the Eastern horizon? Does Maine stand fast in this hour of plots and treason within the free States, to aid bolder but not wickeder plotters and traitors who have been warring upon the Union for three years past?

Traitors stand thick through all the land, and the heart would grow faint at the prospect, were it not that at such a time it would be half treason to quail before the menaces of Conspirators who love their party better than their Country.

Maine speaks first. Will she speak words of Comfort and Encouragement to the Loyal or to the Disloyal?

I have confidence in Maine that she will stand by the Government in its hour of extremest peril.

Suppose we should elect "a peace man," What then?—an armistice of 6 months—followed by the firm Unalterable decision of Jeff Davis and his associates in treason, that they want no peace that does not secure to them the Independence of the Confederate Government. They want no restoration of the old Union, "Or the Constitution as it is, and the Union as it was."

You and I know the men who plunged this country into this war, Davis, Toombs, Slidell, Mason etc.: I could weep over the credulity of honest men who really love the Country, and wish to be loyal to it, who are made to believe that there is a *possibility* of a restoration of the Union by negotiation. The madness of party I fear, will do what open treason could not do,—destroy the Union. Two years ago I took it upon myself to write to Mr. Chase that unless there was more *Vigor* in the management of the war, it would be prolonged until the approach of a presidential canvass when there would be great danger of the people becoming dissatisfied with the Administration, and hopes of a change for the better, trust the Government in the hands of those who have done everything they dare do, to encourage the rebels. I can see that there is a tremor in the minds of our leading Union men. It will become every true man to rouse himself, and appeal to his fellow men as he never appealed before, and rouse the latent patriotism of the Country. It can be done.

I have thought Mr. Lincoln too slow, but the people believe him patriotic and honest and they have demanded his renomination. I have doubted the wisdom of making a nomination until the Sumner campaign was over,—in his election or defeat the Union is saved or lost. If the Democratic party was governed by the purest patriots that ever blessed a land, and succeeded on a peace platform, the Union in my opinion is irretrievably lost.

My hope is this. I cannot believe that the Discovery of this Continent, and the gradual molding of our institutions to be the result of accident. The people of this country are to exemplify the possibility of establishing and sustaining a free *Government.* Sometimes my faith in man's boasted capability to govern himself under such a government, grows weak. Can you strengthen it my old friend?

Henry J. Raymond, Chairman of the National Union Executive Committee wrote:

New York, October 12, '64.
Can you not come into New York and help us during the canvas? We shall have large meetings, intelligent auditors and everything to make your service agreeable and valuable.

The fears which Allison set forth proved to be illusive. Mr. Lincoln was elected easily enough, but after his death, April 15, 1865, the original Republicans were in great uneasiness over the question of the policy of Andrew Johnson who had started as a Democrat. Mr. Washburn had always been a friend of Seward's and if he had sympathized with the efforts of the Republicans in Congress to induce Mr. Lincoln to dismiss Seward, he has left no record of it. On June 12, 1865, George E. Baker from Washington wrote:

Lincoln and Seward never disagreed in but one subject—that was the colonization of the negroes—whether Johnson is to be so fortunate we don't know but I hope so.

BLAINE TO WASHBURN

Confidential   *Augusta, 24 Nov. 1865.*
My Dear Governor: I have not been able to find a day to run up to Portland—though I greatly desire to see you for the purpose of comparing notes on sundry topics both state and national—I expect now to leave home on Monday

next and I would be very glad if you would ride with me from Portland to the Berwick Junction—

In regard to the Governorship, I feel very friendly to Spring—I like him personally—know him to be a man of capacity, scope and integrity and should feel greatly pleased with his elevation to the Executive chair—The only difficulty I see in his way is in Dane coming forward prominently as a candidate by which I should be personally embarrassed—and this section of the state would be hard to control—A collision of this kind must be avoided—It is the interest of Portland to avoid it—and unless it is avoided it is by no means certain that the West would secure the nomination at all—The "far East" has certain schemes on foot and all of Hamlin's followers will be hostile to Spring—and to Dane also—though not in so great a degree—Spring's friends must therefore arrange with Dane *as the first step*—that the latter shall not be a candidate—This settled, my judgment is that Spring will have "a clear coast and an easy sail"—I write this to you in a confidential way though I have no objections to your showing it to Spring if you desire—I presume he counts me among his friends—and he is one of the *very few* in Portland whom I have reckoned as friendly to me—

Let me repeat that the West must not *divide*—Division must be dangerous—*may be fatal.* There has always been a good deal of talk about Kennebec tactics—The only secret we have here is *unity of purpose and union of strength*—The West is entirely welcome to our Patent right—and I commend it most heartily to their adoption at the next State Convention—

I write very hastily—or I would say more—Don't fail to let me see you on Monday at the Depot even if you will not ride with me to Berwick.

When the contest between Congress and the President came, Washburn took sides with the majority of his party whose views the Republicans in Congress interpreted correctly.

JOHN LYNCH TO WASHBURN

Confidential.   *Washington, D. C. Feby 1st. 1866.*
. . .
I write tonight to answer your enquiry as to what I think
of the "signs of the times." Perhaps I feel a little blue
just now, but I must say that if I read the signs aright we
are again to pass through another crisis which will test
our Republican form of Govt. and the virtue of our people
as severely as they have been tested since the Commencement of the rebellion. I hope a rupture may be prevented
by Congress showing a firm and undivided front but I fear
the worst. You have no doubt read Raymond's last speech
and noticed his vote on the Constitutional amendment.
That he spoke by authority, and voted as directed, I have
no doubt. That the Prest is opposed to the Suffrage bill
and to the Constitutional amendment which has just
passed the house, I think there is no doubt. That the
House should pass both of these measures by so strong a
vote, fully understanding the views of the Prest is one of the
hopeful signs of the times. Judge Kelley informs me that
the President is making a direct issue with him in the
matter of appointments and that the Secy of the Treasy
informed him that his appointments were not sent to
Senate, (for his dist.) because the men were understood to
oppose the policy of the President. From these "straws"
you can judge something of how the wind blows.

Yours truly.

But he had a more hopeful view from Seward:

Private.   *Washington, February 15, 1866.*
Present restoration of the Union seems to be the present
policy of the President. It does not yet seem to engage the
action of Congress. My own judgment is that this thing
ought not to be left undone, while I can very well see that
some things which are projected may well be left undone.
Faithfully
Your friend.

From others a different story came.   John Lynch again wrote in a pessimistic way.

Confidential.   *Washington, D. C. Feby 21, 1866.*
Dear Sir: The break has at last come and the President has thrown himself "body and boots" into the hands of the Copperheads. Whatever is intended, this *must* be the result. Third parties cannot exist in these times. The Copperheads can adopt any policy the President may indicate; there is no trouble on that score; but there is one thing they neither can nor will do, and that is abandon their organization or party name. The President with all his power and patronage cannot swallow the Democratic party; it must swallow him and his "conservative friends." There is no despondency here, but a firm determination among the Members of Congress, to assert and maintain the legitimate powers of Congress in the settlement of the questions now agitating the Country.

It is not, as you will see by reading the "veto Message," simply a question as to whether *this* particular bill shall become a law, but whether Congress is a part of the Govt. Notice the monstrous and arrogant assumption, that the Members of Congress represent only localities, (as though the aggregate did not completely represent the whole) while the President is a representative of the whole people, and the peculiar guardian of the rights, and interests of the unrepresented States. This is modest for a man chosen to preside over the Senate, and made President by an assassin. I send you the "Chronicle," by which you will see that Forney is right. If all the Union papers in the country would take the same ground and have the same ring there would be no trouble. We are to have a caucus tomorrow night. I think a Committee will be raised to circulate Documents. One hundred thousand of Trumbull's speeches will be sent to the Country.

I have full faith that Congress will stand by the Country and that the Country will stand by Congress.

BLAINE TO WASHBURN

Washington D. C. 17 March 1867.

Dear Governor: I have yr several favors—and am obliged therefor—You observed of course that the Bill containing Portland appropriations went through without trouble—As the items ran the gauntlet of the Comtee of the whole without challenge, they were of course safe in the House—and this fact I knew would be fully appreciated by you—and hence I did not telegraph anything in regard to final action—

We are in a *Muss* here—and I suppose the rupture between Congress and the Executive will be permanent—I deeply regret it—and yet I do not see how it could have been avoided. The calamity is great—is overwhelming—I am less sanguine or have less faith than you in the future—I do not believe we can carry the House Reps in 40th Congress—The defection in New York is *fearful*—and we shall lose heavily in the states of Ohio, Penna. and Indiana. E. B. (Washburne) says we shall lose *four members* at least in Illinois—others say even more than this—

Your old friend Seward is at the bottom of the mischief—and Congress has certainly not acted with super-eminent wisdom in the way of making up issues for the people.

Regard this as confidential.

BLAINE TO WASHBURN

Washington D. C., 17 March 1867.

Dear Governor: I think [1] Peters will be put on Territories—which is very respectable for a *first term*—Much better deal than I got—My apprenticeship was on Post offices under [2] Alley—The Post offices were not so bad—but Alley!!!

However Peters will have similar grievance on Territories with [3] Ashley at the head!!

[1] John A. Peters, of Bangor.
[2] John B. Alley, a Republican, from Massachusetts.
[3] James M. Ashley, a Republican, from Ohio.

I tried to get him on Foreign Affairs—particularly on account of E. & N. A. R. R.—but the places on that Comtee. were all mortgaged—

I think; at least I *hope*—that we shall adjourn by Friday or Saturday next—possibly sooner—The impeachment humbug is pretty well killed—and with it, its great apostle—Butler. He has fallen very *flat* in the House—even the pages recognize him as a failure—How surely a man gets taken down who essays to lead the House on his first entrance!! Several new Senators are committing suicide in the same way—most conspicuously Drake of Mo.—who is said to be really able—He jumps into the debates as though he thought all the chances of speaking would soon be exhausted.

Hurriedly and very truly.

Hon. I Washburn

P. S. I saw the designs for your two new buildings yesterday at the Treasury—They will be very *magnificient*, I fear extravagantly so!!

J. G. B.

BLAINE TO WASHBURN

Augusta, 12 Sept. 1867.

Dear Governor: Sound as usual. I agree with you entirely! I anticipated rather a *dry year* in '67 and we have realized it—It will be good discipline in many ways and will I am sure be "blessed to us in the edification and building up of the true faith"—I feel, I have for some time felt, that if we should carry everything with a whirl in '67 such knaves as Ben Butler would control our National Convention and give us a nomination with which defeat would be inevitable *if not desirable*—Now Grant looms up as the savior alike of country and party—*a necessity to both* and under his dynasty (the best it will be since Taylor's) such gentlemen as B. B. will not have much show for their schemes of humbug and repudiation.

Can't you drop down and see a body one of these days?

Say come on a Saturday—and bring Madam—and spend
Sunday with us—We can have some quiet talk and will
give you the "stated preaching of the Gospel" with all the
other Churchgoing you desire. . . .

BLAINE TO WASHBURN

Augusta, 4th Nov. 1867.
Dear Governor: I have heard nothing further from you
in regard to that Sunday you promised to spend with me
in Augusta—Can you and Mrs. Washburn come down
next Saturday? We shall be delighted to see you—. . .
P. S. Gen. Saml. F. Hervey is to be in Bangor this week—
and leaves I learn for the West immediately—He is our
Maine member of the National Repub. Comtee. which
meets in Washton. Dec. 11th.—If he does not intend to be
present, I wish he would delegate me to act as his substitute—The Chairman of the State Republican Comtee.
has been selected by other States to serve usually as the
substitute—There are some matters in regard to time and
place of holding National Conventions which Grant's
friends should look to carefully—for that reason I am anxious to have Maine properly represented *on that issue*—
Personally I do not of course care about acting on the
Comtee.—
Would you have any objection to writing Hervey and
suggesting my name as his substitute—in the event of his
inability to be present in person? The suggestion of course
would not come very gracefully from me—and if you have
the slightest objection to making it just drop the matter—
Of course Hervey should not know that I have written
you.

Truly yrs,
J. G. B.

LYNCH TO WASHBURN

Washington, D. C. May 13th, 1868.
Dear Gov.: Yours of the 12th ins. is at hand. The same
feeling of gloom prevails here that you represent as pre-

vailing in Portland. I never knew such a universal feeling of distrust. It is believed that there has been a base betrayal of the party and the country; that there is a scheme on foot to break down the Republican Party and build another on its ruins; that Chase, Grimes and others are the leaders in this nefarious conspiracy. Our friends think they can carry impeachment by one or two votes on Saturday. I fear, however, that the thing was made certain before certain parties ventured upon it and that there is a reserved force that is not known but which will show itself when wanted. I hope I am mistaken.

The responsibility of the whole is credited to Mr. Fessenden with how much justice I know not, although I believe, if he had been known to be for impeachment, there would not have been a Republican vote against it. I don't believe he has been *actively* engaged in organizing opposition. That I think has been done by Grimes. But I think unless it had been understood that he would oppose it, the opposition would have been abandoned. You speak of the evidence being conclusive. There can be no doubt of that, but it is generally thought that the whole thing was predetermined, as a piece of political strategy. If these conjectures are true you see how futile it is to attempt to do anything. The class of men who hold the whole thing in their hands are men who take a position deliberately; counting the cost; and then maintain it. I am surprised that I hear nothing from any meeting in Portland. I understand the men who oppose impeachment say they see no evidence of dissatisfaction or disappointment at the prospect of acquittal. Why don't the people speak? There is no lack of pressure from the other direction upon these immediate judges.

Yours Truly.

WILLIAM SCHOULER TO WASHBURN

Boston, Oct. 26, 1868

. . .

Since the election in Maine I have rested content with the lay of things. I never had a doubt of Grant's election, even if the Democrats had nominated Chase and Hancock, but when they put up Seymour and Blair and rigged up their platform I felt certain of the end. The election shows the democratic party to be a living thing after all, for with bad candidates and bad platform, they have polled an enormous vote.

We are having a slight diversion down in our district (the 5th) between Butler, Dana and Lord. Speaking is going on every night, but it will avail nothing as against Butler. He will be elected largely, though I shall have the privilege of voting against him. The nomination of Dana was a mistake. He is an able lawyer, but he has no warmth of blood which attaches the masses. There was a way to defeat Butler but that way was not followed.

I think we should all thank God that we had such a man spared out of the great war as General Grant. He will save this nation a second time. I regret that Governor Andrew is not alive to enjoy the coming victory and to have taken a place in General Grant's Cabinet. Andrew's love for General Grant was like that of a woman.

This state will give Grant from 60,000 to 75,000 majority. The Democrats are working hard in the two Boston districts where they have a slight show of getting something. It is barely possible that Peter Harvey (Daniel Webster's old friend) may beat Samuel Hooper, but I will believe it when the votes are officially counted and not until then. Bailey the owner of the Boston Herald thinks he can beat Twitchell in the other Boston district, but I don't know anybody else who thinks so, outside of the ten mile circle of the "hub." The democracy are nowhere. John Q. Adams I think will run ahead of his ticket ten thousand votes.

Pardon me for writing you about politics, and hoping soon to hear from you.

I remain Truly Yours.

With the whole program of the radical members of his party he was in full accord. Every circumstance contributed to make him a follower of General Grant. His brother, Elihu, had brought Grant forward, and been the chief agency in affecting his transfer from Galena to the army. Thereafter he stood by him and urged his promotion upon the President at every stage of his military career. He enjoyed, as few others did, Grant's confidence at this time. Israel Washburn believed that Grant was wise, prudent, just and firm, and that the work of the Civil War would be completed in a thorough and lasting manner under his leadership. In the January, 1869, number of the *Universalist Quarterly* he set forth his views of what should be done; and the essay "The Power and Duty of Congress in Respect to Suffrage" discloses admirably the views held at that time by the great majority of the Republicans. The most important measure to be adopted, it said, was "a just, republican, and constitutional rule of suffrage." A law must be passed forbidding any discrimination between citizens in the states on the ground of race or color. Before General Grant's term should expire there would remain neither power nor inclination on the part of any state to disturb such a rule. Men who had enjoyed the suffrage would not part with it. "No man in his senses will believe that four millions of people who have enjoyed the rights of citizenship for four years, can have the most vital of them all taken away in any country in which republicanism has a name to exist." The constitutional power of Congress to prescribe the vote was unquestionable, he thought. To make it was the great duty of the hour. "Colored men are now *citizens*, and if they are to enjoy the rights which were understood to be secured to citizens by the Constitution, they must be allowed to vote on precisely the same terms and conditions as other citizens."

BLAINE TO WASHBURN

Washington, D. C. 11th Feby. 1869.
Dear Governor: Yours recd.—Many thanks.
You can help me with Jno. A. Bingham—who is balancing and wavering. Let him know that I am one of his profoundest admirers, that I have hagged heavy on him etc. etc. This will take John—and you're the right man to capture him. Write him without delay if you feel so disposed.

BLAINE TO WASHBURN

Augusta, 26 June 1869.
Dear Governor: On my return from Bangor yesterday I found yr very kind invitation for myself and Mrs. Blaine to visit the Uplands—I regret very much that it is out of our power to do so—Mrs. Blaine is detained or rather debarred from visiting this summer by the exactions of Mr. Jas. G. Blaine Jr. and I shall myself be engaged all next week.

Later in the season I hope to see you in yr delightful country retreat—Meantime and at any time we shall be delighted to see you and Mrs. Washburn in Augusta— We expect to have an old acquaintance of yours to visit us soon—May Dodge (Gail Hamilton) and I wd be very glad if you could meet her here.

LYNCH TO WASHBURN

Washington Mar. 16, 1871.
You ask my opinion on the Sumner matter. I think it is "much ado about nothing." As a matter of policy it would perhaps have been better to have left Sumner on the Committee and overrode him by a majority so as to have had the real organ of the Committee some other member. That the act was justifiable I have no doubt. Mr. Sumner has a foreign policy of his own which is hostile to that of the Administration. He proclaims in

advance his opposition to anything the Commission, now in session for the settlement of matters with G. B. *may* do, demanding as a condition precedent to *any* negotiations on the subject the withdrawal of the flag of G. B. from this continent. He instructs foreign ministers and diplomatic agts. in opposition to the State Department, and if his instructions are not carried out, uses the influence of his position to defeat their negotiations or the results of them— It appears to me unjust to the Administration to allow this to be done. That Mr. Sumner is bitterly and personally hostile to the Prest. more so than any Democratic Senator, there can be no doubt and I don't see why there would not be the same propriety in continuing a Democrat at the head of Committee on F. R. as in keeping Mr. S. there.

M. W. TAPPEN TO WASHBURN

Concord, N. H. May 16, 1872.
Dear "Israel" ("Of the Lord beloved.")

. . . .

Politics are *muddled.* You say you hope the democrats will nominate Greeley. If I felt that the salvation of the party and the country (and I don't know but it does) depended on the re-election of Gen. Grant I should feel compelled to dissent from your view, and hope that they would *not* nominate Greeley. I think, in spite of all that could be done, if the democrats indorse him, he will carry a large number of republican votes. My own opinion is that he would carry this state. Still it is too soon to predict exactly what the effect would be,—and I don't think many republicans will vote for Greeley if the effect will be to elect a democratic president.

T. J. SAWYER TO WASHBURN

College Hill, Mass. Nov. 30, 1872.
You have doubtless heard with us this morning the sad tidings of the death of Horace Greeley. I know of nothing

more painful. From his first nomination I felt that it would prove his death as a *politician,* but did not think that the disaster was to be so serious and so fatal. Poor man! Never did one make a greater mistake. He was constitutionally unfitted for such a position as he chose to take, and the role he was obliged to play. Then his defeat was terrible, so crushing, that it revealed to him what he probably had never dreamed before, how false his position was and how thoroughly he had mistaken the spirit and purpose of the country. And when the election was over he found himself without friends or a party. He had effectually alienated his life-long friends, and the Democrats into whose society and arms he had thrown himself never loved him, and took him up only to use him, and when this purpose signally failed, cast him aside as they would a worn-out garment. Perhaps it was best that the grave should become an asylum for one who had, in an evil hour, acted a part so unwise, if not false. Peace to his ashes. . . .

PERSONAL PURSUITS

The years of the collectorship wore on without notable event to Mr. Washburn. The position was not a difficult one for a man of method to fill, and his administration was satisfactory to every one. He enjoyed the life in Portland. After leaving Congress he sold his house in Orono and built a handsome brick residence on Spring Street in Portland, which he occupied until his death. Here he had a beautiful library and seldom a day passed, when he was in Portland, that it was not in use. He was a hospitable man and his table saw a constant succession of guests. He liked good eating, was a moderate smoker and often had wine on his table. He kept a horse and carriage and lived as a well-to-do citizen without giving the appearance of being wealthy. When he refused another term as governor in 1862 he had been moved, among other reasons, by the fact that he could ill afford to bear the expense of the office, although from time to time he had made profitable investments. Later, having added to these, he enjoyed an income sufficient for a man without extravagant tastes. He was not a business man, and the money-making spirit was not in him. He had some timber lands and, as we have seen, took an interest in railroad building. After he retired from the collectorship he became president of the Portland and Rumford Falls Railroad, a short line of some 30 miles running from Mechanic Falls to Canton. This had been started some years before and he completed it, but he made nothing from it. When he died the accumulations of his lifetime were an estate valued at about $100,000. He had the enjoyment up to within a few years of his death of perfect health. This was one of the reasons for the good temper which had developed soon after he reached manhood and caused him to look on the bright side of things. His father had been noted as a story-teller and he was a humorist, never neglecting to notice and repeat any peculiar manifestation of human nature which would cause a laugh.

It would be untrue to say that he was not an ambitious man. He strove to succeed, and he wished for a high place and honor; but he was sensitive and proud and would not enter into elaborate and carefully planned contests for public office. Nor would he form alliances with other public men for public office. The party managers found him of no use to them and were of no use to him. To these facts is due, probably, the reason why he missed the great prize of the Senatorship. When he retired from the governorship it was known that he wished to be elected senator. When Senator Fessenden died in 1869 his name was again thought of. He had been the candidate of a number of Republicans when Hamlin resigned in 1861, as he was even up to the time of Mr. Blaine's election in 1876. It was at this time, when the political control of the state was completely in the hands of a few men whom he distrusted, that he seriously considered the project of starting a newspaper to oppose them.

E. B. HASKELL TO WASHBURN

The Herald, Boston, March 23, 1877.
Dear Sir: It will give me great pleasure if I can be of the slightest service to you. I have delayed a little for more accurate information. I am glad to hear your assurances about the Republicans of Maine, for it has seemed as though Blaine strode over the State without opposition; but I know "his tricks and his manners," and I do not

believe they are such as give any public man a permanent
position in the confidence of his fellow citizens. His political
methods do not belong to our native State but to the Pennsylvania school, into which he was born, and of which he is
an advanced pupil. Believing him to be one of the most
dishonest men in public life, I shall be glad to see his power
decline.

In regard to the business of your note, it occurred to me
that the best thing to do, if it could be done, would be to
secure a controlling interest in the Press, which is established and I suppose paying its way at least, and known as
the leading Republican daily of the State. I am told that
Mr. Saml. Spring owns a majority of it. Is he bound to
Blaine? Or if he is, could his interest be bought? On
many accounts it would be better to pay for the Press
more than it is worth than to start a new paper. You have
your audience at once, your business connections, your
advertisers, and so on, with a paper already established.
In starting a new paper, even under the most favorable
conditions, allowance must always be made for a *sinking*
fund, which sinks out of sight while building up a business.
I am inclined to think it would be well to buy the Advertiser, even, if it could be bought for about the value of the
material. It would be a simple matter to enlarge and
change the tone, and you would have *something* to start
with.

Now in regard to the cost of starting anew. . . .

I see by a paragraph in the N. Y. Times that your project is already talked of. I see no reason why a smart paper
in Portland, of the character you propose, should not be
good property. Of course you want a good news managing
editor, and possibly I could help you to such an one should
you require it. . . .

Whatever his reasons may have been he abandoned the
project. In fact soon after he had conceived it he was
deprived of the office of collector of customs and it was
conferred upon Lot M. Morrill who had been serving in

the Cabinet as Secretary of the Treasury. The appointment was made for political reasons and was not excused
on any other score. Mr. Washburn relinquished the office
without a murmur of complaint and went into private life
after a continuous public service of twenty-five years.

He was now sixty-five years old. Five years before,
in June, 1873, his wife had died. She had been his help-
meet for forty years and from the blow of her loss he never
fully recovered. She had gone to Minneapolis to take
care of their son, Charles Fox, who was seriously ill with
typhoid fever. Her son recovered, but Mrs. Washburn
succumbed.

ISRAEL WASHBURN TO ELIHU B. WASHBURNE

Portland July 9, 1873.

Dear Brother: You will doubtless have heard before you
receive this letter, of the death of my darling wife at
Minneapolis on the 30th of June. Others will write you the
particulars of her sickness and death. She died in peace and
with a smile of divine love upon her face—ready to go and
not afraid—She felt that the hour was at hand, but she
feared no evil. A death more happy, more saint-like cannot
be conceived—The radiance upon her face in life and in
death was a foregleam of an immortal and heavenly life.

We buried her last Saturday in the flowers at Mount
Hope by the side of her father and mother.

To me the loss is what no one can conceive. She was my
light and hope and strength, my joy and my pride. I have
never seen such love and sweetness united with so much
practical wisdom and good sense. Such was the rare
beauty of her character and its force, that even those who
knew her but slightly, had such respect and regard for her,
that they feel her loss as a personal one.

It is a great comfort to know how much she was esteemed
and loved.

Ada, Charley, and Maud were with their mother as she

breathed her last. We left Minneapolis Tuesday night, and on Wednesday found Henry at Chicago (his ship had just arrived on a cruise) and he came with us to Orono. He has gone to Erie to bring Belle and the babies who are staying with us for a season. We are now at the Portland home—but how empty and desolate it is without that central light of love and joy that was wont to make it so bright and happy.

Give my love to Adèle—I hope you are all well.

Your affectionate and affected

brother, I. W. Jr.

E. B. WASHBURNE

Israel Washburn kept a commonplace book and journal. In this he put down extracts and sentiments, sayings which pleased him, and made entry of events irregularly. Unfortunately, only one volume has survived, that which he began when his nature was formed, in 1869, and kept up to 1880; but its contents show what were his interests, activities and tastes, and throw light upon his character. Many of the selections he liked simply because of their purport, a striking or epigrammatic truth for example.

"Early marriages and the number of births are indissolubly connected with abundance of food; or, as Burke said, 'Man breeds at the mouth.'" (Emerson.)

"When Lord Mansfield proposed to hold court on Good Friday, Sergeant Davy said, 'there was no precedent since the time of Pontius Pilate.'"

"It is said of John Bright 'that no man has warmer friends or more desirable enemies.'"

Others he put down because they appealed to his sense of humor.

"Curran also spoke of the other world and those he should wish to see there. Madame de Staël said 'that after she had seen those she loved she would enquire for Adam and Eve and ask them how they were born.'"

"Charles Lamb wrote to Tom Hood: 'I design to give up smoking; but I have not yet fixed upon the equivalent vice. I must have said *quid pro quo, or quo pro quid.*'"

"A chap at Bangor says 'it's working between meals that's killing him.'"

Others, and these are the most numerous, are lofty sentiments of optimism and benevolence.

"'We often hear that such or such a thing is not worth an old song. Alas, how few things are! What precious recollections do some of them awaken! What pleasurable tears do they excite! Not only do they purify the stream of life, but they *can delay it on its shelves and rapids, they can turn it back again to the soft moss amidst which its sources issue,*' writes Landor to Forster. How full of truth and beauty are the lines I have underscored!"

"I never knew thee hate!
It is too troublesome, it rumples sleep,
It settles on the dishes of the feast,
It bites the fruit, it dips into the wine;
I'd rather let my enemy hate *me*
Than I hate him." (Landor)

"Omit the negative propositions. Nerve us with incessant affirmatives. Don't waste yourself in rejection, nor bark against the bad, but chant the beauty of the good when the criticism will stop. The affirmative of affirmatives is love." (Emerson)

Add to these some sentiments on patriotism, a poem, "Native Land," in the *Spectator* for August 26, 1876, the chorus running:

"Dear native land, our heart and hand
Are thine on field or foam.
And shamed be he, by land or sea,
Who will not strike for home."

And this:

"Land of the free! Thy kingdom is to come,
Of states, with laws from Gothic bondage burst
And creeds by chartered priesthoods unaccount."
                                        (Campbell)

These were thoughts which Israel Washburn wished to think over, thoughts of a high-minded man, optimistic and benevolent, patriotic and fond of humor without sting. In all the entries there is not one to indicate harsh feelings towards any one or anything.

His enthusiasm as a Universalist took the practical form of active interest in the project of a Universalist College. What was afterwards called Tufts College was started in 1847 by Universalist leaders because of two needs: an educated Universalist ministry and a place where the sons of Universalists could be sent without the danger of influences adverse to Universalism which they encountered in colleges of other denominations. Harvard should have satisfied their desires from a religious point of view, but it cost too much to be educated there, and the proximity to the temptations of Boston was regarded as undesirable. Much of the patronage which Tufts College now receives is from boys who believe—or whose parents believe—that better results are obtained from education in a small college than in a large one; but this was not the reason for its founding. Also, the means of getting from the college to Boston are now so expeditious that it is very little more removed from the temptations of Boston than is Harvard. In the beginning a large proportion of the graduates entered the Universalist ministry, although this is not now the case. All of the promoters of the college were Universalist ministers: Rev. Thomas I. Sawyer of New York, Rev. Hosea Ballou, 2d, of Medford, Mass., and Rev. Thomas Whittemore of Cambridgeport, Mass. The first board of trustees, appointed before the college opened, did not include Israel Washburn; but he was chosen in 1852 when the college opened and served until 1883, longer than any other trustee, and was president of the board in 1873. He received the honorary degree of Doctor of Laws from the college in 1872. When he retired from the collectorship he was urged to be president of Tufts but refused to consider it.

His religion was an expression of his optimism. He went to church every Sunday, usually twice. He would listen attentively to the sermon.

He had a taste in literature, was particularly fond of Burns and other Scotch poets and a number of times delivered a lecture on the Scottish Bards. He liked to quote poetry, especially Burns, Shelley, Wordsworth, and Landor. James Hogg, more read then, than now, but hardly inferior to Burns in Mr. Washburn's view, was one of his favorites. Shakespeare, Cowper, Southey, Campbell, Tennyson, Whittier, Longfellow, and Emerson were others.

His novelists were Thackeray, Dickens, and Scott, but he had a much freer taste in this field than usually belongs to practical American men. He had great admiration for George McDonald. Speaking of *Robert Falconer* he said, Nov. 13, 1870: "What a great book it is! Looking to his insight—his earnestness—his humanity—his power to hit the centre of a great question with a few plain words—he is manifestly, since Dickens, the first novelist of Great Britain." When he was more than sixty years old he read Blackmore's *Mary Annerly*, and admitted it into the circle of his chosen books. The prose of Landor, as well as his poetry, made a lasting impression on him.

Of heavier works he liked Henri Martin's *History of France*, Lecky's *History of European Morals*, Darwin's *Descent of Man*, and John Quincy Adams' *Diary*,—every word of which, in all its twelve volumes, he had read.

Beside the American newspapers and periodicals, he read regularly the *London Spectator* and *Edinburgh Review*.

Although he could not sing nor play any musical instrument he was fond of music, going to the Mendelssohn Club's concerts and recording the pleasure he derived from hearing Ole Bull on the violin. He never missed an opportunity to hear a good actor and even enjoyed the circus. He made no pretensions to possessing an artistic sense, but loved good scenery. He was a member of the Fraternity Club of Portland, an organization which met at regular intervals when the members read papers on serious subjects, and himself, often had material to present.

As before mentioned, Walter Savage Landor made a great impression upon him. The force, dignity, elevation and fearless denunciation of wrong of that erratic scholar appealed to him. Although he was not a reader of the classics, Landor's classicism pleased him. But when he reviewed Landor's works, which he did for the *Universalist Quarterly* in the July number, 1849, the *Imaginary Conversations* from which he quoted most extensively were those between Wilberforce and Romilly on the subject of slavery, and between Melancthon and Calvin, in which Melancthon expounds the doctrine of toleration and general salvation, and Calvin the doctrine of predestination, the former being a part of the Universalist creed.

At The Norlands there was a note-book in which it

was the custom of the brothers to write when they visited the old home. They recorded whatever thoughts or observations interested them. The following notes were entered by Israel:

August 28th, 1879.

"I have been reading a Life of Daniel Webster, by General S. P. Lyman, published in 1852, very soon after Mr. Webster's death.

"It has brought to mind many recollections of this remarkable man. I first saw him in Bangor in the late summer or early autumn of 1835. He was Counsel for plaintiff (with Jonathan P. Rogers) in the suit of Wadleigh vs. Veazie, a case involving the title to the water-power at Oldtown.

"While in Bangor the Whigs tendered him a public dinner at the Bangor House, then recently opened. He accepted the invitation, and I had the happiness—for such it was to the fervent admirer of the great man, to be present. I had been admitted to the bar nine months before, and was a very young lawyer practising at Orono. Edward Kent presided at the dinner, and on his right was the guest of the occasion. On his left, Mr. Webster's boyhood and college friend, the Hon. Jacob McGaw, Hon. Elisha H. Allen seemed to be Master of Ceremonies.

"I well remember the President's introductory speech, and how fine I thought it. Referring to the fact that their illustrious guest had never been called by the nation to its highest place, while small men had been, he thought the fact more to the discredit of the nation than to Mr. Webster, for said he,

'Pigmies are pigmies still though found on Alpes,
And pyramids are pyramids in vales.'

"Mr. Webster in responding to this address, referred to his first visit to Bangor at the commencement of the century, to see his old friend, McGaw, and when, he said, there was no bridge over the Kenduskeg, and he crossed the river on floating logs.

"But he had only got fairly into his speech when a tremendous shout was heard outside, and Mr. Allen appeared at the door and announced that there were thousands of people in the street who desired to hear Mr. Webster, and proposed with his consent an adjournment to the terrace that the larger audience might have the pleasure to hear their distinguished friend. Thereupon the members of the dinner party, followed by Mr. Webster, proceeded (most of them rushed) to the terrace in front of the hotel, where the speech was concluded.

"I remember the effect made upon me by the closing paragraphs. After referring to the numerous abuses of the Jackson party, dwelling upon their causes and consequences, he straightened up, raised his voice to its fullest and richest tone. How clearly do I see him now in his blue coat and buff vest—saying, ' But after all, but after all, gentlemen, this country can endure a great deal of bad government—it is so young, so full of resources, so strong, I see her yet in spite of the maladministration, to which I have alluded, like a stately ship making her way

'Against the Wind, against the tide,
Still steady with an upright keel.'

" I did not see Mr. Webster again till, I think, 1847 or 1848. I had occasion to attend the Circuit Court in Portland as counsel for the defendant in the case of Burnham vs. Webster. The defendant was Colonel Ebenezer Webster of Orono, a relative and old friend of Daniel Webster, and who had been interested with him in real estate in the province of New Brunswick. Mr. Webster attended that court to argue the case of Williams vs. Veazie, before Judge Story.

"I had not seen him until one morning I encountered him at the library door, and I think that I never saw a human figure that impressed me so strongly—so unexpected was the meeting, and so majestic, so grand and Jove-like was his form. He did not know me, of course, but I could not help knowing him. There was but one such form on all

the earth, and there never would be another; for the
die made for one casting only, was broken in moulding
Webster.

"But in a day or two, Mr. Josiah H. Little of Portland,
one of Mr. Webster's personal friends, called upon me and
said that Mr. Webster had heard that I was in town and
would like to see me in respect to some of his business
matters with Colonel Webster, whose son-in-law he had
understood I was.

"Accordingly, not long afterwards I accompanied Mr.
Little to Mr. Webster's boarding house, Miss Jones'
corner of Park and Congress Streets where we found him
in his stockings, toasting his feet. Hastily putting on his
boots, he began his enquiries about the Province property,
in which I informed him I had become interested. I
explained to him the situation, and he said he had hoped
there was some 'spes recuperandi.' He thought it might be
for his interest to make some contribution and come in for
some share of the property with me—his rights having
been forfeited. I consented readily, and as I was going to
Boston on the adjournment of the court, he invited me to
call on him, at his office in Court Street, where he would
talk the matter over at more length.

"I did call on him and we made arrangements which
led to correspondence for the next year or two, and finally
to a transfer of a share in lands to him, which he afterwards
assigned to his son Fletcher but which I subsequently
purchased from the latter.

"At this time I met Fletcher Webster and also Mr.
Choate, and was very kindly and flatteringly introduced
to them by Mr. Webster. I remember that Mr. Choate
had come in to see about an exchange of books that had
been agreed upon between them. Mr. Choate was to have
some law books in exchange for those of a political
character.

"Among the volumes embraced in the transfer were
some of the Chancellor d'Angepeau; I remember Mr.
Webster speaking of the author as having been referred
to and praised by John Quincy Adams in his address to

Lafayette on his departure from the United States, during Mr. Adams' presidency—

'Go thou beloved stranger, to that beautiful
France, the nursing mother of the twelfth
Louis and the fourth Henry, the land of Bayard
and Coligny, of Fenelon and d'Angepeau.'

"I did not see Mr. Webster again till December 1851, when I went to Washington as Representative to Congress from the Penobscot District. Webster was Secretary of State in President Fillmore's Administration. But the 'seventh' of March speech had been made—the Administration was conservative and 'cotton,' and there was a great gulf fixed between him I had almost worshipped and myself. I was fiercely liberal and 'conscience.'

"His position was before the world, and mine was not unknown to him. So our relations thereafter were friendly and respectful but not intimate and cordial. This condition of things was a great grief to me, but I could not help it—and I would not budge a hair's breadth for all the favours and all the blandishments which I knew awaited only my acquiescence in the policy of the Administration.

"The last time I met Mr. Webster was a few weeks before his death. I shall not soon forget the occasion or how he appeared. I was passing up C. Street in Washington about nine o'clock of a bright moonlight night, when I met the Secretary locked arm-in-arm with a gentleman whom I did not recognize—but the deep sad eyes, and the haggard and deathstruck look which Mr. Webster wore, painted themselves upon my mind with a distinctness, which death only, will be likely to efface."

August 29th, 1879.
"In February, 1848, Sidney (Washburn) and I visited Washington. We passed a day or two in New York enjoying the Astor House, and its incomparable host, Charles Stetson. At Philadelphia the United States Hotel was our home, at Baltimore, Barnum's. For companion between the cities we had Booth the Elder.

"While at Baltimore we heard that John Quincy Adams had fallen in a fit at his seat in the House of Representatives. He lingered for a day or two and died in the Capitol. I saw his remains lying in state there, and we attended his funeral which took place at the eastern portico of the Capitol, and was attended by an immense concourse of people.

"We stopped in Washington at the National Hotel. During the recess of Congress occasioned by the death of Mr. Adams, Abraham Lincoln, who was a representative from Illinois, visited us at our rooms and told us of his overland visit that day to Mt. Vernon. He staid nearly two hours and was very pleasant.

"We were in Washington one day after Congress resumed its sessions. I should have said on a previous day, that I then saw Mr. Webster in his seat in the Senate. I saw also Mr. Calhoun and listened to a bright and good-natured tilt between him and Willie P. Mangum of North Carolina, in which the advantage seemed to be with the tall Senator from the old North State.

"Mr. Calhoun was a man of marked personal appearance—with strong incisive features, a talking eye, and a head of long, thick, brushed-back or standing-back gray hair.

"I was much impressed with the refined and courteous appearance of Mr. Berrien, Senator from Georgia. J. W. Bradbury and W. B. S. Moor were the Senators from Maine, and the latter who lived at our hotel, was very civil to us, as were also Mr. and Mrs. John P. Hale of New Hampshire who were likewise stopping at the National. I remember hearing Charles P. Ingersoll and R. C. Schenck in the House, and that I thought Mr. Schenck one of the most ready and forcible speakers I had ever heard.

"We did not see Mr. Clay in Washington though he had recently been there. He was not then in the Senate. But on our way home I attended a Hebrew's Ball in Philadelphia that I might have a glimpse of my great political idol—if idol I ever had. I was there introduced to him, but never saw him again in life. He was member of the Senate when I entered the House—but was unwell at Ashland. He came to Washington in June 1852, and was in the Senate but once before he took to his rooms at the National Hotel never to leave them alive. He died in a few weeks and his funeral equalled in respect, in ceremony and in numbers attending it, that of Mr. Adams four years before.

.   .   .   .

"Mr. Adams' decease preceded the three memorable years by which were bounded the mortal lives of the great triumverate, of whom Buchanan Read wrote after Mr. Webster's death,

'The great are falling from us—one by one,
As fall the patriarchs of the forest trees;
The wind shall seek them vainly, and the sun
Gaze on each vacant space for centuries.

So, Carolina mourns her steadfast Pine,
Which like a mainmast towered above her realm;
And Ashland hears no more the voice divine,
From out the branches of her stately Elm.

And Marshfield's giant oak, whose stormy brow
Oft turned the ocean tempest from the West,
Lies on the shore he guarded long—and now
Our startled Eagle knows not where to rest.'

"Sometime, about midway in the '40's, perhaps, John Quincy Adams, accompanied by his son Charles, visited Halifax, going out by a Cunard steamer from Boston, and returning overland via St. John, Fredericton, Houlton and Bangor. I happened to be at the Bangor House when they arrived there. An evening reception was improvised at which the citizens of Bangor were introduced to Mr. Adams by Ex-Governor Kent.

"John Quincy Adams' Diary has recently been edited by his son and published in eleven volumes. . . . It is a testimony to the greatness and to the infirmity of human nature.

"Soon after our September election in 1860, Mrs. Washburn and myself visited Mr. and Mrs. Charles Francis Adams at their home in Quincy,—a quaint, low-studded house, of broad dimensions, more than a hundred and fifty years old, which had been the home of two presidents. Through Mrs. Adams' kindness in showing its treasures, we were made to see, or to think we saw, more of this nation's history than could be found in any other house in the land."

Less than a year before he died, Mr. Washburn made this entry in the book:

August 13th, 1882.

"This is a glorious day. To look out from the western piazza upon the mountains is a blessing.

"The same sunshine, the same sky, the same clouds, mountains and valleys as fifty years ago are here—but most else how changed! The big brook is dwindled, the fish brook is a figment, the houses and barns have changed, the boys have become men, and the old men sleep with the fathers."

CLOSE OF LIFE

The last activities of Israel Washburn's career were colored by his complete disgust for the corruption in official life. He wrote:

To Elihu B. Washburne

Portland Friday Dec. 26, 1873.

Dear Bro. . . . I returned from Washington Wednesday the 24th. The President had gone to St. Louis with Col. Dent's remains and I did not see him. Such a cowardly set as is in Congress I never saw. They want the pay unbeknown to the people, but how to do it, is the rub.

J. G. B. is evidently troubled about something. He was *not* "mellow as a pear" nor did "he go in and light the gas."

There is a most miserable ring and the people are getting tired of them. What will come, or who, only a wiser than I knows—I am much as Har. Hersey described himself on a memorable occasion. One thing is apparent, the thieves are all . . . and as they are loud, earnest and numerous, the latter are much assailed. But the Spaniard has a saying that may help them out. Time and I against any two. . . .

I sent you a card picture of poor Maud. . . .

Congress is in bad repute—It will not come to specie payment, nor will it do anything good. . . .

To Elihu B. Washburne

Portland, Jany 3, 1874.

Dear Brother: Nothing new politically or otherwise— There is to be a crumbling of the power of old leaders— In Me. there is understood to be an alliance offensive and defensive, the high contracting parties being Hamlin and Blaine and all the Congressmen including Morrill are supposed to revolve around these principal luminaries. How the scheme will work time will disclose. There are heard some mutterings, but whether they are to increase to thunder or die away into sheet iron echoes, I am not wise enough to predict. They may slide along unopposed, or their pathway may be filled with rocks and stumps.

ISRAEL TO ELIHU

Portland, April 24, 1874.

Dear Bro: The veto of the inflation bill was a great act, and has done the President more good that any other act of his entire administration. The political atmosphere is clearer and the financial has improved marvellously. What the Logans and Butlers will do I know not, but I do know that they cannot harm the President. . . .

There are no new signs of importance in the political world that I have observed, save those occasioned by the veto.

Perhaps Morton may undertake to rally, under the flag of expansion, a party to his support. We must wait till after the adjnt. of the present Congress before we can see much of "the lay of the land."

On July 4, 1874, Mr. Washburn delivered the address at the unveiling of a soldiers' monument at Cherryfield. The note of triumph which he held was typical.

"By constitutional amend'nent and the amelioration of public opinion, slavery has been made legally and practically impossible in this country—the slave of other days has been recognized as a citizen, and his inalienable and fundamental right of suffrage secured beyond danger of abridgment or loss. He has taken his seat in the halls of legislation, State and National. Schools and seminaries of learning have been opened to him; the church receives him, and his claim to all that man may claim has been allowed; for I regard the passage of the civil rights bill as beyond doubt. His neighbor of another race, so long his master and tyrant, has been enfranchised, too, and from a bondage scarcely less unhappy than his own,—the bondage of prejudice, contemptuousness and injustice. All the States that were in rebellion have been successfully reconstructed, and avenues to prosperity, unknown and unhoped for in the earlier times, have been opened and are being rapidly occupied. A neighborly feeling—is not returning for it had never existed—is growing up between the North and South; men of either section understand and respect each other, as they could not do so long as they were members of conflicting societies and warring civilizations."

He depicted the consequences of the war:

"The war with its disturbing influences, the changes in habits and occupations, its vast expenditures, its unavoidable employment of unworthy and selfish men at times, its relaxation in manners and morals, left an inheritance of many dangers. Soldiers of fortune, adventurers, and rascals, discover in the opportunities and tendencies of such seasons, manifold avenues to speculation and fraud, and they are swift to occupy them. While the patriotic and true are engrossed with the settlement of great questions, with vital necessities, with the duties of repair and restoration, the selfish and false are busy with their schemes of greed and plunder. Familiarity with large sums encourages a liberal arithmetic,—where the carcass is, the vultures gather. When vast national expenditures are unavoidable corruption festers, and theft and plunder hold carnival; men become giddy, impatient, excited. They cannot wait for slow gains, or descend to small things. Details are pitiful, and the homely virtues disgusting. Industry is a jade, economy a by-word, and honesty a fool. Looseness in manners, profligacy in life, faithlessness to obligations become so familiar that they cease to shock or disgust the average man and woman.

"There is cause for alarm. Danger is everywhere in business, in society, in the noiseless walks of private life, as well as in the wider theatre of public affairs.

"Of what avail the sufferings and the sacrifices of the dreadful years from which we so lately came, if these things are to go on? But they must not go on. The people must call a halt, and they will. Did I not believe it I should despair of the country. Economy, retrenchment, reform, responsibility, and purity must be the popular watchwords. . . .

"Our work is first and mainly at home, with ourselves and our ideals. With right thinking we must expect wise acting. If we are slaves to wealth, extravagance, and show—if we look with foolish eyes upon their possessors and exhibitors as the fortunate and happy ones of earth, careless of means by which they rose,—if we think that fraud and falsehood may be winked at when successful, we make reformation and improvement impossible. The work, then, must begin with the people and *now*. . . .

"In an address in which I wish to be practical, I seek, rather than avoid the consideration of topics that are near at hand and the expression of thoughts that are trite so that they may be timely and true. For our business is in the present and our duties are directly before us. The debt is due today and its payment cannot be postponed. We cannot deal with the needs and dangers of the next generation but we can with those of this. If we do what is required in 1874, 1875 will be relieved of tasks and burdens that might be too great for it to perform or bear.

"Looking then to the questions that demand immediate attention, we see directly before us that of *reform in the civil service*. It is one of the most difficult problems before the country. How to secure faithful and efficient service; and how to hold the power of official patronage within due limitations and restraints, and yet keep up a wholesome interest in public affairs, are questions that have taxed the earnest and thoughtful consideration of the best minds in the country for many years. It is also a subject as vast as it is difficult. The appointees of the federal government are not as in the time of Andrew Jackson, a handful, but scores of thousands. There can be no question that one of the chief perils of the nation arises from the relations of the civil service to the country—from the manner of its constitution, and the political or rather party work which an appointment to office is understood to imply to those in whose interest or by whose procurement it is made. It is a question that must grow into the first importance and continue to be agitated and discussed by intelligent and patriotic citizens until some practical and efficient solution has been reached, and it should be our purpose to give hospitable reception and a fair trial to every plan for reform that presents a reasonable promise that it may be successful,—for it is only by practical tests, carefully and patiently applied, that the final discovery can be effected.

"Among the dangers too obvious to be overlooked, and which should awaken the serious apprehension of the country, is that resulting from the general and apparently irresistible tendency of things in the direction of *centralization*.

"Educated in the specious school of the Virginia abstractionists, many men of acute rather than strong minds, speculators and theorists—especially after the subtle intellect of Mr. Calhoun discovered that the cause of slavery would be served by it—became believers in, and champions of the dogma of State Rights, and so far did they go in their denials of the legislative power of Congress, and in their restriction of the functions of the general government, that their affirmative and vehement claims of the right of any state, at any time, when it saw fit, to secede from the Union, was not only a logical deduction from these positions, but its exercise, conceding their soundness, would have been matter of but little practical importance to the nation, stripped as it would have been, of nearly every essential of sovereignty.

"These opinions, which, from their association with the slavery controversy, were rapidly propagated, and came to be widely held in all parts of the country, found their logical expression in the attempt at secession, and in rebellion.

"It will not seem strange that after such efforts as the country had occasion to make to put down a rebellion organized and pushed in the immediate interest of slavery, and on the theory of State Sovereignty, there should be a strong reaction towards power and centralization in the General Government. There is unquestionable danger that this movement of forces and tendencies to the centre may go unchecked until all substantial power and authority shall be absorbed in the nation, and the States shorn of their most necessary political functions.

"I confess that I look upon the disposition of Congress to extend its jurisdiction over questions and concerns heretofore acknowledged by all parties, to pertain, rightfully and exclusively, to the states, with unaffected alarm. Congress is almost daily legislating upon matters where the right would have been promptly, not to say indignantly, repudiated by such broad constructionists as Mr. Clay, Mr. Webster, Mr. Mangum, Mr. Evans, and Mr. Clayton.

"The nation is becoming everything, the States nothing.

"For all ills and evils, for all inconveniences and accidents relief is sought at Washington.

"Whatever State legislation, or individual or corporate enterprise and capital are inadequate to accomplish, or unwilling to undertake, the federal government is confidently asked to promote.

"Among the most wholesome and effective means of staying this rapid and appalling march of centralization, will be the inflexible and persistent requirement by the people of the practice of *economy* and *retrenchment*. Necessary in themselves, they are indispensable to a true adjustment of the proper relations of the national and State Governments to each other. Centralization, with its hundreds of millions for yearly disbursements, must breed carelessness and profligality, while vast and loose expenditures feed and strengthen centralization. A terrible peril—insidious, fascinating, but inexorably fatal, lies in this source and reservoir of corruption, the Treasury. Fifty years ago, aside from the public debt, the entire payments of the government scarcely exceeded ten millions in a year, where now they are two hundred millions.

"A strict limitation of appropriations to constitutional objects,—to cases where the power is clear and the necessity unquestionable, an education of the people to the constant inquiry whether the appropriations are in all cases within the scope of congressional power, and to a vigilant scrutiny of details, with a practice of holding members to a rigid accountability for their votes, are duties in the performance of which the people may do much towards discharging their obligations to those who preserved for them the government under which they live. I have sometimes thought that a provision for the publication in the newspapers of the several States of all the items of appropriation and expenditure by authority of Congress, so explained in detail as to be easily understood, would be wise and salutary. It is, I imagine, truly necessary to bring the attention of the people to these things and lead them into the habit of classifying and examining all items of expenditure, to effect a reform in the manner of dealing with the people's money that will largely protect the Treasury from spoliation, and the people from the arts of influence of corruption."

The speech was an able one and showed that Mr. Washburn's mental powers had expanded. It is doubtful whether there was any public man in Maine at the time who could have given a fairer presentation of the state of the country and the evils confronting it.

This year (1874) was published the volume *Notes, Historical, Descriptive, and Personal, of Livermore, in Androscoggin (formerly in Oxford) county, Maine,* by Bailey and Noyes, at Portland. It comprised some 169 pages, written without attempt at literary style or scientific arrangement, but giving a great deal of valuable information about the early history of the village, the early settlers and their families, its industrial development, churches, politics, and military characters. Although it appeared anonymously it was written by Israel Washburn and shows that he had minute knowledge of all that concerned his ancestral birthplace and a great attachment to it, as well as an unselfish willingness to spend his time and energies in a labor of love.

A few years later Mr. Washburn made his most important and elaborate contribution to historical literature in his paper on the North-Eastern Boundary, read before the Maine Historical Society. The paper was read on May 15, 1879, and may be found in the Society's Proceedings for 1881, Volume VIII. The Webster-Ashburton treaty had been concluded in 1842, and Mr. Washburn remembered all the circumstances leading up to it and the mortification of his state at what she considered to be a betrayal to Great Britain by the loss of territory which she had always claimed and valiantly contended for. Washburn's presentation of the facts was masterly and his arguments difficult to answer in so far as they pertained specifically to the Maine boundary.

Elihu wrote to him from Philadelphia, December 1, 1881.

> Dear Bro: . . . I have read your paper on the North Eastern Boundary with a real interest. You have performed a great service in the interest of history, but in doing so have made disclosures that must mantle the cheek of every son of Maine with shame and indignation. The arrogance and insolence of England in all that matter makes the blood boil. And then old Webster sold you out lock, stock and barrel. One strong, bold, fearless man from Maine on the Commission to make the Treaty could have knocked the whole thing higher than Gilderoy's kite. But in the end they took to the timber, including my old friend John Otis.

When he retired from the collectorship, Washburn settled down with his two daughters, Ada, a young lady and Maud, a young girl. The two boys, Captain Israel Henry Washburn of the Marine Corps and Charles Fox Washburn were established in life, the latter, as we know, living in Minnesota. Their father's robust health gave promise of long years of further usefulness.

However, on Thanksgiving day, 1882, he returned from church to lunch at half-past two o'clock apparently perfectly well; but after lunch he came into his library and complained of feeling ill. The doctor was called and it was supposed he had merely contracted a bad cold, but he was never well again. He soon realized that his ailment was serious, being a chronic inflammation of the bladder, and he devoted himself from that time on to efforts to recover. In the spring his Portland doctor advised him to put himself under the care of the famous Dr. Weir Mitchell at Philadelphia, and he went to that city in April with his second wife and his daughter, Ada, taking apartments at the Lafayette Hotel. At first his ailment seemed to yield to treatment and he was hopeful of recovery, but early in May he grew worse and the disease got beyond medical control. He suffered great pain, but bore it manfully. He sank into unconsciousness on May 11th and died May 12, 1883, his wife and daughter being the only persons present at the time, except the nurse.

His body was taken to Bangor and buried on May 23, in Mt. Hope Cemetery near that city, by the side of his first wife. An eloquent funeral oration was pronounced by his friend, the Rev. Amory Battles.

ELIHU B. WASHBURNE

ELIHU BENJAMIN WASHBURNE

THE CAREER

Next to Israel, a year and a half his junior, was Algernon Sidney Washburn and three years his junior was Elihu Benjamin Washburne. (Early in manhood this latter added the final 'e' to his surname to bring it more nearly into assimilation with the spelling which had prevailed in England.)

In 1874, being then American Minister to France and fifty-eight years old and not pressed by public duties, Elihu Benjamin Washburne while sojourning at Arcachon, France, and at Carlsbad, Bohemia, wrote an autobiography for his children of which the following is an abridgment.

I was born in Livermore, Maine, on September 23, 1816, being the third son and child. I think it was in the spring of 1823 when I was seven years old that my father took me to Raynham, Massachusetts, to stay for a year with my grandfather and grandmother Washburn. We went to Hallowell and there took the schooner *Superior*, Captain Butler, to Boston. I remained somewhat over a year at Raynham and have not a single pleasant recollection of my stay. My grandfather and grandmother were quite old and their children were all grown up. Their youngest son, Eli King Washburn, and his two younger sisters, Lydia and Cornelia, took care of the house and farm. All of them were staid and serious people, kind enough in their way, but without any warm or genial side for a child who had been in a measure thrust upon them and who was naturally full of life and longing for sports. My grandfather was a type of the New England character of

155

the time of the Revolution. He was descended directly
from the pilgrims and he had the characteristics of the
Puritans. He was tall, large-framed and straight as an
arrow. He was a well-to-do, independent farmer, industrious and frugal. He added to an inflexible honesty the
sense of justice and his name was a synonym for truth and
honor. But as I recollect him, he was a man stern and
severe, talking but little, abrupt and sometimes vehement
in speech. Having been a soldier in the Revolution, he
enjoyed great prestige and was honored by town offices
and by being a representative of the great and general
Court of Massachusetts. To him there was no nonsense
in life; he never unbended. I soon found that I was to be
made useful to this household and I was put to such work
as a lad of seven or eight could do, gathering chips, carrying wood, picking up stones, driving the cows to pasture
and doing "chores" generally. I went to school for a
few weeks in the winter and the summer, but I was a
stranger and was not regarded kindly. I shall never forget the brutal beating given me by the master, a man
named Williams, for some trivial offense. Lonely and un-
friended the sad and heavy months wore on until finally
my father came to take me home. He had come from
Livermore with a horse and chaise and we drove back,
being three days on the way; the distance from Boston to
Livermore was one hundred and eighty miles. We arrived
at home about midnight of the third day and I remember
the joy of my poor mother at seeing me again. Having
been so far from home I was a sort of hero to my brothers
and the boys of the neighborhood. It was considered a
great thing for so young a boy to have been to Boston.
The next few years were spent at home. I heard a great
deal of discussion of religion, politics and other serious
subjects in my father's store. He took the New England
Galaxy, founded and edited by Joseph Tucker Buckingham, afterwards the editor of the Boston *Courier* and a
well known politician, also the Hallowell *Advocate* which
was left at the store every week by the post rider, Uncle
Jed White, who came on horseback and left the mail.

The papers were anxiously awaited and read eagerly. There was a good circulating library in the town and I read all the books of history and biography and many romances. We had three months of school in the summer and three in the winter, but I never went to school in the summer after I was thirteen. Nor did I make as much progress at winter school as I should have done, for my thoughts were full of athletic sports and I had formed the idea of going to sea. One day I drew a picture of a ship on my slate and wrote under it "The ship *Hero*, Captain Washburn, bound for a whaling voyage to the Pacific Ocean." I forgot to rub it out, and the boys saw it and made fun of me. This caused the sea-going fever to abate and finally it passed off.

For many years my father used to take a drove of cattle in the fall from Livermore to Brighton, the nearest market for Boston. In 1828 he took me with him. We were nine days on the road and I enjoyed it very much. During these years my brothers Sidney, Cadwallader, and I were made to work more or less on the farm but Israel escaped for he was employed as a clerk in the store. There he had opportunity for reading and study and for argument with the people who came to the store. In 1829, I think it was, misfortune lowered over our house. Trade had been diverted and times were hard. My father was unable to meet his payments, the sheriff attached the store and everything was sold except what the charity of the law exempted for the family of the unfortunate debtor. The little homestead of sixty acres, was mortgaged to my father's brother, Reuel Washburn; and no one can estimate the value of Reuel Washburn's advice and protection at this time.

Among the debts my father owed was one of twenty-five dollars to a neighbor whom we called "Uncle Lovewell." He was very illiterate, deaf as a post and never performed any manual labor, but such was his thrift and skill in getting money that he became one of the wealthiest farmers in the town. He lent money in small sums on good security and always regretted that the laws were not more severe against the debtor class and that "Monarch laws," as he called them, had been abolished. As my father could not pay the money he owed Uncle Lovewell it was agreed that I should work it out at five dollars a month. I began on April 19, 1830, and for five long months I worked on that hard and sterile farm to pay off a twenty-five dollar debt. I was called up every morning at sunrise and worked until sunset through all the days of summer. No slave boy under the eye of a taskmaster ever worked harder. The living was none of the best. In haying time we used to have tea at four o'clock in the afternoon and then work till night when we would have a bowl of bread and milk.

At this time our family was very, very poor. Besides my father and mother we were ten children to be fed and clothed and it all had to come out of the unwilling acres of the little farm.[1] My father being a merchant, or rather a "store keeper," as he was called in the country, had never been habituated to manual labor, and now he went cheerfully to work on the farm to put bread in our mouths. But the great burden fell upon my mother. In the presence of our adversity her great qualities of courage, energy and management developed. When I think of her labors, her anxieties, her watchfulness, her good and wise counsels and her attention to all our wants my heart swells with emotions of gratitude towards her which no language can express. Born in Livermore at an early period of the settlement she had had few advantages of education, but she was possessed of a quick and rare intelligence and excellent common sense. She always read the newspapers and was greatly interested in public events. Though firm and resolute she was one of the most tender-hearted, most sympathetic and most charitable of women. She was a devoted wife, an affectionate mother, a loyal friend and a good neighbor.

After my summer's work at "Uncle Lovewell's" I returned home in order to go to school during the school months, but there were so many mouths to feed that I

[1] Mrs. Washburn's very small income was a material help at this time.

was sent to a neighbor's where they wanted a boy to do "chores" for his board. Witnessing the poverty and struggles of my parents I determined to shift for myself. From the time I was fourteen I was not only not an expense to them, but my various little earnings went to help support the family. I went to school one winter at the "Intervale," working for my board with my Uncle Nathaniel Benjamin, my mother's brother, and I worked for him on his farm more or less the following summer. He and his wife were always kind to me. They had children about my age, the household was a jolly one and I had a good time. The next year I hired out to Jonathan Lovejoy whose wife, Ruth Benjamin, was my mother's sister. They lived in East Livermore in a mean part of the town called "Tobacco Street." The farm was of fair size, but the house was small, old and comfortless. It had only one story and an unfurnished garret, where I slept close under the roof. I can recall many of the neighbors. There was Dr. Niles, the horse doctor, old John Young and his son "little John," who was as worthless as his father and never would go to school. He had arrived at manhood and did not know how to read or write. He is the only man I ever knew in Livermore who could not read or write. A more distant neighbor was "Grandpa Sias," who was a Hessian, brought over by the English to fight against us in the Revolution. He remained in the country, married and settled down, and I believe was a good citizen. His grandson, John Sias, was of my age. He moved to California and when I was in Congress wrote to me. The summer was a dreary one. I worked hard and was homesick. Mr. Lovejoy, with whom I worked, was never inclined to talk. I dug up stumps, drove the oxen to the plow and harrow, planted and hoed potatoes and corn, spread, raked and loaded and stowed away hay. I was not quite strong enough to mow and pitch, but in most kinds of work I did the labor of a man and received a boy's wages. My Aunt Ruth was always kind to me and often tried to alleviate my task. She had a true affection for me and in after years when I used to visit Livermore I never received from any one a warmer welcome than I received from her. She was a noble woman but her lot in life was hard.

I think it was in the summer of 1832 that I worked for my Uncle David Benjamin. In the spring of that year I worked for a while in Isaac Fuller's brick yard in East Livermore. About this time I tried ineffectually to get work in a rope walk at the "Falls." I have pleasant recollections of the summer's work at my Uncle David's. I always worked well and faithfully wherever I was, but I had a great distaste to farm work and longed to get something to do which would be more congenial. I had read the life of Dr. Franklin and took a great notion to be a printer as he had been. I wrote to J. and W. E. Edwards, publishers of the Portland *Advertiser* and asked if they did not want an apprentice, but they did not reply. Then I went down to Portland and boldly entered the *Advertiser* office, but they had all the apprentices they wanted. I think this was in the winter of 1832–33. I returned home with a heavy heart. I did not dare to aspire to be a clerk in a store and I had no taste for any trade but that of a printer. Israel then had a place as clerk in a store at West Waterville, and Sidney was in a store at Hallowell. I chafed at the idea of being obliged to return to farm work.

On the last of May or beginning of June, 1833, being at my Uncle Morison's in East Livermore, I took up the *Christian Intelligencer*, a Universalist newspaper, published by James Dickman, at Gardiner, Maine, and edited by William A. Drew, an old friend of our family, and read this advertisement: "Wanted, an apprentice to the printing business. Apply at this Office." Here was my chance. I returned home at once and told my mother, and the next morning I started for Gardiner on horseback. It was thirty miles distant and I must go and come in a day as I could not afford the expense of staying away for the night. I had just enough money to pay my ferriage over the Androscoggin River, for my dinner and for "baiting" the horse. Before noon I was in Gardiner and presented myself at the *Intelligencer* office. I was accepted as an apprentice until I should arrive at the age of twenty-one. I was to have my board and twenty-five dollars a year to clothe myself. By two o'clock I was on horseback again and arrived home at midnight. My mother used to tell how I started off that morning before sunrise.

Now had come a new departure, and I felt that I was starting out in the world to seek my fortune and would never return home to live. My mother prepared my slender outfit and it was packed in a small wooden trunk. Early in the morning of June 12, 1833, my father and I started for Gardiner and by noon I was delivered over and that afternoon became a "printer's devil." I found the work much easier than working on a farm.

I was contented and pleased with my trade, and I had leisure to study and read. I read all the exchanges and contracted the habit of newspaper reading which has never left me. I made a resolution, which I have kept, not to drink, smoke or play cards. I am satisfied that I learned more in the year I was in the *Intelligencer* office than I ever learned in any year of my life. But matters did not go well with our publisher and he kept falling behind. My personal expenses at this time were literally nothing and I sent home more than half of the twenty-five dollars I received every year. My mother made and sent me nearly everything I wore. In the summer of 1834 the *Christian Intelligencer* failed and I was left without a place and without money.

I returned home and determined to prepare myself to teach school the following winter and in the spring I would take up the printing trade again. I went to school at East Livermore and worked for my board with my uncle and aunt Lovejoy. For three months in the winter of 1834–35 I kept the district school at Proctor in Hartford, Maine, being paid ten dollars a month and "board around." For a short time in the fall of 1834 my uncle Reuel Washburn took me in his law office and taught me Latin. I was eighteen when I began to teach school. I boarded for a week at one place and then moved on to another. I was treated with deference, as a man, for the first time. My time was up March 1, 1835, and I received my three months wages in three ten dollar bills. I disliked teaching more than anything I had ever done. My great ambition was to be a printer in the office of the *Kennebec Journal* at Augusta of which Luther Severance was the editor, but there was no vacancy, so I went to school at the Maine Wesleyan Seminary, a Methodist institution, still in existence, at Kent's Hill, Readfield. After being there several weeks I was offered a place in the office of the *Working Men's Advocate*, Belfast, Waldo County, and went to work on April 11, 1835. It was a shabby, one-horse establishment and I determined to leave as soon as I could. In the course of two weeks my father wrote to me that Mr. Severance had written he would like me to come to live with him, to work in the *Journal* office and receive forty dollars a year for clothing besides some spending money and pay for extra work.

Sometime in the early part of May, 1835, I started as an apprentice in the *Kennebec Journal* office. Mr. Severance was a practical printer and set up his own editorials. He was a quiet, conscientious man, of remarkable intelligence, of plain appearance, tall and spare with red hair. I never knew a more honest man. Though revered by the Whig party he never sought office. In the summer of 1835 he went to report a convention to nominate senators for Kennebec County and when he returned to the office I asked him who had been named. "Two men and a boy," he replied, "and I am the boy." He was afterwards elected to Congress and, in 1844, General Taylor, I think, made him commissioner to the Sandwich Islands, but he returned in a few years to Augusta where he died horribly of a cancer in the face. The state legislature met at Augusta in January, 1836, and as my head was always full of politics I managed to see many of the members.

But serious troubles were now coming upon me. I had not been many months in the printing office in Augusta when I began to feel the effects of the change from the active out-of-door life of the country to the confined life of a printer. A hernia began to develop and the physicians whom I consulted decided it would be impossible for me to continue at my trade, for the constant standing at the case would always aggravate my difficulties. So I was compelled to abandon the trade which I had chosen for myself and had spent two years in learning. I have always loved a newspaper office. There is an intelligence and excitement about it which are attractive to me. I have not forgotten how to "stick type," and when making my congressional campaigns I would "show off" in the offices of country newspapers by taking a composing stick, going to the case and setting up a few lines. There is no humbug about the trade of a printer. A man may be a bogus lawyer, doctor or clergyman, but he cannot set type unless he has learned the art and mastery of printing.

On Wednesday, April 6, 1836, I bid a final adieu to the *Journal* office and to printing and went back to Kent's Hill Seminary. I had determined upon another career— that of the law. But it would require a long preparation before I could enter upon the study of that great profession, and I was dependent upon myself alone. I had $33.88 coming to me when I left Mr. Severance, enough to carry me through school for one quarter and leave a little over. This session I had an attack of the measles and was taken home, and it was some time before I could return to the Seminary. I was greatly exercised to know how I could earn money enough to go on with my schooling after the money which Mr. Severance had given me was gone. I had a horror of school teaching. After the school closed I remained at Kent's Hill and earned enough at haying to pay my board while I kept on with my studies. In the middle of August, my cousin Samuel B. Morison, who had a situation in the post office at Hallowell under Dr. Amos Nourse, the postmaster, gave it up and I took it. I boarded as a student with Dr. Nourse and had only to clothe myself and pay a small sum for tuition. Dr. Nourse treated me with respect and became my steadfast friend. He served as senator from Maine for a short

time when I was in the House. I got along very well
during the winter of 1836–37, studied Latin and French,
attended lyceum lectures and made general progress.
Hallowell was then a high place. No town in New England of the same population held so many distinguished
men. There were at the bar William Emmons, Samuel
Wells, Henry W. Paine, William Clark and Sylvanus W.
Robinson, all men who would have been distinguished
in their profession anywhere. John T. P. Dumont was
another. He was more of a politician than a lawyer, but
was probably the most eloquent and captivating public
speaker that the state has ever seen. The Rev. Dr. Shep-
ard, a man of great ability, preached at the Old South
Church. Doctors Hubbard and Nourse were physicians
whose fame extended far and wide. There was an English
colony, the Vaughans, Merricks and others who were
rich and aristocratic. Then, there were many sea captains,
some retired and some still at sea,—all with fine houses,
men of character, courage and intelligence. There was
great political excitement in the town in 1837 and my
studies suffered by the attention I gave to politics. I
wrote occasional editorial squibs for William Noyes who
published the *Chronicle*, the Whig paper. Jeremiah Loth-
rop was then living at Hallowell. He was a tremendous
Whig and my friendship for him dates from that time.

After studying for sixteen or seventeen months I felt
that I must begin my law studies, and towards the end
of 1837 entered the law office of John Otis. He was a
true friend. He not only took me in his office, but I
boarded with his family and he advanced me money for
my expenses. Afterwards he advanced more to help
pay for my education at the Cambridge Law School and
in a law office in Boston, and after I was admitted to the
bar helped me to buy some law books and to go West. He
never asked for any security or appeared anxious for
repayment. Not long after I was settled in Galena I paid
him all the money he had advanced with interest. I was
his friend till his death. I think the last time I saw him
was in Washington when he was a member of Congress.

Thus my three best friends, Mr. Severance, Dr. Nourse and Mr. Otis were all afterwards in Congress. I also received financial help at this time from my uncle, David Benjamin, and Col. Dumont, both of whom I repaid with interest.

The Maine legislature met in Augusta in January, 1838, and the Whigs elected Elisha H. Allen of Bangor speaker. I thought I could get the position of assistant clerk at two dollars a day. I went to Augusta and attended the Whig caucus where my name was presented, but another was chosen. I sneaked out of the caucus and took my way on foot to Hallowell. Samuel S. Benson, of Winthrop, was the secretary of state and my friends insisted that he should give me some writing in his office which he did grudgingly, but it did not amount to much. The next time I met him both of us were members of Congress and we were on an equal footing. I pursued my law studies diligently through the winter and into the summer. Politics ran high, however, and Mr. Otis's office was a rendezvous for the Whigs and the discussions and the interest I took in politics interfered with progress in my studies.

About the middle of the summer I went up to Raynham to visit my relations and read law. One day when walking from my uncle Edward's to my grandfather Washburn's I was seized with a severe pain in my right hip. I had felt the pain before slightly and thought it would pass off. On the contrary, it continued and increased. It was evidently an attack of "hip disease," foreboding the most serious consequences. The thought of being thus stricken down and becoming an invalid and perhaps a cripple for life depressed me dreadfully. All my relations at Raynham showed me great sympathy. There was nothing for me to do, however, but to return to Hallowell and seek Dr. Nourse's advice. Though he applied remedies I grew worse, and finally could only hobble about with the aid of a cane. I attempted to pursue my law studies, but my mental and physical sufferings were great. The doctor finally concluded to try the severe remedy of a seton on the hip. I think it did some good, but I still suffered.

And then, in the winter of 1838–9 the time had come for me to make another departure. I had been over a year in the law office of Mr. Otis and I had determined that I must have a year or more in a law office in Boston and at the Cambridge Law School. Through the kindness of friends I could see my way clear in the matter of funds. I left Hallowell in the dead of the winter when the weather was fearfully cold. From Hallowell I took the stage sleigh at four o'clock in the morning and went through to Portsmouth, New Hampshire, that day, arriving at nine or ten o'clock at night. The next day I went to Salem where I took the railroad to Boston, this being the first time I had ever travelled on a railroad. I entered the office of Derby and Andrews to study till the term of the law school at Cambridge should begin. The firm did a large business and I learned a great deal about office practice and went a great deal into the courts to see how cases were tried. There were great judges on the bench and the Suffolk bar was at the zenith of its glory. When I entered the law school the two professors were Mr. Justice Story and Simon Greenleaf. The students came from all parts of the country. Among them were Charles Devens, afterwards on the supreme court of Massachusetts and attorney general of the United States, Richard H. Dana, James Russell Lowell, Charles A. Peabody, afterwards a leading lawyer in New York, and William M. Evarts. I was at the law school and in the office of Derby and Andrews for about fourteen months. I studied diligently and made fair progress, but my hip troubled me a great deal. I consulted Dr. Hewitt and under his advice bathed my leg and hip in strong decoctions of bark, but I did not think I was benefited. I thought the seton inserted by Dr. Nourse which had healed up did me good, so I inserted with my own hand six small setons and kept them running for a long time. The scars still remain. The setons seemed to draw away the inflammation and the disease gradually disappeared. Still I suffered more or less pain in walking for two or three years.

It was impossible for me to pursue my law studies longer. I had incurred debts and obligations which weighed heavily on my mind and I was unwilling to tax still further the kindness and generosity of my friends. My brother Cadwallader had gone West in the spring of 1839 and was living at Stephenson, now the city of Rock Island, Illinois. I made up my mind to go West too. First I would join Cadwallader; but my inclination was to settle in Iowa, which had been admitted a territory a year before. It was important, however, that I should be admitted to the bar before leaving Massachusetts as that would give me a certain prestige and enable me to be admitted at once in any other state. Before I could be admitted in Massachusetts I must pass an examination before a judge of the supreme or common pleas court. I determined to try an examination before Judge Wilde of the supreme court, an able and upright judge, but of the old school, with very set notions. When he had been admitted to the bar a candidate for admission had to be "college learned" and must have studied law for three years; or if he was not "college learned" he must have studied for seven years. I had procured satisfactory certificates from Judge Story and Dr. Greenleaf, that of Judge Story being particularly strong, and with these documents I went before Judge Wilde. He questioned me as to how long I had studied law, what college I had been to, etc. I told him, but added that I was going to the far West to practice law. I saw that I had made no impression on him and that he thought I had not studied a sufficient length of time to justify his giving me a certificate of admission. He plied me vigorously with abstruse questions intended to catch me and I was not surprised when he told me that he did not find me entitled to a certificate. This was, of course, a grave disappointment, but I immediately bethought myself that there were other judges in Massachusetts besides Judge Wilde, and I resolved that after studying a little longer I would apply to one of them. It was not long before I was emboldened to present myself before Judge Strong who was holding the court of common pleas in Midale County. I kept my own counsel and never told a human being about my disastrous repulse by Judge Wilde. Judge Strong was an old man, as I now remember him, and was from the western part of the state. His heart and sympathy had not been frozen by the east winds at Boston. His reception was reassuring. There was as much difference between it and the reception Judge Wilde had given me as there is between an ice house and a room with a genial fire. He read my certificates, asked about my studies and where I was from, and then he examined me. I answered his questions satisfactorily and he gave me a note to the clerk of the court ordering him to make out a license for me to practice law in all the courts of Massachusetts.

The time had now come, the last of February, 1840, when I was to go West. I had money enough to pay all my bills and my expenses to the North West. Once there I must begin earning a living at once. I feel grateful for the kindness of my brother Sidney while I was in Boston and Cambridge. He was always on the lookout to serve me. I am grateful to all my relations at Raynham.

On March 2, 1840, I took the train from Taunton to Mansfield and connected with the train from Boston to Providence where I took the boat to New York. In New York I had my life insured for the benefit of my creditors. I determined to go West by way of Baltimore so as to visit Washington. I left New York late in the afternoon and arrived at Philadelphia at eleven o'clock at night. The next morning I left Philadelphia at eight by rail and reached Baltimore at three in the afternoon. At four I left Baltimore by rail for Washington and arrived at half past six. I stopped at the American House, near the Capitol, and paid $8 per week for board. The hotel was kept by a man named Beers who continued to keep it for some years after I came to Congress. I was in Washington for a week and never have I been so much interested. I was excited at what was going on in Congress, and I regretted that I could not be in both Senate and House at the same time.

George Evans was the representative from the Kennebec district. I had known him well in Hallowell and went to see him. He took me to the White House and introduced me to President Van Buren. The President was a little, dapper, Dutch-looking man, with a little bald head, small features, but bright and intelligent countenance. He was courteous and polite but somewhat reserved in his manners as it appeared to me.

Having no more time or money to spend in Washington I left there on Wednesday, March 11, 1840, taking the railroad to Frederick, Maryland, which was as far as it went. We there took the stage to cross the Allegheny Mountains and tremendous staging it was. There was a great deal of travel and there were opposition lines. The consequence was that we travelled at great speed and made no stops except to swallow hasty meals. After being on the stage for two days and nights we arrived at Wheeling, Virginia, on Friday at noon. As good luck would have it the steamboat *Reporter* was at the landing ready to start for St. Louis. It had cost me twenty-one dollars to go from Washington to Wheeling and Captain Caldwell was taking passengers on the *Reporter* from Wheeling to St. Louis for eighteen dollars and finding them. Leaving Wheeling on Friday we reached Cincinnati at half past eight Sunday morning and I presented several letters which Richard Houghton of the Boston *Atlas* had given me. I was kindly received, and on Tuesday morning Mr. Whiteman, a prominent merchant in Cincinnati, took me to see General Harrison. Being an ardent Whig I was enthusiastic about him. We knocked at the door and the general himself answered our summons. I described him at the time in a letter to my brother as, "a hard-faced, keen, eagle-eyed, grey headed old gentleman—frank, plain, simple, cordial, ingenuous." I went on: "We sat down and talked about half an hour upon various subjects, but mostly on politics. His voice is very fine and his conversation chaste and pure to a remarkable degree. You only want to see him and talk with him to become satisfied that he is the man for the people." While I was in the city talking with the future President, our steamboat departed for Louisville and left me behind. Fortunately, the steam packet, *General Pike* was about leaving for the same port, so I got aboard of her and easily overtook the *Reporter* before she left Louisville. Then we went rapidly down the Ohio. Some distance below Evansville, Indiana, when going fast, the main shaft of the engine broke, tearing up the cabin and creating great confusion among the passengers. The boat would have to wait until a new shaft could be made and sent down from Evansville. The passengers could wait till the repairs were made or receive back part of their passage money and go on by another boat when it should come along. I determined to go on. Before long a large New Orleans boat called *The Tarquin* came and several of us got aboard for Cairo. We arrived there early and went ashore. And what a horrible place it was—half overflowed, with a few scattered buildings, infested with river thieves, gamblers and cut throats. The hotel was a small, two-story frame building, quite a distance from the landing, and thither we went to await a boat for St. Louis. The first one to come was the *Otter*, a new boat on her first trip, being brought from Pittsburg, owned by the Harrises from Galena and commanded by Captain Smith Harris. She was crowded with passengers, notwithstanding that her cabin was unfinished. We were packed like sardines and slept on the main cabin floor. She had not much power and made slow headway against the currents. We were three days in getting to St. Louis. I found St. Louis very interesting. The French character and aspect of the place had not then worn off and the French element predominated. It was a busy, stirring place, with many steamboats at the levee loading and discharging cargoes. I looked for a boat going to Stephenson and Davenport but there was none going above the lower rapids. The *Burlington* was going as far as Keokuk the

next day so I took passage. Then I went into the town
to see Nathaniel Holmes with whom I had been to the
law school in Cambridge. He took me "Away out of
town," as he called it, to see the foundation of a tremendous hotel they were building. It was the Planter's House
on Fourth street. The *Burlington* got to Keokuk in due
time. There was nothing there but a string of log cabins
under the bluff, occupied by Indians, half-breeds, traders
and groggery keepers. There were half a dozen drunken
squaws parading up and down the bank of the river,
yelling and hooting like mad. Fortunately, the *Ama-
ranth*, Captain Atcheson, was just ready to leave Keokuk
for Galena. She was the crack boat of the upper Mississippi of that day and Captain Atcheson was the prince
of steamboat captains. We stopped at all the towns on
our way up. Burlington was the most considerable of
them, and there I met James W. Grimes, afterwards
governor of Iowa and United States senator. At this
time all the people along the river depended upon the
boats for their news, and as political excitement ran high,
when a boat came in sight, the whole town rushed to the
landing to see who was on board and get the news. We
arrived at Stephenson where my brother Cadwallader
was, at four or five o'clock of a pleasant afternoon. There
was a big crowd on the levee and straining my eyes I saw
him—a tall, spare green-looking young man with a gray
plush cap. I remained several days with him and made
many acquaintances. He was then reading law with an
old friend of ours from Maine, Joseph B. Wells, afterwards lieutenant governor of Illinois. The supreme question with me was where to locate.

Here the autobiography breaks off.

Cadwallader had told Elihu that Illinois was a better
place to settle in than Iowa and that the most promising
locality was in the northern part near the Mississippi
River not far from the Wisconsin border at a place called
Galena where lead mines had recently been opened.

Elihu went to Galena arriving there on April 1, 1840. They had told him in Stephenson that there were eight or nine Democratic lawyers in Galena, but only one Whig lawyer and that political feeling was so strong that the Whig litigants would choose a lawyer of their own political faith if they could. On April 1, 1871, in Paris, Washburne made this entry in his diary:

"It is thirty-one years ago this day since I arrived at Galena. I was a passenger in the little stern-wheel steamboat *Pike*, Captain Powers. We arrived at the levee before daylight, and when I got up in the morning it was bright and clear, . . . The mud in the streets knee-deep, the log and frame buildings all huddled together; the river full of steamboats discharging freight, busy men running to and fro, and draymen yelling. Those were the golden days of Galena."

Washburne determined to settle in Galena almost immediately after he had reached the town. He rented two rooms for ten dollars per month, which he shared with Horace H. Houghton, editor of the Whig paper, Houghton paying three dollars and sharing his bedroom. He found a boarding house where he paid four dollars per week. It was a log cabin and his office on Bench street was built partly of logs, being on the second floor with three windows, and furnished with a table, three chairs and a Franklin stove. He had the building whitewashed and wrote home that he was "very respectably situated." On Monday, April 6 (five days after his arrival) his sign as a lawyer was out. He thought Galena "a horrid rough place," but the lead mines made a place of business where there was much money in circulation, and lawyer's fees were high. The population was 4000 with about a dozen lawyers. "The people" said Elihu, "are a litigious set."

Within a month he had clients and had done more than enough business to pay his expenses; also he had made two or three political speeches. He had three cases at the first term of court held in Galena after he settled there. As early as May 2, 1840, he was ready to send money home to his brother Sidney in Boston. His practice was of a varied character; for example, the defense of a member of "the Bellview gang" for stealing, for which he received a fee of forty dollars and the defense of a burglar which carried a fee of twenty-five dollars. The thief was convicted but the jury disagreed about the burglar. He was engaged in a case of some importance with Charles S. Hempstead, one of the leading lawyers. The other lawyers were men of talent Washburne thought, but some were bullies, gamblers and drunkards. He attended the Episcopal church in Galena because it was the best in the town. Very soon after he had settled he liked Galena. He found its society pleasant and even thought it gay and fashionable.

So his career was fixed and thenceforth law and politics eng.ossed his life, until the politics crowded out the law. He had business before the Supreme Court of the United States four years after his office had been opened in Galena. In 1844, three years after he had settled at that place he was a delegate to the Whig national convention at Baltimore and presented Henry Clay's name as the candidate for the Presidency. In 1848 he was the Whig candidate for Congress and was defeated. In 1852 he was a delegate to the Whig convention which nominated General Scott for the Presidency. In the same year he was elected a representative in Congress. His majority was only 286 votes; but it rose at successive elections until in 1860 it was 12511. A change in the districting of the state then reduced it to 3711, and in 1868 it was 9200. He served in Congress for nine successive terms, for eighteen years, and became the "Father of the House." He was chairman of the Committee on Commerce for ten years and from 1867 to 1869 chairman of the Committee on Appropriations. He was a member of the joint Committee on Reconstruction after the Civil War and chairman of the Committee of the Whole in the impeachment of Andrew Johnson, President of the United States. At various times movements were made to make him senator from Illinois. The first one was in 1865; the last in 1879, when David Davis, an Independent, was elected. The belief was general at that time that if the regular Republican candidate, General Logan, had withdrawn from the contest Mr. Washburne would have been chosen. As early as 1875, his friends proposed his name as that of a suitable candidate for the presidential nomination from the Republicans, and in the convention of 1880 some forty delegates voted for him. In 1874 when a change in the head of the Treasury Department was about to take place the Secretary of State, Hamilton Fish, and the Secretary of the Navy, George M. Robson asked Mr. Washburne to become Secretary of the Treasury, but he positively declined for reasons of health and from family considerations. In 1876 several Illinois newspapers proposed him for governor of Illinois, and his name was brought forward for that post on several succeeding occasions. He retired from the post of Minister to France in 1878, having been continuously in the national service for twenty-six years. Upon his retirement he changed his residence to the city of Chicago and interested himself in literary and historical pursuits as well as politics. He was president of the Chicago Historical Society from 1884 to 1887.

ESTABLISHMENT AT GALENA

Elihu Washburne honored his father and mother. He did not attribute his hard youth to any dereliction on the part of his father and in reality there had been none. The father's pecuniary misfortunes were as unavoidable as the blindness which came upon him and rendered him helpless during the last years of his life. Elihu's contributions to the support of the old parents were regarded by him simply as a duty.

Maine was always the center of his affections. He had never been outside of the borders of that state and Massachusetts till he was twenty-four years old. Back of him lay generations of New England stock. In Illinois he was an active member of the organization known as "The Society of the Sons of the State of Maine" which had as its object "to revive and perpetuate the memories of our early homes and native state." Hardly a year went by that he did not revisit the home of his birth and youth. He had a restless life—from the East to the West, and in the West, from Galena to Chicago; more often in Washington than in Illinois; eight years in Europe, from Paris to Bohemia; ever moving, hardly spending six months continuously in one place in the whole of his life; but in whatever place, the mining town, or representing a Western constituency in Washington, or in foreign capitals and health resorts, always a son of New England, formed upon a New England model, steeped in New England traditions, talking, acting and thinking as a New England man. In all essential particulars he was as much a son of Maine as his brother Israel who lived his whole life within fifty miles of the place where he was born.

He cast in his fortunes with a conglomerate community. Galena, when he went there, presented many varying types of humanity. There were the miners, Americans, Germans, Swiss, good men and bad men and all rough men; there were the free-living lawyers,—a lawyer in those days and those communities was not expected to be of Puritanical habits;—there were the sturdy pioneers like himself who had gone West to succeed and would have succeeded anywhere. To these should be added the floating adventurers who liked change and excitement, and the criminals who found a good field for operation among miners and in a new community where no one knew anything of his neighbor's past.

But there was a little group of cultured people also. Washburne spoke about the women and complained that he missed some gayety because he could not dance. A few years before his arrival a traveller who visited Galena illustrated the variety which constituted its social life by saying that he had met J. P. B. Gratiot's wife who was born and educated in Paris, Henry Gratiot's wife who was born and educated in Connecticut and Mrs. Croonce who was born and educated in London.

When Washburne attended his first term of court in Illinois he was associated in one case with Charles S. Hempstead and this was the beginning of a fateful connection. Hempstead was the oldest member of the Galena bar and had more cases on the calendar of the court than all the other lawyers combined. He had partial paralysis of the fingers of the right hand and wrote with difficulty. In the fall of 1840, he proposed to Washburne to take a desk in his office, board in his family and in return assist him in writing. He would also turn over to Washburne some of his smaller cases. Accordingly, the log boarding house and the half-log office were abandoned and Washburne went into the office of the first lawyer of the vicinity, a man of high character, of influential connection and of large experience. After remaining with him for a year Washburne's practice had so far increased that he found it to his advantage to open a separate office. He formed a partnership with Hempstead again in 1845, however, and continued it for some years after he had been elected a congressman.

Charles Hempstead was the brother of that Mrs. Henry Gratiot who was described as having been born and educated in Connecticut. Henry Gratiot had died in 1836 and his widow and her eight children, four boys and four girls, were living at Gratiot's Grove, a primeval wood with a wide expanse of rolling prairie around it, situated a few miles north of Galena at "Gratiot's Survey," the best known of the lead "diggings." The Grove was actually in Wisconsin, but at the time of the settlement it was commonly supposed to be in Illinois. The Gratiots were a famous family. The first one to come to America was Henry Gratiot's father, Charles Gratiot, who was born in La Rochelle, France, in 1753, but, being a Huguenot, fled to Switzerland, whence he came first to London, then to Canada and then to the Illinois region. There he became one of the best known of the early fur-traders. He was a patriot during the Revolution and performed important services for General George Rogers Clark. Soon after the Revolution he went to upper Louisiana and settled in St. Louis. There he married Victoire Chouteau, a member of one of the French families which had founded that town. Two of Charles Gratiot's sons, Jean Pierre

Bugnion Gratiot and Henry Gratiot, went to the new
lead mines on the Mississippi River in 1826 and settled
at the Grove which became known by their family name.
One reason why they left St. Louis was that they wished
to live in a place where there were no slaves. Thirteen
years before, on January 21, 1813, Henry Gratiot had
married Susan Hempstead in St. Louis. She was the
daughter of Stephen Hempstead of Connecticut, a
soldier in the Revolution, who had served at Bunker Hill
and as sergeant in the company of Nathan Hale. Stephen
Hempstead's son, Edward Hempstead, was the first
delegate in Congress from the newly organized territory
of Missouri and consequently the first representative
in the national Congress from the country west of the
Mississippi.

The rest of the story so far as it concerns us is soon told.
Young Washburne, as a member of Edward Hempstead's family, was thrown with the Gratiots, and met
Henry Gratiot's third daughter, Adèle, who was born in
Galena in 1826, being probably the first white child born
in that town. When Washburne first saw her she was
only fourteen years old, but girls were called women at an
early age in those days. She had been educated at a con-
vent of The Visitation and had lived in St. Louis with her
aunt, often visiting Madame Chouteau, another aunt, a
lady of importance, one of those who gave the French
atmosphere to the place. Madame Chouteau, it should be
remarked, was a Catholic, but Henry Gratiot's daughter
was a Huguenot and, following her mother's church, was a
Presbyterian.

Five years after he had met her, on July 31, 1845,
Adèle Gratiot and Elihu Washburne were married at
Galena. It is recorded that Madame Chouteau insisted

that the whole of the bride's trousseau should come from Paris.

Their union lasted for forty-two years, for all of her womanhood and for nearly all of his manhood. He was a masterful man, controlling those about him, driving ahead on the way he had marked out for himself, self-reliant and determined. He was not under the influence of anyone except his wife who had much to do with the directing of his career. It was on her account he studied French history, mastered the language and went as Minister to France, that he admitted into his mental outlook an entirely new and liberalizing element. Even in the family, French was always spoken. In fact, he fitted himself to be the husband of a half-French woman almost as much as environment had fitted him for a son of Maine. No personal trait of Washburne's is as outstanding as the devotion he felt and showed for his charming wife. She was his chief correspondent, and he, who was not a man of gentle ways, could write to her only in gentle tone. (Each of the letters quoted here contains some tenderness which has been omitted as the writer would have wished that it should be.)

Because Washburne had married a daughter of the Gratiots and Hempsteads, Thomas H. Benton in the House of Representatives showed him special consideration when he entered Congress in 1852. Everything connected with Adèle Washburne's family and history was of interest to him and a source of pride. Soon after she died he put up a memorial window to her grandfather, General Charles Gratiot, the friend and compatriot of General Francis Marion, in the Huguenot church in Charleston where General Gratiot had lived for a time. Thomas H. Benton gave Washburne a sketch of Edward

Hempstead he had written in 1818, a year after Hempstead's death. Washburne printed this in 1875 with an historical sketch from his own pen of Charles S. Hempstead who had died December 10, 1874. Later, he made an address on Edward Hempstead before the Missouri legislature on the occasion of the presentation to the state of a portrait of Hempstead painted by Gilbert Stuart, the portrait being the gift of Mrs. Washburne's cousin, Edward Hempstead of Chicago. In 1884 he gave to the state Historical Society of Wisconsin, on behalf of his wife, a portrait of Henry Gratiot and made an address before that society, giving the historical facts concerning the career and services of the more conspicuous members of the Gratiot family.

The first two sons of the seven children who were born to Elihu and Adèle Washburne were named for his wife's family, also his two daughters. The first was called Gratiot, the second Hempstead, the third William Pitt, the fourth E. B. Washburne, Jr. (born 1857, died 1862), the fifth Susan Adèle, the sixth Marie Lisa, and the seventh E. B. Washburne, Jr. Of his children Washburne was very fond although all had to bend to his will.

Mrs. Washburne's influence was not necessary to preserve the religious principles of her husband. They belonged to his up-bringing and youth and were deeply rooted in a nature which clung tenaciously to the early training. These principles were broadly Christian, for the church of his childhood and youth had been Universalist. As we have seen when he first went to Galena he attended the Episcopal church because he happened to like it, but after his marriage he went to the Presbyterian church with his wife. In Chicago they were a part of Dr. Swing's congregation, and after Dr. Swing ceased to be a Presbyterian they attended his Independent church. Washburne never belonged to any particular denomination and was never a churchman in the same sense as his brother Israel.

In 1837 (October 3) when he was at Hallowell he wrote to his brother Sidney: "But this going to the theatre is devilish bad business for young men, and I hope and pray that you will curse and quit it forthwith. As for myself, I would as soon think of going to his Satanic Majesty as going there. *The theatre is no place for young men.* Mark those words." He modified these views as time went on; in fact, after the Washington life began he went to the theatre often; and we find him, after his return from Paris, giving a letter of introduction to friends in Paris to Miss Mary Anderson, the actress, who was making her first visit to that city, the request for the letter coming from Colonel Tom Ochiltree of Texas. In his autobiography he stated that he neither smoked nor drank alcoholic liquors. This was literally true as to tobacco, but after he rose in the world his table was like that of any other man of his class, wine was served and he himself drank it moderately.

The world was before Elihu and Adèle Washburne when they married. He was making a living—that was all—and she brought him a desirable family connection but no fortune. Yet they faced the future without fear. He was an intrepid man and she never had a doubt that he could do anything which he set out to do. She was well-educated, intelligent and blessed with intuitive tact. She accepted any place in which she might be living with quiet adaptability. In appearance she was French—a very pretty woman, small and slight with dark brown, almost black eyes, soft black hair, regular features and clear white complexion.   She was a woman of gentle manners and quiet dignity, loving her home, adoring her children, waited upon by servants completely devoted to her.

PRE-WAR POLITICAL ACTIVITIES

The following extracts of letters selected from a great number are sufficient to illustrate certain facts of Washburne's political career before the Civil War. He took an absorbing interest in political affairs before he was of age; he was a Whig but became a Republican as soon as that party was organized; he was a contemporary of Abraham Lincoln in the politics of Illinois; he was active in the anti-slavery propaganda after the Kansas question came up; he favored the nomination of Lincoln for the Presidency. After his election to Congress in 1854 his progress as a public man of national importance was steady and uninterrupted. It culminated in 1880 when a few of his enemies prevented his nomination for the Presidency. His rise was not a sudden jump into prominence, but came gradually because of a growing impression that he had become familiar with public questions, that he was industrious and effective, that he was conscientious and honest and that his views of public policy were those which the majority of the people held.

Washburne's first committee service was on the Committee on Manufactures; by 1856 he was chairman of the Committee on Commerce; at the same time his brother, Israel, was chairman of the Committee on Elections and Cadwallader was on the Committee on Military Affairs. Elihu remained chairman of the Committee on Commerce for thirteen years, when he became chairman of the Committee on Appropriations. The House now recognized him as one of its leaders.

He wrote to his brother, Algernon Sidney:

Hallowell, Sept. 19, 1837.

This is a day of jubilee—the big guns are proclaiming in tones of thunder the prostration of loco-focoism, while the bells speak out in a very manner that Maine is regenerated. Will yᴏu believe it, that old Maine has burst the ignominious thraldom of Jacksonism and now peers out as the brightest star in the whole political firmament. *It is even so*—Maine has gained herself unfailing laurels, by achieving one of the brightest victories ever recorded. What do you think now, after telling me so many times that there was no possibility of carrying the good old State of Maine. Never mind—that was only *"Love's labor lost"*—Edward Kent is Governor and Gorham Parks is defeated—Glory enough this for a thousand years. Keep it to the credit of old Maine.

To W. H. HERNDON

Private.   *House of Reps. April 28, 1858.*

. . .

The events here for the last week, the defection of the Douglas men and the almost certain passage of the Lecompton swindle, has, I hope, opened the eyes of the country to the fact, that the only reliance is upon the republican party and all we have to do now to secure a complete triumph in our State is, to act with energy and discretion.

. . .

In all my correspondence I have insisted that we must stand by our principles and our men, and as for Senator, I was for Lincoln against the field. That the Republicans were bound to stand by him by every consideration of honor and fair dealing,. has always been my position, and it has been known to be my position. It is generally known where *I am*. If I am for a man I am *for him*, and if against him, I am *against him*.

And yet standing as I do stand in these matters, I have not felt it necessary to protest in every letter that Douglas should not work with us, but in this great fight, operating so vastly to our benefit, I have said, God speed him. I am rejoiced to see him laboring so manfully in a direction to make some amends for the injury he has brought upon the country. He is doing a grand service for the republican party, and for one, while he pursues his present course, I shall not lay a straw in his path. He is fighting this Lecompton swindle in all its phases, with boldness and determination. If things go on, as it now seems inevitable, if he be not with us, a vast number of his followers will be, and hence I cannot see the wisdom of abusing either him, or them, as matters stand now. I have no fears that the republican party is to be swallowed by them. I say leave open wide the doors and invite all to come into our platform and greet them with kind words. Our party is not so large but what it will hold a few more.

I have marked this letter private, but you are at liberty to show it to Lincoln if you think proper.

January 10, 1859. Washington, D. C.

To————————.

My dear Sir: I enclose you herewith a prospectus for the "National Era." This paper is not only the best representative of the living and genuine principles of the Republican Party, but it is also a paper to distinguished literary merit as well as one of the very best family newspapers of which I have any knowledge.

At this time when great efforts are being made to get up an organization in opposition to the present democratic organization which shall ignore the great *anti-slavery* idea upon which the Republican Party was founded, it is vastly important to have a paper circulated among the people that will uphold the standard of principle and not yield it to every suggestion of temporary success. I am anxious to see the "Era" circulated in every neighborhood of our Congressional district, and I would regard it as a personal favor if you would exert yourself to get up as large a club of subscribers as possible in your vicinity and forward the names as directed in the prospectus.

To Mrs. Washburne

Thursday, Nov. 14, 1860, Home.
I got home last night from Springfield. I spent night
before last with Mr. Lincoln and his wife and had a very
pleasant and satisfactory interview. I found Old Abe in
fine spirits and excellent health, and quite undisturbed by
the blusterings of the disunionists and traitors. You
would pity me if you only saw the piles of letters I am now
having. Although I write fast it will take me all day to
answer those I have received since Monday. . . . . .

To J. W. Shaffer in Freeport, Ill.

Washington, D. C., April 4, 1860.
. . .
The results in Conn and R. I. put a new phase on matters.
It must now be patent to every sagacious man that we
cannot elect Seward, and some other man must be nominated at Chicago. I do really hope things will be so arranged
that you or Turner will be the delegate from our end.
Don't make much talk before hand or commit yourselves
for or against anybody. With a *proper* candidate, and
either of you know who will be a proper candidate, the
triumph is an absolute certainty. With an *improper*
candidate our defeat is equally certain. But all this is
private talk to you—I believe we agree exactly.

To Mrs. Washburne

(March 1861) Sunday morning.
Well, Old Abe rather came it over the Baltimore Plug
uglies, and got here yesterday morning, without being
known to anybody but Seward and myself. I went down
to meet him, but Seward was not there, and so I took him
into a hack and went to the hotel. He is very well, considering how much he has been jaded and worn down.
Mrs. Lincoln came last night. I shall not express my
opinion of her until I see you. . . .
It is not to be supposed that his continuance in Congress

was effected without difficulty; on the contrary, every nomination he received required a great deal of manœuvering, negotiation and struggle on his part. His district was not different from other lively political districts; it was a nest of ambitious, scheming politicians, honest and dishonest, fair and treacherous, and self-seeking to a man. It would require more space than the subject justifies to tell the story of the hundred plans which were hatched to defeat his nomination and the hundred plans which he devised to overcome them. The innumerable undercurrents of Illinois politics have no abiding interest. Before Lincoln became President, Washburne had no federal offices to bestow among his friends, except a few minor positions at the Capitol, for the executive power was in the hands of his political opponents. After Lincoln's election, however, there was a plentiful flow of federal appointments made at his request. He did not neglect his opportunities in this direction. There was no civil service commission in his day and no pretense of making federal appointments to office for merit alone; political considerations entered into all of them. As a friend of Lincoln, Washburne's recommendations were apt to be effective.

The directions which his career in Congress took became clearly defined as his service proceeded. His first act was to introduce, on December 13, 1853, a resolution to the effect that it was the sense of Congress that the federal government had authority under the Constitution to build railroads through the territories. Seven months later, July 24, 1854, he introduced a resolution designed to prevent the absorption of public lands by a railroad in the territory of Minnesota. Fourteen years later, on November 26, 1867, he asked the House to resolve that there should be no further appropriations of public lands to states or corporations for building railroads; that all public lands should be held for private sale by the government to actual settlers. His efforts in this direction had been unremitting. He furthered the building of the Pacific Railroad. He was in favor of every measure which looked to the development of the western country, and he watched jealously the efforts of the railroads to take more than they were actually entitled to from the public domain. On March 6, 1854, he carried through an amendment to the homestead law which permitted aliens who had made declaration of intention to become citizens of the United States to take up public lands on the same footing as citizens. In his speech on this measure he said he thought that persons of color also should be allowed to take up public lands. His watchfulness over the interests of his own state especially and of the Northwest generally was incessant. Improvements of the navigation of the Mississippi, the salaries of territorial officers, establishment of additional mail routes, the admission of Minnesota as a state in 1858 were a few of the many measures in this direction which he advocated with zeal. When the tariff bill was up in 1857 he spoke on February 14 in favor of continued protection of the lead mining industry. His speech showed exhaustive knowledge of the subject and its development in Illinois. He became known as one of the business members of the House and his work on the Committee on Commerce looked to business results.

March 10, 1856, he had printed an important report from the State Department on foreign commerce. This was the inauguration of the series of publications known as *Commercial Relations of the United States with foreign nations* and of the *Consular Reports* which have played an important part in the development of our foreign commerce. His service as chairman of the Committee on Appropriations came after fourteen years in the House when he had probably a greater knowledge of the government's business than any other member. It was then that he became known as the "Watchdog of the Treasury," guarding the public purse as jealously as if it had been his own, and gaining a reputation in the country at large of being the foe of all who endeavored to obtain or use the government's money wrongfully. The expenses of the government while he was in this important position were very great because of the necessities arising from the Civil War. Those expenses had allured many men into embracing false schemes of finance by substituting promises and notes of obligation for actual money, but Washburne stood firm for orthodox currency, and on December 15, 1862, introduced a resolution that it was the sense of the House that no law should be passed changing the requirement that interest on the public debt should be paid in coin.

Into the controversial political affairs of Congress Washburne plunged with keen relish. On April 5, 1854, he made a set speech on the Kansas-Nebraska bill. It was a straightforward defense of the Missouri Compromise and its inviolability. He gave the usual arguments for the right of free soil, but added that the bill violated our treaties with the Indians by not safeguarding their territory to them. He instanced the unhappy fate of the Winnebagoes who had been driven from their land. Evidently his mind reverted to the experiences of Henry Gratiot. The Nebraska speech was the first of many political speeches by Washburne, and as time went on he engaged more in the rough and tumble fighting of congressional debate.

Here is one and an extreme example of the practical rough and tumble to which the debates sometimes degenerated, the account being contemporaneous.

"On February 9, 1858, Keith of South Carolina rushed belligerently at Grow, of Pennsylvania, and received a blow from someone else which knocked him down. Southerners and Lecompton men then dashed to the rescue and prominent in the melée were Washburne of Illinois and Washburn of Wisconsin. Barksdale of Tennessee had hold of Grow, when Potter of New York struck him. Barksdale thought it was Elihu Washburne who had struck him and struck at Washburne. Cadwallader Washburn ran to protect his brother and seized Barksdale by the hair. Barksdale's hair was a wig and came off in Cadwallader's hands. This incident was so funny that they all stopped to laugh and the pause put an end to the riot. Cadwallader restored Barksdale's wig to him and in his excitement Barksdale put it on wrongside foremost."

In the prolonged contest over the Speakership in December, 1855, Washburne was on his feet constantly and showed shrewd parliamentary resources. When Lincoln was nominated to be President in 1860 Washburne made a speech in the House (May 29) on Lincoln's personal history and public record. He had known him, he said, since he went to Illinois in 1840. The speech was long and contained little about Lincoln which is not known to everybody, but at the time it was made, Lincoln was not well known in the East and the words must have been useful in spreading information about him. Washburne was not given to long speeches, however, being incessantly engaged in the regular business of Congress.

When he became by longer service than any other member the "Father of the House" the dignity of his position was second only to that of Speaker. He administered the oath of office to the Speaker, three times to Schuyler Colfax and once to Blaine. When each session began he moved the formal notification to the President and Senate that the House was in session and he was always appointed chairman of the committee which conveyed the information by word of mouth to those coördinate branches of the government. To an American public man there are few positions more conspicuous and powerful than that of a recognized leader of the House of Representatives and that position was Washburne's from the time of the Republican ascendancy in 1861 till he resigned on March 6, 1869, to become Secretary of State in the Cabinet of General Grant. In consequence of his long service his friends in Illinois began to examine his career systematically. The Chicago *Tribune* printed an article in 1864, when it was hoped that Washburne might be promoted to be a senator from Illinois, which was copied by other papers. It mentioned his being "Father of the House" and probably the most influential member. Whatever he did, he did with his might and had a way of succeeding in whatever he undertook. Nervous energy, a strong will and knowledge of the rules had made him an effective member. He had battled for Grant and procured for him the leadership of the army, crushing the rebellion.

Shortly after Grant's election, George Alfred Townsend ("Gath") gave an impressionist picture of Washburne in his Cincinnati paper.

"Here is E. B. Washburne," he said; "a broad-shouldered, good-bellied, large, and yet a thin man. He leaves a plump impression upon your mind, while you admit his lankness. You say to yourself, inwardly, when he has gone—The model is Yankee, but the cargo is Western. The man was meant to be lathy, and longitude 'chucked' a good deal of corn and pork into him. His age is beyond fifty; say, for an impression, fifty-four. His hair is gray; he dresses plainly; he has a very impulsive manner, accompanied with a look almost of fanaticism out of large lightish-gray eyes. He wears no beard, the expression of his face in repose is rendered almost untranslatable by his intense industry, which, being of a nervous sort, keeps him screwed up to a headlong gait all the while. He never listens to hear his own brother speak more than a few minutes, being brimful of things to do and say, and the lines across his forehead deepen and thicken as he scratches away with a pen, tears the wrappers off newspapers, whistles for a page, leans over backward to talk quick and nervously, jumps up to object or interject remarks, and now and then stops when at work to blow off like a steam engine, with his hands behind his head, clasped. Directly he is up yonder in the diplomatic gallery, talking to a lady; again down in Downing's restaurant, taking provender. A horse and buggy comes with him to Congress every day; his house is up near Gen. Grant's and close by St. Aloysius' church, in the new suburban part of the city, and there he lives with his family and his rich brother, Cadwallader Washburn, the General, of Wisconsin."

He went on to describe him as having all the best New England traits—"He does not drink a drop of liquor; he never smokes. He has an affection of the kidneys, which sometimes gives him exceeding pain, and is probably the cause of his testy exhibitions of temper."

He spoke of the family: "His love of his birth-place and his honor of his father and mother, are unostentatious and profound. He and all the boys go home every year, sacredly, to see the old gentleman, whose hair is white as snow, but who looks like the father of generations to be. His is a fine face, well-featured, with each faculty expressing its acuteness in the dignified totality. The old gentleman has been photographed, with his remarkable brood of boys around him—a regular old Priam in the midst of his household of Trojans.

"Of these boys, the ex-Governor of Maine has been said to be the ablest; the young ones are coming along vigorously. They love and strengthen each other up, though each is independent as a wood-sawyer."

They had paid their father back, he said, by building him a fine house.

Washburne he said was "an educated, independent and scrupulously honest man, a watch-dog, indeed, over the public money, and a man of moral courage, used to saying 'No' with two o's to it.

"He is opposed to giving any more land to the Pacific railways believing them to be corrupt from scalp to bowels. He is opposed to giving away land any way, and money more, except on the homestead principle. He is perfectly reckless of the effect of any economy upon the fortunes of his party, and would have seen Gen. Grant defeated without remorse rather than to have voted for any popular corruption. He has not one friend in this city among the Speculators, ring makers and place seekers, and these constitute the bulk of the town. All of these would be so glad to see him go away that they would labor with the corrupt Senators to get him confirmed for any executive appointment. . . .

"What does Washburne want? I don't believe that Gen. Grant knows; I don't believe that Washburne has

made up his mind. I don't know that he wants anything.
His friends are Dawes, of Massachusetts and Allison, of
Iowa, and only one or two more. Among the citizens here
he has made few acquaintances. He is a very plain man,
with a comfortable home, up to the eyes in public business,
and he has no design to be driven away from Gen. Grant,
whom he likes and admires. His family, I have heard,
wish to go abroad, where Mr. Washburne has been already for his health's sake. His wife being French by
descent and scholarship, might like to go to Paris. If
this be the case, and Grant wants to send Washburne
there, I suppose that Gen. Dix could be called home, and
might possibly go in the Cabinet, though he is up in years."

The *New York Tribune* gave another picture more
minute and less highly colored. "He had a broad high,
square forehead with projecting corners at the temples.
His hair was iron gray, worn long, half rolled under at the
ends like a Southerner's or a man from the rural districts.
The ears were large, the eyebrows not very heavy presenting a straight line near the nose. The eyes were large
and full, though deepset, of blueish gray and shining like
diamonds. The nose was prominent. The cheeks were
slightly sunken, of pale freshness. The mouth was large,
the lips thin and compressed, forming almost a straight line
across the face. His dress was plain but he wore a stock
instead of a neckerchief. His voice was full and deep, his
style of speaking easy and offhand and more convincing
than that of any other member of the House. He was
earnest and forcible in his expressions and went into an
argument or a debate with honest enthusiasm and thrill-
ing excitement. His gestures were wild in the extreme but
not ungraceful. Socially he was a gem of rarest price."

To these descriptions should be added that he was five

feet ten and a half inches tall, that his hair had been a sandy brown before it became gray, that his complexion was rather dark, that his hand was short and broad, and his feet small and well proportioned and that he wore well-fitting boots, being, in fact, proud of his feet. His clothing was of broadcloth, blue or black, cut in the fashion of the day, the same one year with another.

Mrs. Julia Washburn, his cousin's wife, went to a reception at the White House in 1876 when Grant was President and saw Elihu Washburne enter the room and heard the people say, "No one has filled a room as Washburne does since the days of Daniel Webster." His manners were cordial and easy, but he was always impressive. He was a great talker.

WARTIME SERVICE

Every measure designed to prosecute the war vigorously was favored by Washburne. He was one of the staunchest supporters of the administration. He criticized none of its measures and went along with it and the majority of his party in his opinions and his actions as a representative. He watched over the interests of Illinois troops and Illinois officers especially. He did not try to transfer his services to the field. His brothers, Cadwallader and Samuel were in service, Samuel in the navy, a lieutenant on a gunboat called the *Galena*. He himself was content to do his share towards saving the Union, in Congress. In fact, his physical condition was such that he could not have held a commission in the army. But he actually did see something of war.

To MRS. WASHBURNE

Washington, D. C. July 18, 1861.
Yesterday was one of the most interesting days I ever passed. As I wrote you yesterday morning, I went out with the advance of the grand army on Fairfax Court House. Four of us, Gov. Lane and Mr. Colfax of Indiana, Mr. Hill of the N. Y. Tribune and myself took a carriage and started at 5 o'clock in the morning. After proceeding on the "sacred soil of Virginia" about 10 miles we overtook the advancing column at the place where they bivouacked the night before. The column extended three or four miles, and it was the most exciting scene I ever witnessed—a great army on its march to the battle field. There were the two Rhode Island Regiments, with their white forelocks and red blankets on their backs—their bright bayonets gleaming in the hot sun. Then followed the long

trains of heavy artillery, some immense guns requiring eight horses to haul one of them. The New Hampshire Regiment followed, a splendid body of men; then came the regiment of Zouaves, with their red breeches making a magnificent appearance; then a splendid company of U. S. Flying Artillery; then a whole regiment of regular U. S. Infantry; then the U. S. Marines, and the rear followed by four companies of regular U. S. Cavalry. There were also other regiments, and then such a host of baggage waggons, carriages, ambulances, etc. as you can hardly conceive of. They would not let our carriage enter the column, and as I could not stay in the rear, I started on foot for the head of the column, marching with the soldiers. Col. Marston of the New Hampshire Regiment lent me his horse and I rode forward to within 100 yards of the very front of the advance, where the commanding Genl. McDowell and his staff were. The enemy had felled large numbers of trees across the road in these different places to impede our march, but the soldiers, with their axes soon cut them out of the way. Within about two miles of the Court House we drove in the enemy's picket guards. Now it became vastly exciting, as nobody knew whether we were to have a fight, or a foot race. Skirmishers were out on all sides to look for masked batteries and pit falls, and we moved forward very cautiously. Soon we came in sight of the entrenchments of the enemy. For a long distance this side, they had thrown down all the fences, and cut down all the trees, so that the range of their guns could not be interfered with. One column with fixed bayonets and at a quick step pressed on, but the bird had flown. The cavalry had taken to their heels three hours before—had left their camps and run like white-heads. The entrenchment was about half a mile from the village and had been put up at vast labor. The embrasures were all filled in with sand bags, one of which, marked "Confederate States," I have got as a trophy. The rebel troops evidently left in a hurry. An officers' camp was found with breakfast all set and the table left in that way. Passing by the entrenchments the troops moved quickly into the village, the men cheering and the bands playing. Soon the four companies of cavalry which had been in the rear, were ordered up to give chase to the flying rebels, and it was a grand sight to see four hundred of them dash through the main street of the town at a gallop. It reminded me of the charge of the cuirassiers of Nansonsty and La Tour D'Auvergne which we read of in the wars of the great Napoleon. The troops soon began to scatter about the town and I blushed at the scenes of pillage and robbery on every side. Houses were broken into and completely gutted. At the little village of Germantown, two miles beyond Fairfax, six houses were burned. Our soldiers exhibited a most revengeful spirit. Fairfax Court House is quite a village,—30 years ago it must have been quite an important place. It is situated on uneven ground and is full of shade trees. It is now the very picture of desolation. Nearly all the people had fled, expecting there would be a great battle. There are some fine houses there and handsome yards. Having seen all there was to be seen, and more particularly the star spangled banner flying from the court house, we started on our return home—distance 18 miles—and arrived at dark, worn out with fatigue and hunger.

.   .   .   .

MEMORANDUM FOR MRS. WASHBURNE

July 20 '61, 4 P. M. Went to McDowell's head quarters—found there McDowell, Col. Burnside and James B. Fry together with Genl. Wilson. McD. and Burnside were apparently in consultation about a forward movement—McD. stated to us his embarrassment—troops leaving, their time being out, etc. etc.—supposed the enemy to be in very large force and appeared to be a good deal discouraged and in low spirits. The whole interview impressed me that the crisis is a most serious one. This mem. is made in Col. Keyes' camp.

TO MRS. WASHBURNE

Washington, D. C. Monday P. M. July 22, 1861
I wrote you this morning only a brief and a sad word about the terrible battle of yesterday. I had had but a

little sleep for three nights and been in a state of constant excitement for two days. I am now somewhat rested and will proceed to give you a little history of what I saw. I wrote a hasty line on the field Saturday P. M. and sent you. After closing that letter I went about a good deal among the camps. I went to the tent of Genl. McDowell and had quite a conversation with him. I never had much of an opinion of him as a General, and I left his tent with a feeling of great sadness and a sort of a prescience of coming disaster. He seemed discouraged and in low spirits, and appeared very doubtful of the result of the approaching conflict. That was a bad symptom. As night came on I went into the miserable, straggling old village of Centreville and found a place to stay with a decayed Virginia gentleman. All we could get to eat was some poor bread and poor ham. The troops were under marching orders for two o'clock the next morning to advance to the field of battle. I laid down to rest with feelings such as I had never before conceived. The thought of the inevitable contest of the next day and of the untold results to follow it, oppressed me heavily. I slept a few hours and before daylight I was up to see the march of the troops. They poured along in one continued stream for many hours, and the earth fairly shook beneath the heavy tread of nearly thirty thousand troops, as they poured down on what is called the "Gainesville road," toward the battle ground. About 5,000 went on another road, in the direction of Manassas Junction, and a reserve of 4,000 was left at Centreville, commanded by Col. Blenker, a dashing and brilliant German officer, reminding one of Eugene Beauharnais or Poniatowski. By eight or nine o'clock the whole army, except the reserve, had passed thro' Centreville and was out of sight. From an eminence in the village the whole country round about could be seen, but it was so broken and there was so much timber, no movements of the army could be seen except by the clouds of dust which it raised wherever it went. About nine o'clock, Mr. Daily, Delegate from Nebraska, and myself took our horse and buggy and

went to the head of the left column, which was the small
column of 5000 men. Nothing could be seen from there.
Two batteries had been placed on a hill which were being
discharged into a wood in the direction of the enemy. This
was intended as a mere feint to draw the attention of the
enemy from the heads of the two other columns where the
real attack was to be made. While loitering about at the
head of this column, the battle commenced at the head of
the centre and right columns. To get on to the centre
column we had to return from where we were back to
Centreville, two or three miles, and then down the Gainesville road, where the main body of troops consisting of the
right and centre had passed in the morning. We left
Centreville to go down this road about half past twelve
amid the terrific roar of cannon in our front. We pressed
on by countless numbers of baggage waggons. Soon we
met a poor fellow being led away by two of his companions.
He had a ghastly wound in his head received in a charge
upon the enemy. These men could only tell us that a
battle was raging in our front, but did not know how it was
going. We continued on and on, till we came to a wood on
one side of the road, and some farms on the other side,
where the houses were turned into hospitals. Beyond,
along the road, there was heavy timber on both sides.
Continuing down this road we came to Schenck's brigade,
a part of which had been in the battle, but had then drawn
back to protect the point where they were stationed. While
there we could distinctly see the enemy as it was driven
across the road. The firing at this time was tremendous—
the booming of the artillery and the rattling of the musketry surpassed anything you can conceive of. While standing with the staff of the brigade a courier came riding up
and delivered a message from Gen. McDowell, saying that
the "day was ours and that the enemy was on the retreat."
Then we set up a shout that would have done you good to
hear. But yet the firing continued, and it would seem that
the retreat of the enemy was only falling back to get re-
enforcements. After this the firing continued heavier than
ever, particularly of musketry. I moved still further along

the road and looking through two points of timber I distinctly saw the enemy. I went back to Genl. Schenck and asked him to ride along and take a peep at them himself. Just at this time a scout came up and announced that the enemy was in musket shot of us. Genl. Schenck then advanced and formed his brigade in battle array on both sides of the road in the fields (for we had then come out of the timber) and he put some cannon in position on a little eminence of ground. They then commenced a few discharges of cannon, which were answered by a masked battery of the enemy by a few shots. At this time we only considered this a sort of "side show," believing the main battle had been won. The balls of the enemy during this last firing whistled over our heads pretty sharply. About four o'clock we turned about and made our way back to the top of the rise of ground where the hospitals were, having no idea that the enemy was near us, and resting in confidence that the day was ours. We came along more to get some water than anything else, for I was literally famishing from thirst. But not one drop could we get, and I said to Mr. Daily we must go back towards Centreville to get water. At this time there were a good many straggling soldiers passing along by us, but we had no idea of any disaster in the rear, for there was no panic among the soldiers who were passing. Mr. Daily and myself then started off in our buggy, and before getting far along we overtook a poor wounded soldier shot through the leg. He begged a ride of us, but as three could not ride in the buggy I told him to get in and take my seat and I would walk to Centreville—some two miles and a half. They had but just left me when I beheld a perfect avalanche pouring down the road immediately behind me. *It was the retreat of the army.* Never before had I such feelings. I had read of wars, and retreats and routs, but I never expected, or wanted to live to see my own countrymen retreating before an enemy. On they came, baggage waggons, horses, carriages, foot soldiers, cavalry, artillerymen, pell-mell, helter-skelter. A perfect panic had seized every body. The soldiers threw away their guns and their blankets and divested themselves of every encumbrance. Officers, I blush to say it, were running with their men. At this time Genl. McDougall, of Colorado, came along in his carriage, and I got in with him and we rode on to get at the head of the retreating force. We stopped our carriage and got out and tried to rally and form the men, but we might as well have attempted to stop the current of the Mississippi with a straw. I had a revolver in my coat pocket, but unfortunately my coat was in the buggy with Daily, and I was in my shirt sleeves utterly without arms. We then pushed on to Centreville and there I seized a gun and attempted to raise a sufficient force to stop the retreat, but that I could not do. I stood almost alone in the road, threatening to bayonet every cowardly soldier who was running away. But I was soon overpowered and had to move on. Daily had continued on with the buggy, leaving me to get along the best way I could. I soon came across some acquaintances and got a ride. Presently I met Daily coming back after me, and I again took a seat and we came in to Washington, arriving between twelve and one o'clock at night. Up to our arrival here, I did not believe there was any general retreat of the army, but I only thought that the particular force where I was, had been panic stricken. But I found on my arrival that it was general. I immediately went to see Genl. Scott and found him surrounded by the President and Cabinet, and a more sober set of men I never before met. They had just got a dispatch from McDowell announcing the retreat. It now appears that Daily and I had not left the hospital *three* minutes before a charge of the enemy's cavalry was made right up through the timber into the road, and the very spot where our buggy was standing. They seized a large number of prisoners. Of course, *I* was not among them. It would have been rather a serious joke to have been carried off to Richmond at this season of the year. One of our members, Mr. Ely of New York, I am afraid was taken. The last man I talked with before leaving the hospital was Senator Foster of Connecticut, and he only got away in season to escape, leaving his carriage behind him to be seized by the rebels.

I only lost a comb from my coat pocket. There is great excitement and alarm felt here, and a great many persons will leave, particularly ladies, and it is well enough they should, as the war about here is to be more fierce than ever. The city, however, will be held. If the rebel forces had been sufficient I really believed they could have moved on here this morning and taken the city. It is too late now. Our folks are recovering from the effects of the panic and defeat, and will be prepared to give bigger fight than ever. We will whip the traitors yet. Their barbarities towards our wounded will arouse a spirit of vengeance which will not be appeased till their leaders are all hung and their followers are driven into the gulf.

The giving of battle at the time it was done was a grave mistake. The whole movement was against the judgment of Genl. Scott, but the clamors of presumptuous ignorance induced him to yield. I heard him this morning tell the President that he (Scott) was a coward for yielding to this clamor, and that the President ought to dismiss him for it.

I could tell a great deal more, but I have no further time to write. You will read further particulars in the papers, perhaps now with the more interest since I was on the spot. So good bye for to-night.

To Mrs. Washburne

Washington (May 17, 1862.) Evening, Tuesday.
I wrote a line from the House to-day. I now write this in my new quarters, which I like very much so far—that is, for an hour. Last night I went up to see old Abe, and after I got through I thought I would pop in and see Mrs. Old Abe, particularly as she was so gracious when I saw her last September. I found her holding her hands all alone in a great big room in the great big White House. She received me very cordially and rather reproached me for not having been more friendly. She well knew the reason. She was very much affected when she spoke of her boy that died last winter—that the house seemed to her like a tomb and

that she could not bear to be in it. He was the favorite
child, so good, so obedient, so promising.

To Mrs. Washburne

Washington, D. C. Sunday morning 25th May, 1862.
How do you all find yourselves this most lovely Sabbath
morning! The air here is cool and pure and all nature smiles
in loveliness. Who would think the country was torn by a
terrible civil war. What a year we have passed thro', and
who on earth knows what may be in the future. God alone
knows. Since I have commenced this letter, the mail brings
me a letter from Genl. Grant and one from John E. Smith.
The General is deeply wounded by the infamous attacks
upon him, but he writes like a true and noble man. Mr.
Rogers of N. Y. writes me that he has just received a
splendid Panama hat, and that he is going to send it to
Genl. Grant of whom he is a great admirer. . . .
The news this morning looks badly all round. The
driving back of Banks is bad. I do wish McClellan would
move his boots. But we must be patient, long suffering
and slow to anger.

To Mrs. Washburne

Sept. 1, 1862.
Yesterday was a day of unheard-of and terrific anxiety
here among all loyal people. There is no doubt but our
arms met with a terrible reverse on Saturday. We were
driven from the ground leaving our dead and wounded to
the enemy. It is all the fault of McClellan, ... He
refused for two days to send re-enforcements after he was
positively ordered and then refused to send supplies to our
starving army. It is thought, now that Pope is re-enforced
there will be another fight to-day. Unless Pope attacks
and whips the enemy, he is among the "played out"
generals. Geo. Hamilton left Pope's head quarters yesterday noon. Our army was all there safe, and without
demoralization. Halleck has ordered Pope to fight to-day.

I must stay here till this thing is settled in some way for it would be cowardly to run when there is any danger.

I have to stop in Phila. to get clothing for our regt. and then my committee will be in N. Y. for a few days, and then home, home, home. . . . .

To Mrs. Washburne

West Point, Cozzen's Hotel, Sunday, Sept. 7, 1862.
As I had to remain over in N. Y. Sunday, I thought I would run up here last night and pass the night with Genl. Scott. I found him at this hotel and very well for him. I passed the evening in his room talking over the affairs of the country. While alarmed and somewhat depressed, he is not despondent. He says we can subjugate the rebels. This morning the news is brought to us that the rebels are in Maryland in force, and that surprised and disappointed him very much. He thought they could not get over. It seemed to affect him very much indeed. He has a very poor opinion of our generals about Washington. He speaks in the very highest terms of Gen. Grant, who he says has displayed great vigor and sagacity.

I have never before had such feelings of despondency as now. It seems to me that our beloved country is in the most desperate peril, and if something be not done at once to stem the tide, may God have mercy on us. I fear there is no more happiness or prosperity for us or our dear, dear children. The future has an awful look, and I never before yearned so to be home. I shall make short work of our committee business in N. Y. and start directly home. This is no time for business. It is now eleven o'clock and I leave for the city in a half an hour and will mail this there and perhaps add a word.

E. B. W.

To Mrs. Washburne

Monday Morning, Oct. 6, 1862.
On river bound from Memphis to Cairo.
I left Helena on Saturday night last and hope to be at Cairo to-night, where I shall mail this letter. I regret to

say I found Cady very feeble—emaciated by disease, labor and care. His position as commandant of the post is a very laborious and important one. Helena is pestilential and horrible. He has lost 30 pounds since he has been there. Our brave soldiers have been dying like sheep there and the horrors of that command are enough to make the most obdurate heart bleed. What I have seen on this trip makes my heart to sink within me. Inefficiency, drunkenness, debauchery, semi-treason, rule the hour in the Arkansas army. God only knows what will become of us. I go straight to St. Louis to see if I can get a short leave of absence from Genl. Curtis for Cady, in order that he may recruit. His trouble, a chronic diarrhoea. I have no word from you since I left home two weeks ago to-night. Hope to hear something at Cairo.

I shall get home as soon as possible, as I learn that they are making an effort to beat me by an "Independent" dodge. How I wish I were out of all this and could only be at home but it is no use. My country claims all I have both of service and money. . . .

Washington City Dec. 14, 1862. Sunday
My heart is so heavy with anxiety this morning that I am almost unable to write at all. The great battle is going on so near here, upon which may hang all the destinies of our country, and our own happiness, and the happiness of our children. To say nothing of the vast sacrifice of lives of noble men, of the anguish and sorrow and tears. It is enough to appal the stoutest hearts. I went up to see the president last night, and we went over to see Genl. Halleck and get the latest news. I considered it bad, and came back to my room with a heart sinking within me. The battle is going on today, but it is no use for me to write about it, as you will get all by telegraph before this reaches you. May God, in his infinite mercy, vouchsafe to us a victory. A defeat, I fear, will end us. With a triumph of the rebels of the South, the rebels of the North will rise up, and loyal and union men will have to go under.

Memo.
May 3, 1864
Left Washington this morning at 9.45 and arrived at Culpepper C. H. Va. at 3.25 P. M. and proceeded immediately
to Lt. Genl. Grant's Head quarters. I met at Brandy
Station, Col. Dent, member of his Staff who had first
delivered Burnside his orders. I am accompanied by Mr.
Wm. Swinton of the N. Y. Times. I found the Genl. and
his senior aid Col. Comstock in the General's room, quietly
reading the newspapers. The Genl. developed his entire
plan to me and his reasons. The movement takes place at
midnight tonight. The weather promises well. . . .

May 4, Culpepper
8 A. M.
The movement commenced at 12 last night. The orders
were not given till dark. So quietly was all done that the
people of this village had no idea of what was going on till
they arose this morng. when they found all the troops had
quietly left.

I went to bed last night a little before midnight. Passed
the latter part of the evening in Rowley's tent in conversation with Genl. Grant, Rawlins Duff and Rowley. Our
conversation turned on politics and war, discussions of
individuals and the prospects of success, etc.

Germanna Ford
1 P. M.
We left Culpepper at half after seven and came by
Stevensburg and reached this Ford at 11 ¼ A. M. and here
found a crossing had been effected without difficulty and
nearly all of the 5th Corps (Warren's) over. The troops
are all coming up magnificently. Hauled up at Meade's
Headquarters
   2d Corps Hancock
   5th   "   Warren
   6th   "   Sedgewick
Genl. Grant selected his headquarters in an old vacant
house about ¼ mile from the ford, and it afforded us a

splendid view of the troops as they passed in one continued stream all the afternoon. At this time the three corps above named are all over, but their trains are to come over to night by the "Culpepper Mine Ford" about equi-distant between Ely and Germanna Ford. Hancock's Corps has crossed to-day at Ely Ford. The day has been beautiful indeed. The distance from Culpepper to this Ford is 13 miles. At Stevensburg we fell in with the Column of Sedgewick, moving on.

May 5

Lodged in the old abandoned cottage—in the garret with Grant and Rawlins.—Got up at 3 A. M. and breakfast at 4. Bivouac fire in front of the house, around which we all gather after breakfast. Head quarters train leaves at 5 but the Genl. and Staff remain till Burnside comes up. Splendid morning. 8–5 A. M. Burnside's force just come in sight coming down to the ford on the other side—one division.

8.15 A. M.

An officer from Meade has just dashed up to our head quarters with despatch stating that enemy is forcing the battle in his front and that he has ordered Warren to attack at once.

9.45

Arrived at Meade's H. Q. near an old building erected for crushing gold.

10.45

Officer just arrived at Meade's Hq. from Plank Road 3 miles off—also says enemy in small force on that road, Getty's division ordered out immediately.

12.15

Heavy skirmishing fire in front at this moment

12.45

First Cannon shot in front just heard
2d Cannon   "

1.10

Started with the Genl. and staff towards the front. The firing was very heavy—the skirmish had become a battle. We met many wounded men coming in. We started on our return to H. Q. and came by where Genl. Warren was. He said his whole corps was engaged and that on the right a brigade in Griffin's division had been badly handled. The Genl. then galloped to H. Q. to give further orders.

2 P. M.

A lull in the fight—little less firing. 100 prisoners come in. Report that we have lost two guns and Capt. Winslow killed.

3 P. M.

Genl. Griffin has just come to H. Q. and represents that he has had terrible fighting and that after having driven the enemy ¾ mile was driven back. He represents his loss as very severe. Warren's corps has been badly shaken so far to-day.

3.15

Meade orders a general attack by all the corps as soon as possible.

4.15

Hancock has just opened heavily on our left.

4.30

Started at once to where Hancock was going in. When we got there the fight was terrible and Hancock was hard pressed by the enemy. The road was completely blocked up by wounded and stragglers as we returned to H. Q.

5 P. M.

Wadsworth's division has just been ordered to push out from the centre and attack the enemy on his flank and rear.

6.30

Warren has again attacked the enemy from the centre.

8.30
No particular result from the above attack.

9 P. M.
The result to-day seems on the whole favorable. Just at night Wadsworth's division fell on Wilcox's division Hill's corps, and drove them a mile. That was a grand movement and it was directed by Genl. Grant. Wadsworth has behaved nobly to-day. I lodge in the General's tent.— Meade has been in and is in good spirits. The whole wing is to move simultaneously at half past four in the morning. Took 700 prisoners to-day.

Friday Morning
May 6
Clear and beautiful morng. Awakened at 4 o'ck. Sit down to breakfast at 4 ½ and at 4.45 the ball was opened by what is considered an attack on our right. At 5.10 we attacked them on the whole line.

6.40
At this moment the fire has slackened. We are all sitting about the bivouac fire.

6.45
Hancock sent word he has advanced two miles and that Birney has taken a line of rebel rifle pits with the enemy's colors. Longstreet is just heard from as being in with his corps.

7.00
Genl. Warren has just come into H. Q. We have just heard hearty cheers from our men on the left.

8.00
Went over to the head quarters of Burnside's second division, which is moving across to Parker's Store in the Plank Road. Returning it was as quiet as a Sabbath morning for ten minutes. Then a most tremendous fire on our right.

8.10

A monstrous fight raging on our right. It is the attack of Sedgewick on the enemy in his front.

8.50

A perfect lull in the battle. It is the lull before the storm. We are not apparently maintaining our earlier advantages. Wadsworth falling back, but contesting every inch of ground.

9.00

Couriers from Sedgewick bring report that his third attack on the front has been repulsed.

9.15

Wadsworth's Division seems to have been driven out of the timber into the open field in plain sight. We do not know what it all means. Genl. Grant has gone out in that direction. It is feared it may be serious. Meade has gone there.

9.45

The mystery still continues and no one about H. Q. can tell what it means our troops being out of the timber. Our artillery is taking up positions on the hills about H. Q. as if apprehending an attack.

10.30

Mystery is explained. The Brigade stampeded and came out of the woods without any enemy behind them. Genl. Grant has just returned from Hancock and reports all satisfactory and thinks Hancock is gradually driving them.

11.30

Heavy firing on our left and it is believed Burnside is engaged. I leave the head quarters in the grove on the hill and come down in the ravine to the ambulance to get some rest.

12. M.

It is reported that Hancock is being driven back slowly and is getting behind entrenchments on the "Brook Road." Stragglers are coming from that direction in great numbers.

1 P. M.

It is true—Hancock driven back and his left turned. It is an awful moment.

1.30 P. M.

Burnside has just commenced a furious attack on the flank of the enemies right. An immense column from Warren is moving forward to reinforce Hancock.

2 P. M.

Genl. Wadsworth's son just came to H. Q. to report the death of his father. The report is thought to be unfounded.

3.30 P. M.

A complete quiet has prevailed for the last hour. There is no doubt of the death of Genl. Wadsworth and that his body is in the hands of the enemy. His fall has created a profound impression at H. Q.

4.45 P. M.

Heavy attack on Hancock again.

5.15 P. M.

The enemy has broken through Hancock's line. The rebels have evidently the best of the fight to-day thus far. It looks gloomy enough at this time and there are long faces about the H. Q.

5.25 P. M.

Genl. Grant has just left the H. Q. with an orderly and gone in the direction of the left.

5.45

An officer from Hancock says he repulsed the enemy instead of having his line broken. It was a brilliant affair and we all feel better. The day will close not so disastrously to us as we apprehended. Genl. Meade shows the true patriot and the persistent soldier. He says the hopes of the world rest upon our success and that he will fight so long as there is a man to stand up.

7.30 P. M.
The enemy has flanked Sedgewick and getting between us and the river, threatening our supply train and our colored troops.

10 P. M.
Lt. Genl. Grant who went out to see about the disaster having just returned, tremendous firing was again heard on our right and terrific cheering of the enemy. We are in great doubt what it means, but it would seem very serious and it is impossible to tell what it will lead to.

May 7, 1864
Pleasant but a little hazy.

5 A. M.
All quiet up to this moment. An officer from Meade brings intelligence of enemy massing on Hancock's front. We have contracted our lines very much. A lot of colored troops are taking a position immediately in our front.

5.15
Firing just opened on our front very heavy. Artillery— about the first artillery firing we have had.

6 A. M.
The firing turns out to be the enemy feeling Warren, who opened on them with his artillery and they left. Meade has just been here and thinks the main attack will be on Hancock's left. Hancock has borne the brunt of the fight so far and nobly has he sustained himself.

7 A. M.
Broke up H. Q. and move to other side plank road.

9 A. M.

Entire quiet since the dash on Warren this morning. Reports come in from Hancock and Burnside that the enemy is evidently falling back. It is impossible to tell what it means. Burnside and Warren have both been to H. Q.

10.30 A. M.

Just come back from Hancock and he thinks the enemy has left his front. Coming back I hear heavy firing from Warren's front.

2.30 P. M.

No fighting to amount to anything thus far. Mr. Dana Ass. Sec War has just arrived with news of Butler's landing at City Point.

5.45 P. M.

We are getting already to start on a night march towards Richmond. Firing has just commenced on Warren's left.

7.10 P. M.

The firing not very heavy and as the sun goes down a three days fight closes—one of the most desperate of the war. The troops are full of enthusiasm.

8 P. M.

Genl. Grant and staff mount and start "onward to Richmond."

8.30 P. M.

Arrive at Genl. Hancock's H. Q. to wait until Warren's Corps shall come up.

11 P. M.

Leave Hancock's H. Q. and march with the column preceded by cavalry.

May 8, 1864
Todd's Tavern
6 A. M.

Reached here this morning 1.45 and sleep on a blanket in the tavern. Much disappointed as we awake to find so

great a delay in the troops getting up. Great apprehension
that Hancock who has the rear, will be attacked.

10.30 A. M.
Piney Branch
Church Head Quarters

We left H. Q. at Todd's Tavern and came over here where
we shall remain the most of the day. There has been sharp
skirmishing in front—rebel cavalry trying to keep us back.
The weather is very hot and the troops have marched all
night and are too much fatigued to advance further without
rest. We are all feeling pretty well, yet we do not know
what is to come as we have no knowledge of the enemy's
movements. We think we have the inside track to Richmond.

11.00

Heavy firing towards Spotsylvania C. H. The enemy's
cavalry are making a stout resistance there it is thought.
Sedgewick's corps is up on another road.

12 noon

Genl. Wilson sends word from Spotsylvania C. H. that
he is being driven back slowly by two divisions of Longstreet's corps. This shows that the enemy is ahead of us.
Orders are given to mass our forces and check him if possible
before he is supported.

3 P. M.

Break up our H. Q. at Piney Creek Church and come
toward Spotsylvania C. H. and stop in the woods to get
information.

5.16 P. M.

The first gun in front.

5.20 P. M.

The attack opens slowly only a few guns fired. Now a
lull.

5.30 P. M.
No further firing in front.

5.40 P. M.
Skirmishing with musketry just begun.

6.07 P. M.
The attack seems to be a fizzle,—only a little scattering fire.

6.30 P. M.
Heavy firing again commencing in front.

6.45 P. M.
Report that enemy is being strongly entrenched.

6.50 P. M.
A most tremendous musketry fire has just opened and a furious attack.

7.30 P. M.
Genl. Grant and staff have just come in from the front and report failure to carry enemies works.

Monday morning. May 9, 1864
8 A. M.
Indications that the enemy are to attack Hancock this morning. Grant and Meade have just left Head Quarters to visit the different Corps.

10 A. M.
A staff officer of Sedgewick has just come to H. Q. and reports him mortally wounded by a rebel sharp shooter. No fighting to-day so far. He who talks lightly of war, knows little of war. Genl. Grant not yet returned to H. Q.

11 A. M.
The dead body of Maj. Genl. Sedgewick has just past our H. Q. to the rear, escorted by his staff. It was a sad

sight. His loss is irreparable, as he was a most brave and skillful soldier possessing the entire confidence of his troops.

5 P. M.
No fighting along the line to-day till this moment a brisk cannonading and musketry is heard on our right—supposed to be Hancock attempting to get over into the Block House road.

6.05 P. M.
Genl. Grant has just returned to H. Q. Hancock has carried the Block House road.

6.50 P. M.
Just as we were sitting down to our supper a big engagement opened over on the line of the road just taken. The firing is very heavy indeed—a portion of Warren's and Sedgewick's divisions were ordered to the attack.

8 P. M.
Although the firing was heavy, there were no decisive results, though we drove them a little. The advantage gained by Hancock is very decided. On the whole, the results of to-day are favorable and all are feeling well at H. Q. We should all feel better were it not for the death of Sedgewick.

Tuesday morning May 10, 1864.
6.30 A. M.
We are just up this morning and have as yet no reports. The weather is cooler this morning. There were two alarms last night by firing on Hancock's line.

9.45 A. M.
Scout has just come to H. Q. from Washington bringing intelligence that Butler has whipped the enemy badly at Petersburg and is advancing on Richmond and that Sherman has whipped the enemy at Dalton and Tunnel Hill. Rowley and I start to find Genl. Grant at Hancock's H. Q.

10.10 A. M.

We came to their H. Q. on the full jump with the news. I getting in ahead and announcing it to Genls. Grant, Meade and Hancock. Genl. Meade is just issuing a general order announcing the fact to the troops.

11.00 A. M.

Have just returned to H. Q. from Hancock.

11.45 A. M.

A heavy engagement has opened on our right and centre. The artillery and musketry is heavy. This is the sixth day of fighting.

12.30 P. M.

The battle still going on. Genl. Grant and staff have just returned to H. Q. and they report Wright and Warren going in.

1.45 P. M.

The fighting continued on our right very heavy. A general attack is ordered along the whole line at 5 P. M.

3.05 P. M.

The fight is going on with great vigor in Hancock's division and has been—for half an hour very heavy.

6 P. M.

Genl. Williams just come into H. Q. and says the enemy is advancing in the rear of our camp and is within ¾ of a mile of us. This is reported to him by one of our signal officers.

6.30 P. M.

Rode out to the front. The attack which was to have commenced at 5 has just commenced along the whole line with the most terrific fury. Genls. Grant and Meade and staffs accompanied by such others of us as desired to go, rode on to a ridge in front of the timber where the battle was raging. It was at its heighth just as the sun was going down. The roar of musketry and cannon and the cheers of our men as they rushed to the charge made an impression never to be effaced. It has been a day of continuous fighting and our losses have been heavy, but we have gained decided advantages. Just at night Wright took a brigade of rebel prisoners.

Wednesday morning. May 11, 1864
7 A. M.

Raining a little this morning. Col. Porter came in from Burnside's corps this morning and reports that it made a good advance yesterday P. M. getting within a quarter of a mile of the Court House. Our loss yesterday is estimated at 3500 in killed and wounded, 25,000 men have been placed hors du combat since we started.

9.45 A. M.

Left this morning for Washington.

10 P. M.

Arrived at the War Dept.

To Mrs. Washburne

In the Field, Near Spotsylvania, Va. (May 9, 1864)
We are in the midst of terrific events. This army has now been fighting for four days, on its advance to Richmond. It fought three days at Wilderness and then started in a night march towards R. the enemy having commenced a retreat. They got ahead of us about two miles from here near Spotsylvania Court House, and the result was a hard fight all day, but without material results to either party. Both lost heavily—our killed and wounded something like 2000, and that of the enemy quite as heavy. We took say 100 prisoners. This morning the enemy is in all its force in our front and we are likely to have a big battle to-day. It is fighting, fighting all the time and the most desperate and terrible of the war. The imagination cannot paint all

the horrors that are around us. It is war, on the greatest scale the world has ever seen. Our army train would reach from Galena to Freeport. Our men generally have fought nobly and displayed prodigies of valor. What is in store the good God only knows, but I have unbounded faith the movement we are engaged in will substantially succeed, but war after all is a game of chance.

Meade is a great general and has fought his army well, but after all Grant is the great head and soul of the army, and without doing any injustice to any one I can say I fully believe this army would have been defeated before this, and in its retreat had it not been for him. He is in capital spirits and seems to have no doubt of success.

The weather is intensely hot here and all is dust and smoke. I stay with the General in his tent.

I cannot begin to give you any idea of all I have seen during the last four days. When you think of all that depends upon our success here it is enough to wring every heart with anxiety. The great day of battle at Wilderness was Friday, and twice during the day we were on the eve of defeat and rout. Such a long and awful day I never went through before in my whole life and hope never to see another.

I think we have now three men to Lee's two.

All Galena friends here are well. I send this by a courier through the enemies country and with not more than half a chance it will ever get through.

You can show this to friends, but dont have it printed,

P. S. Monday P. M. Since writing this Genl. Sedgewick, one of our best generals, has been killed by a sharpshooter.

PERSONAL OBSERVATIONS

Galena, Ill. April 3, 1865, 5 o'clock, P. M.
Left for the front. Arrived at Washington Thursday morning Apl. 6, and left same evening for City Point.— Arrived at City Point Friday P. M. at 2.30. Went on board *Mary Martin*, remained over night.

Saturday morning, Apl. 7, 1865

Left City Point for the front—Genl. Grant's head-quarters, supposed to be near Burksville. Arrived at Petersburg at 10.45 A. M. Past in sight of Fort Stedman which had been captured by Gordon's rebels. Called on Genl. Hartsuff who is in command. Then called on Maj. Genl. Warren. Met Roger A. Pryor in the street and had a long conversation with him. He talked very freely and frankly on the situation, looking upon the rebel cause as hopeless. He said he was satisfied before his return from the North that the rebellion would have finally to succumb to the great power and resources of the north and so advised Jeff Davis and his other friends, whereat they accused him of having become demoralized. Rode out through the works about Petersburg. Saw the Burnside mine and went into Fort Mahone, which was captured by our forces Sunday morning about 2 and also went into Fort Sedgewick, our fort right opposite Mahone. Both strong works, but Sedgewick vastly the strongest. Our military men express surprise at the want of strength of the rebel works as compared with ours. Yet the rebel works are strong and the whole country about Petersburg is dug up.—This is quite a large place, fine streets and stores, but all closed. Train has already been detained here for five hours.

Left Petersburg, 4.15 o'clock P. M.

Arrived at Ford's station South Side R. R. at 6.30 P. M. Met there Genl. Patrick just from Burksville and gave me information from front.

11 P. M.

Arrived at Maj. Genl. Wilcox's head quarters.

Sunday, April 9

Left Genl. Wilcox at six o'clock A, M. arrived at Wellville Station at 8 A. M. Found here Lt. Col. Green 37th Wis. Vol., the regiment that first entered Fort Mahone.

Nottoway Court House. Arrived here at 10 o'clock. Miserable, forlorn, dilapidated straggling village of fourteen families. The county only gives about three hundred votes.

Rail-road stations from Petersburg to Burksville,
    to Sutherland
    Ford's
    Wilson's
    Wellville
    Black's & White's
    Nottoway C. H.
    Burksville
Arrived at Burksville April 9, 1865, 12.30 o'clock P. M.
Nearly dead—having ridden thirty miles in five hours.
Met Genl. Birney at Nottoway Court House who gave us
intelligence of breaking up generally of rebel forces. Waiting for ambulance to go to Farmville, as I cant ride horseback any further. At Burksville saw five splendid Arm-
strong guns captured from the Johnnies, specimens of
British neutrality.
    Arrived at Farmville at 10.30 P. M. Very hard ride from
Burksville in ambulance.—Found Lt. Genl. Grant had
left.

Sunday Morning, Apl. 10, 1865

Remained over at Farmville in ambulance last night—
rained all night. After a breakfast of pork, hard tack and
tea got under way at 7 A. M. for the extreme front. Farmville is a town of 1800 people and on the Appomattox the
South Side Rail-road crosses here by the "High Bridge," a
considerable portion of which was burned. The other
bridge was burned and we crossed by a pontoon.
    At 11 o'clock we arrived at one mile from the "New
Store," the horses very much jaded, for the roads are
horrible. It still rains. We stopped at a farm house, the
owners having left home leaving the old negroes here in a
state of utter destitution, nothing in the world to eat.
Buckingham is the man's name. One mile from New Store
met soldiers who gave us first information of the surrender
of Lee's army, at one P. M. heard the news.
    Arrived at Meade's Headquarters at 4.15 P. M. three
miles from Appomattox C. H.
    Arrived at Genl. Grant's head quarters at 9.50 P. M. and

am to remain with him in his tent over night. Found all the staff here who greeted me with great cordiality and kindness.

Tuesday morning

Left Genl. Grant's head quarters at 7 o'clock for Appomattox C. H. where we arrived at 11 A. M. Met Custer and Sheridan as we were starting out. Custer's men bore 31 captured rebel flags. Went right into the rebel camp and rode all through it. Met there L. Q. C. Lamar of Miss. Ex M. C. and saw the following rebel generals, R. E. Lee, Longstreet, Anderson, Ransom, Benning, Alexander, Picket, Heth, Wilcox, Pendleton, Gordon, Perry.

At six o'clock I saw the final surrender and stacking of arms of Gordon's entire corps, consisting of ten thousand men. The whole body was addressed by Gordon and when he concluded, the last ditch was reached and the arms stacked and the Johnnies marched off to the tune of Dixie played by a band. Got chips from the apple tree under which Lee surrendered to Grant. I stay at Gibbon's head quarters to-night.

Wednesday Apl. 12, 1865

I make this memorandum on the piazza of the house where all the capitulation papers were signed. For hours the rebel prisoners have been filing in front of the door, having laid down their arms. They are marching off under command of their officers. They are a terrible looking set.

Gov. Wise just came up the steps upon the piazza, a poor, old, dried up man, with white whiskers and long grey hair, a grey old over coat and a shabby cap. Three rebel generals are going along with our escort, Wilcox, Gordon and Alexander. Have just seen Wilcox division of the late A. P. Hill corps lay down their arms. Bartlett's division of the 5th Corps were stretched out in line of battle on both sides of the road and the rebels marched between them until they covered the whole front, where they halted, deposited their flags and stacked their arms.

The following named generals on our side were the commissioners to carry out the terms of the surrender. They signed their names in the room where Lee wrote surrender to Grant in the house at Appomattox C. H.

W. Merritt
Bvt. Maj. Genl.
Comdg. Cavalry
Mid. Mil. Div.

John Gibbon
Maj. Genl. Vols.
Comdg. 24th Corps.

Chas. Griffin
Bvt. Maj. Genl;
Comdg. 5th Corps

J. B. Gordon
Maj. Genl.
C. S. A.

The house where the surrender was made is owned by Wilmer McLean who has lived here for two years. He came from Prince William Co. Va. near Blackburns Ford where Beauregard had his head quarters at the battle of Blackburn's Ford, July 18, 1861. About a dozen families reside at the Court House. Wilmer McLean (signature).

Left Appomattox C. H. at noon, with my escort, for Farmville. I had the escort from Lt. Genl. Grant's head quarters, consisting of Capt. C. B. Atchison, Lt. Taylor and ten dragoons. The following rebel generals were in our party, wishing the benefit of our escort to Burksville

Maj. Genl. J. B. Gordon
"   "   Cadmus Wilcox
"   "   Alexander

About six miles from Appomattox C. H. met Maj. Genl. Fitz Hugh Lee and staff on their way to surrender to Genl. Gibbon. Reached Farmville at 9 o'clock P. M. and remained over night, at the house of Dr. Wood.

Thursday Morning April 13, 1865

Left at 9 A. M. for Burksville. It had rained very hard all night and the roads are frightful. Overtook nearly all of Meade's army on their way back to Burksville. We passed very near the place where Col. Washburn 4th Mass. Cavalry was wounded. Genl. Wilcox showed me the house to which he was taken after being wounded and where he saw him. Arrived at Burksville at 1.30 P. M.

Left Burksville by rail at 11 P. M.

Friday morning, April 14, 1865

Delayed on the train last night. Only reached City Pt. at 2 P. M. Left for Richmond at 6 P. M. on the steamer Thomas Collier No. 2.

Richmond, Va. Apl. 15, 1865. 6 o'clock, 45 M.

Arrived. Landed at Rocket's in the rain.

In Richmond all day and left at 5 P. M. for Point of Rocks Hospital where I saw Col. Washburn who had been wounded at High Bridge. Then dropped down the Appomattox to City Point, where we arrived at 10½ P. M. I had retired for the night before reaching there. Capt. Atchison went ashore to enquire at telegraph office for a despatch. Returning, he aroused me and informed me of the shocking intelligence of the assassination of the President and of Gov. Seward and son. I immediately ordered the boat to start for Washington.

Sunday Morning, April 16, 1865

Arrived at Old Point at 6 A. M., coaled and started for Washington at 8 A. M. Arrived at Washington Monday morning.

To SECRETARY STAUNTON

City Point Apl. 14, 1865

I send you the farewell address of Lee to his army which I obtained a copy of at Appomattox C. H. just before I left there day before yesterday.

E. B. Washburne

To Mrs. Washburne

On Genl. Ord's boat Silver Star,
bound from Richmond to Washington.
Sunday Apl. 16, 1865

After leaving City Point for the front a week ago yesterday, I had neither opportunity or convenience for
writing you, but I kept a journal so that I could hereafter
give you a full account of my trip. I got back to City
Point on Friday P. M. and started at once for Richmond at
which place I arrived the next morning. I spent yesterday
till five o'clock P. M. in R. where Genl. Ord was kind enough
to give me his boat to take me to Point of Rocks to see
Frank Washburne, who had been badly wounded. Charley
Atchison came along with me. We found Frank doing
very well, though very weak. He was wounded in one
of the most desperate cavalry fights of the war and received
his wounds in a hand to hand encounter. He had a pistol
ball shot through his cheek, knocking out three teeth and
then going down into his lungs. He spit it up after it had
been there eight hours. Another bullet grazed his neck and
he received a ghastly sabre cut over his head from which he
lost a great deal of blood. He is not believed to be now in
any danger, but it is a marvel he was not killed. He was in
good spirits. Dr. Fuller was with him, he will start for
home in a day or two.—We left Point of Rocks at ten last
night and stopped at City Point to see if there was anything
for me there. Charley went ashore and I went to bed. It
was our intention to come to Norfolk last night and spend
to-day with Sam, as Genl. Ord had given me control of the
boat. I was feeling well and in the highest spirits. I had
seen so much of the final scenes of the rebellion and peace
seemed so near. But alas! how soon my joy was to be
turned into unspeakable sorrow. Charley returned to the
boat and awakened me to tell me of the shocking news of the
assassination of our God-given and beloved President. It
completely unmanned me. I immediately gave orders to
start the boat for Washington and we shall reach there
about midnight to-night. God only knows what is now in

store for our unhappy country. I have been abed all day, having no heart to get up and write or do anything. I am tortured by the most cruel anxiety to know all the particulars. I will write more to-morrow after arriving at W. . . .

To Mrs. Washburne

Washington, Apl. 18, 1865, Tuesday
We are to be longer delayed than I had supposed. The remains will not start from here till Friday morning, and then we go by N. Y. and shall stop along several days on the way. It will be ten days before we shall reach Chicago. The remains of the President are lying in State at the White House, and the crowd going thither is immense—stretching nearly from Willard's Hotel to the White House. . . .

EARLY CONTACT WITH LINCOLN AND GRANT

Elihu Washburne knew Abraham Lincoln from the time that he first went to Illinois but he was not thrown with him intimately until both were attending the session of the Supreme Court of Illinois at Springfield in the winter of 1843–44. In the library of the court in the evenings the lawyers were wont to gather for social purposes and there Washburne heard Lincoln tell his amusing stories surrounded by his congenial friends. They met again at the River and Harbor Convention at Chicago in July, 1847. It was then that Washburne heard Lincoln, who was only thirty-six years old, called "Old Abe" and, himself, ever afterwards called him "Old Abe." He described his appearance at that convention. "Tall, angular, and awkward, he had on a short-waisted, thin, swallow-tail coat, a short vest of the same material, thin pantaloons, scarcely coming down to his ankles, a straw hat, and a pair of brogans with woolen socks."

Washburne went to Washington in 1847 to attend to business before the Supreme Court when Lincoln was in Congress, and as he was the only Whig member from Illinois, Washburne passed much of his time in Lincoln's room. Afterwards they corresponded on political matters. In the spring of 1849 Washburne was again in Washington and saw more of Lincoln and went with him to the inaugural ball of General Zachary Taylor. Washburne supported Lincoln in his candidacy for the Senate in 1855 and although Lyman Trumbull was chosen by Lincoln's advice the latter felt grateful to Washburne for standing by him. He wrote him a long letter describing the contest and concluded thus: "With my grateful acknowledgments for the kind, active, and continual interest you have taken for me in this matter, allow me to subscribe myself,

Yours forever,

A. Lincoln."

Washburne came to be recognized in Congress as the friend of the new President and as a consequence his prestige greatly increased. When the electoral vote was counted on February 13, 1861, Washburne was one of the two tellers on the part of the House. After the election there was fear for the safety of the government in consequence of the threatening language of the Southern members, so the Republican members of the Senate and House appointed a committee of two to take measures to guard against hostile plots. Grimes of Iowa was the Senate member and Washburne the member from the House. They kept in communication with General Scott, and Kennedy, the chief of police of New York, sent them several of his best detectives. As the time for the inauguration approached another unofficial committee was formed to look after the safety of the President-elect, Seward acting for the Senate and Washburne for the House. They received information believed to be authentic that a plot had been formed to assassinate Lincoln when he should pass through Baltimore on his way to Washington. It was therefore arranged that he should come at an unexpected hour. Accordingly he was at Baltimore before daylight travelling on a regular passenger train and arrived in Washington at a very early hour on February 24. Seward and Washburne had agreed to be at the station to meet him, but Seward was late, so the only person to welcome the new President to Washington was Washburne. He took him in his carriage to Willard's Hotel.

It is probable that there was no member of the House whose voice was more influential at the White House during Lincoln's administration than Washburne's. It was in reply to Washburne's inquiry that Lincoln said, as early as October, 1863, that he was willing to serve for a second term.

Private and confidential
Hon. E. B. Washburn
    Executive Mansion, Washington, Oct. 26, 1863
My dear Sir:—Yours of the 12th has been in my hands several days. Enclosed I send a leave of absence for your brother (General Cadwallader Colden Washburn) in as good form as I think I can safely put it. Without knowing whether he would accept it, I have tendered the Collectorship of Portland, Maine, to your other brother, the Governor. Thanks to both you and our friend Campbell (Thompson Campbell) for your kind words and intentions. A second term would be a great honor, and a great labor, which together, perhaps, I could not decline, if tendered.
                                        Yours truly,
                                            A. Lincoln

To Mrs. Washburne

    Washington, D. C. Dec. 6, 1863, Sunday morning
. . . We had the caucus last night and I declined to be a candidate (for speaker), all of which you will see in the papers before this reaches you. . . .
"Old Abe" has a well developed case of varioloid. I was with him an hour and a half the other day and we went over many things. He did what he said he had done to no other person outside of his cabinet, he read me his message. The Madam was very gracious when I saw her. . . .

To Mrs. Washburne

Washington, Sunday Morning, Dec. 20, 1863
. . . The President has confided to me the getting up of
the medal to Genl. Grant, and I go up to the Governor's to
talk about the emblems and devices we shall have on
it. . . .

To Mrs. Washburne

Washington, D. C. Sept. 11, 1864, Sunday
. . . Things are moving on finely in the political world.
The Copperheads seem to be in a great snarl. Little Mac
don't seem to go down very well with the real rebels, but
they will have to swallow him. But we shall beat them any
how. You will have seen the excellent letter that Genl.
Grant wrote to me. It is doing a great deal of good. . . .
If we can only get through this Presidential election and
save the country, I shall feel like a new man.

To-morrow is the Maine election, and if that only comes
out right it will be the first gun to knock them. . . .

More of a factor in Washburne's career than his relations
with Lincoln were his relations with Grant. He and
Lincoln were coadjutors in Illinois politics and in carrying
on the war, and they were mutually helpful to each other,
but the burden of the obligation was on Washburne's
side. In the case of Grant the burden of the obligation
was on the side of Grant who owed more to Washburne
than he did to any one else.

Soon after Lincoln issued his first call for volunteers to
suppress the rebellion, on May 3, 1861, a Union meeting
was held at Hanover, a small town near Galena, and Washburne arranged to go to it with John Rawlins, a lawyer in
Galena, and W. R. Rowley, the clerk of the circuit court.
Both were afterwards generals in the war and Rawlins

became Secretary of War. It was suggested to Washburne
that they should take with them Rawlins' neighbor,
Ulysses S. Grant, who was a graduate of West Point.
Both Rawlins and Rowley knew Grant, but Washburne
did not know him. He had been a clerk in his father's,
Jesse Root Grant's, leather store for about a year. Washburne knew nearly everybody in Galena and everybody of
consequence, but the obscure clerk had escaped his notice.
So Rawlins and Rowley introduced Grant to Washburne
and Grant agreed to drive the party of four over to the
meeting at Hanover with his horses. He was made chairman of the meeting, and after it was over, as they drove
home, he told his companions that, as he had been educated by the government, he considered that the government had a right to his services, and if war broke out he
intended to offer them. West Point graduates were rare
in Jo Davies's county; in fact, Washburne did not have
another constituent, in all probability, who had been an
officer in the regular army.

A few days after the Hanover meeting Washburne and
several others went to Springfield to consult Governor
Yates on military measures and carried Grant with them.
The governor welcomed him and appointed him a clerk in
the adjutant general's department. On June 21, 1861, at
Washburne's request, Lincoln appointed him colonel of the
21st Illinois volunteers. On August 7, at Washburne's
instance, he was appointed a brigadier general of volunteers, the commission being dated back to May 17. On
February 16, 1862, at Washburne's instance, he was
appointed a major general of volunteers. All his other
appointments came with Washburne's assistance. He
introduced and carried through the bill creating the rank
of lieutenant general. The story of Grant's gratitude can

best be told by the extracts from some of his letters to Washburne.

Under date of September 3, 1861, he wrote:

". . . In conclusion, Mr. Washburne, allow me to thank you for the part you have taken in giving me my present position. I think I see your hand in it, and admit that I had no personal claims for your kind office in the matter. I can assure you, however, that my whole heart is in the cause which we are fighting for, and I pledge myself that, if equal to the task before me, you shall never have cause to regret the part you have taken."

Under date February 21, 1862, he told Washburne he had asked his brother, C. C. Washburn, to take a place on his staff, and added: "I feel very grateful to you for having placed me in the position to have the honor of commanding such an army and at such a time. I only trust that I will not disappoint you."

He repeated this phrase again; invited Washburne to be his guest and told him his military plans. He asked his assistance with the War Department constantly. On December 12, 1863, he wrote: "I feel under many obligations to you for the interest you have taken in my welfare." At another time he said he was very grateful to the citizens of Illinois in Jo Davies's county and to Washburne in particular.

On November 9, 1865, he said: "I will be in my new house by Christmas. Without furnishing the fourth story I will have abundance of room for myself and friends. If Mrs. Washburne comes on to visit Washington this winter bring her to our house."

From Headquarters, August 16, 1866, he wrote that he would be at Galena when the election took place, but thought it improper for an army commander to take a part. He added: "Your friendship for me has been such that I should not hesitate to support you for personal reasons, on the ground that there is no one who cannot recognize great acts of friendship."

ENDORSEMENT OF RADICAL PARTY

Washburne, having witnessed the surrender at Appomattox and having attended the funeral of the great President, took up the work of rehabilitation of the Union with his party friends in Congress. He would have championed Lincoln's conciliatory plan of reconstruction if Lincoln had proposed it, and if there had been a split on the question between Lincoln and certain radical members of his party (as there would have been) Washburne would have stood with Lincoln and so would the majority of his party. Washburne did not want a split with Andrew Johnson.

He wrote to Mrs. Washburne.

Washington, D. C. Jany. 7, 1866, Sunday Morning
. . .

I was quite busy in running round yesterday. I saw the President and found him very well and he talked very well indeed. I hope and believe there will be no split between him and the Congress. I also saw the General and all the staff and all are well and made many kind inquiries about you. I expect the General every minute to call for us to go over home with him. . . .

When the bill to admit Nebraska as a state, the object of which was to add more votes to the Republican majority in Congress, came before the House, Washburne moved, on January 1, 1867, to lay it on the table. When his party associates remarked that this would kill it he replied: "I want to kill it and to kill all such bills." There were reports that he had become one of the President's party and several of his friends wrote to him in some astonishment at the news. On November 25, 1867, a resolution to impeach the President being presented to the House, Washburne voted against it and it was defeated. But as the tide turned more strongly against the President he turned with it. His correspondence was all with anti-Johnson men, many of them Republicans who were holding office in the Southern states. They related to him the ill-treatment which the negroes and all Union men were receiving. He was appointed one of the joint committee of the House and Senate on reconstruction and concurred in the reports of the committee. In Congress great importance was attached to his views, not only because of his commanding position among the leaders but because he was supposed to be the mouthpiece of General Grant. He was regarded as the ordinary medium of communication with General Grant for all sorts of purposes, military and civil, and his mail was full of letters containing information or requests which were intended for the great man.

As time went on and radical vindictiveness towards the South on the part of the majority in Congress was met by maladroit defiance on the part of the President the atmosphere became surcharged with feelings of hatred towards the President. All of Washburne's friends joined in the chorus of denunciation of the President. Grant and the President became bitter enemies. It was impossible to be a friend of Grant and of Johnson at the same time. Washburne was never a moderate man. He was for or against a measure or a man with all his might, and he was now against Andrew Johnson and his policy with all his might. Every measure leveled against that unhappy man he now favored. He wanted him impeached; he wanted him convicted. When a resolution was offered giving the thanks of Congress to General Hancock for his conduct as military governor at New Orleans, Washburne offered a substitute "utterly condemning the conduct of Andrew Johnson acting President of the United States" for removing General Sheridan from the military governorship of that department and the House adopted the substitute. Later, in a speech he attacked the President with peculiar rancor. "His whole official career as President," he said, "has been marked by a wicked disregard of all the obligations of public duty and by a degree of perfidy and treachery and turpitude unheard of in the history of the rulers of a free people; his personal and official character has made him the opprobrium of both hemispheres, and brought ineffable disgrace on the American name." He wrote of him privately as "the bad and faithless man at the head of the government."

When Thomas Turner who was a candidate for Congress against him in 1867 proposed a public debate with him he replied:

"Before accepting your invitation, I wish to know from you what Congress you are a candidate for? If you are a candidate for the Congress to be composed of Northern Copperheads and Southern Rebels, which it is semi-officially proclaimed that President Johnson is to recognize, to the exclusion of the constitutional Congress of the United States, then I desire to say that I am not a candidate for any such Congress, and that I do not propose entering into a canvass for any office for which I am not a candidate.

"If, on the other hand, you will certify to the people of this district that you are a candidate for the legal and constitutional Congress of the United |States, and for a member of that House of Representatives for the Fortieth

Congress which shall be called to order, according to the established precedent, by the Clerk of the present House, and to which no member shall be admitted without taking the 'iron-clad oath' of loyalty, and that you will repudiate the illegal and revolutionary Congress which President Johnson proposes to recognize then I have to state that I will accept your invitation with great pleasure."

Members of the ruling party in Congress competed with one another in phrasing violent abuse of Andrew Johnson, and Elihu Washburne deserved one of the prizes. History now delights to honor the men who opposed the impeachment of Andrew Johnson, who opposed his conviction and who recognized that his position was right and the position of Congress was wrong. But at the time these men were in the minority and especially in the Republican party they were overwhelmed by the bitter sentiment on the other side. Washburne's fierce attacks strengthened his hold on his party at the time and never in his subsequent career were they a source of weakness to him. When the impeachment trial was in progress he sent this telegram to a Republican convention which met in New Hampshire to put General Grant in nomination:

"Bingham is making a splendid speech. All looks well. The Constitution will be vindicated, and the recreant put out of the White House before the end of the week."

RELATIONS WITH GRANT AND LAST PERIOD OF CONGRESSIONAL ACTIVITY

With General Grant's nomination for the Presidency Washburne's congressional career entered upon its final phase. He introduced a bill to make the telegraph a part of the postal establishment to be operated by the government. His speech was carefully prepared and he arrayed all the arguments in favor of the measure with his usual ability. He co-operated in the project with his brother Cadwallader, but neither of them could awaken much popular interest in the subject. Joseph Medill, the editor of the *Chicago Tribune*, always the friend and advocate of Elihu Washburne, explained to him one cause of the apathy. The newspapers thought it probable that the especially low tolls which the telegraph companies granted to them would be raised if the government owned the telegraph lines. Relatively few people used the telegraph and no glaring abuses had resulted from the private ownership, so in spite of Washburne's efforts the proposal for government ownership made no headway.

He encountered a different popular temper when he rose to warn the country against official extravagance and corruption. Here he pointed to that which any man could see and of which all men were ashamed. The indignation against those who had brought scandal upon the government was intense and the mouthpiece of this indignation was Washburne. The praise which he received after his speech of January 6, 1869, which was his last in Congress, would have turned the head of a less seasoned politician. One correspondent wrote: "You must be constantly

239

occupied in keeping at bay the human wolves who are sneaking about the government treasury. Such vigilance and bravery will bring their reward sooner or later. I have for a long time feared for your health. If that should fail, I don't know who would fill the breach." Another said: "We consider you as the man of the people." Another said that he must on no account leave Congress, that the country could not spare him. The favorite expression was to praise his "noble stand against extravagance and corruption."

The speech which called forth these encomiums was one of a number of the same tenor, denouncing the subsidized railways, government contractors, speculators in the rise and fall of the value of gold, lobbyists who were urging corrupt measures upon Congress. He began his speech by saying that the war was now over and the reconstruction of the South had been accomplished. A loyal administration was about to come into power. Therefore it was a time when the country should turn its attention to its internal affairs,—to taxes, economy, railroads and telegraphs, to dishonest office holders and all others who were plundering the public treasury. General Grant had been elected, he said, not only because of his great services in subduing the rebellion, but because the people believed him to be an honest man who would administer the government without fear or favor. A new departure in administration was absolutely necessary. The demoralization incident to the great expenditures of the war, with immense contracts, inflation of the currency, speculation, sudden fortunes, widespread extravagance and corruption must be met and the subsidized land-grabbing railroads, grasping monopolists, gamblers, lobbyists and bribe-givers who were fattening upon the government must be driven away. The first necessity was to keep all expenditures down to the lowest possible level.

He could not have chosen a theme more in harmony with popular desires. Moreover, his long record was in harmony with his words. At this time there were few men in the country who stood higher with the public than Washburne did. All the signs of the successful man surrounded him. His offices were crowded with suitors for his favor, flatterers fawned upon him, half the letters he received were from strangers who were attracted to a famous man, and, surest sign that power was believed to lie in his hands, hundreds of people asked him to get offices for them. The requests took a wide range from small clerkships to assignments upon the staff of the general of the army.

In the midst of it all, when the echoes of the retrenchment speech were still sounding, Mr. Washburne was taken seriously ill, and, on the eve of the inauguration of the new President, for the whole month of February, 1869, he was confined to his bed or his house. He had been seriously ill the year before; he had spent the summer of 1867 in Europe in search of health. His friends and relations now urged him to take a rest. E. H. Gratiot wrote from Belmont, Wisconsin, Feb. 22, 1869:

"I hope you will give up your work for a while and after the inauguration will come out with Adèle and recruit up again."

But there were other things for him to do and however much he may have needed rest there was none of it in the future as there had been none in the past.

General Grant heard the news of his election to be President at Washburne's house in Galena.

Elihu wrote to Mrs. Washburne the day of the election:

It is very quiet so far to-day, and it is now just after dinner. The weather is pleasant, and voting is progressing very well. We hope to beat the coppers in this town of East Galena, but you will see long before this reaches you how it is. The Genl. was in my library an hour before dinner, calm as a summer morning. He will probably leave here for W. Thursday evening. The telegraph operator is over from Chicago and the wires are already in the library ready to tick out good news. About eight o'clock this evening we shall begin to get something, I hope. . . .

Genl. Rawlins will stay at our house to-night and Mr. Allison will be over to stay to-morrow night. . After to-morrow I must dismiss politics from my head and look after business.

We had a splendid meeting last night at the Court House and kept it up till near eleven o'clock. John Rawlins made a fine speech. . . .

Again that evening to Mrs. Washburne

6 P. M. Nov. 1868

You ought to be here this evening for you would enjoy it. The telegraph machinery is all in and I am writing at the table where the instruments are in front of the window that looks out on the porch. The operator is here and we are waiting for the returns to come in. Augustus and Anna have come in and now we all go in to tea. Now we all come out from tea into the library and the telegraph ticks away, but as yet brings no news. We expect the General in soon; also Ben Campbell, Felt, Nate Corinth, Badeau, Isaac N. Morris and Comstock. Morris is a friend of the General from Quincy. It has been a very rainy day and disagreeable. . . .

To Mrs. Washburne

Galena, Wednesday morning, 9-½ o'clock November, 1868

The little old library looks like a Committee room of Ward politicians this morning. . . . It was very exciting receiving returns. After success seemed to be assured, the

Lead Mine Band came over and gave some music and we felt pretty foxy. The General staid till about one o'clock this morning. You will see all the returns before this reaches you. The General was very cool, yet anxious. . . . What a terrific contest we have had! It has come out right, but what a narrow escape.

The election to the Presidency of General Grant was a fateful event in the career of Elihu Washburne. It was felt at once that the great friendship which Grant bore him, the great debt which Grant owed him and his long and useful career in public service marked him as the coming man in the new administration. There were rumors that he was to be the Secretary of the Treasury, that he was to be Secretary of the Interior, that he was to go as Minister to England. Some of his friends begged him not to leave the House, asserting that he would be more useful to the country there than he would be elsewhere.

The selections for the Cabinet were kept a profound secret until the nominations were sent to the senate the day after the new President had been inaugurated.

One story current at the time was that Washburne had no desire to be Secretary of State and was surprised, when, sitting in his committee room on March 5, a page handed him the list of the Cabinet nominations and he saw his own name at the head. Cabinet offices are not, however, usually conferred in that way. The construction of a Cabinet is an elaborate process involving discussion and consultation; and it is improbable that Washburne did not know that he was to be the Secretary of State.

Why did he accept the office? His health had been bad all winter and was still uncertain. He had no desire to put it to the strain of performing the duties of a cabinet officer. Did he desire merely the compliment of being named for the highest office in the President's gift? Perhaps he did. There is no way of testing the question. In itself it was a barren compliment, however. His name is on the list of the Secretaries of State—that is all. His fame derived no addition from the fact. Did he desire the office so that he might have greater prestige when he went as this country's representative to a foreign power? This seems not improbable. All the accounts of him which were written in Paris after he became Minister there laid stress upon his intimate relations with President Grant and the fact that the President had shown the regard in which he held him by appointing him to be his Secretary of State. He did derive added prestige as Minister from the preliminary appointment in the Cabinet.

As for his qualifications to be Secretary of State, we can pass the matter over. He had not been especially concerned in the nation's foreign affairs during his public service; but he was not himself conscious of a lack of the qualifications necessary to manage them. He had the self-confidence of an ambitious, successful man. Whether he would have made such a notable record as Secretary of State as Hamilton Fish made is an idle speculation. He was a man of many resources which developed as occasion called for them.

Historians have generally assumed that Mr. Washburne's appointment as Secretary of State was merely intended as a compliment and this may have been the reason why it was made. Another reason which has been given by the critics is that he sought the office so as to appoint his political friends to offices in the foreign service; but this reason is both absurd and false—absurd, because no man of Washburne's intelligence would have hazarded his standing before the public by a course which would certainly have met with public reprobation, and false because, as a matter of fact, he made no appointments.

Washburne was commissioned Secretary of State, March 5; on March 10 he wrote to the President resigning the office; on March 15 his successor, Hamilton Fish, took the office over. Washburne held it for exactly ten days, five of which were by sufferance while he waited for Mr. Fish to come on from New York and claim the office to which he had been appointed and confirmed. The official record shows that in those ten days twenty-two nominations to foreign positions were sent from the State Department to the Senate. Only one was the nomination of a citizen of Illinois; not one was a nomination in which Washburne had any special concern. Further than that, he announced publicly as soon as he was made Secretary of State that he would merely receive the papers of applicants for office and file them for his successor to consider—that he would not consider them himself— and this announcement was printed in the newspapers.

Washington, D. C., March 10, 1869

To the President,—

When you did me the honor to confer upon me the appointment of Secretary of State, I felt constrained to state to you that my health would prevent me from holding the position for any length of time. I am already admonished that a proper discharge of the duties of the office would involve more labor and responsibility than I am willing to undertake in justice to the public interest and myself. If convenient and agreeable to you, I would be glad to have you name my successor at as early a moment as you deem practicable, and you will please consider this as my resignation, to take effect as soon as my successor is qualified and ready to enter upon the discharge of the duties of the office.

I need not add here, Mr. President, how gratefully I

appreciate the distinguished honor you conferred upon me by inviting me to become one of your constitutional advisers.

Had circumstances permitted it, I should have been pleased to have been associated with you officially, and to have aided you as far as in my power in carrying out your views in the administration of the Government upon the principles of honesty, retrenchment, economy, public faith and exact and equal justice to all.

I have the honor to be, very respectfully, your obedient servant,

E. B. Washburne

THE PRESIDENT TO WASHBURNE

Washington, D. C. March 11, 1869

Hon. E. B. Washburne

Dear Sir: Your resignation of the office of Secretary of State, with reasons for the same, is received. In accepting it I do so with regret that your health will not permit you to continue in the office or in some cabinet position. Our personal relations have been from the breaking out of the rebellion to the present day, and your support of me individually and of the army and its cause, such that no other idea presented itself stronger to my mind, on the first news of my election to the presidency, than that I should continue to have your advice and assistance. In parting with you, therefore, I do it with assurance of continued confidence in your ability, zeal, and friendship, and with the hope that you may soon be relieved from the physical disabilities under which you have labored for the last few years.

Very truly yours,
U. S. Grant

MINISTER TO FRANCE

Then, as we know, he accepted the office of Minister to France. The letters to his wife, shortly after his arrival there, show how much he wished her to participate in his official life.

Legation des Etats Unis
Paris Le 13 June 1869, Sunday morning

Last night attended my first State Dinner at Lord Lyons. There were fifty guests. The dinner was given in honor of the Queen of Holland. The hotel of the British Embassy is one of the most splendid in Paris. The English Government keeps it up in most magnificent style. The drawing rooms, the dining room, the garden, the verandahs, are indeed splendid. I can hardly describe the gorgeous appearance of the table decorated with the most exquisite flowers. The dinner was served with all the elegance that taste and money could secure. We sat down at half past seven and made comparatively short work of it. We were through at nine of the o'clock. I like that better than the way in Washington of sitting three and four hours at the table. I can tell of but few of those who were present, for here in society they never introduce people, except for some special reason. I was, of course, introduced to the lady whom I escorted to dinner. She was La Baronne Waetcher, the wife of the Würtemburg Minister, an American lady, and very pleasant. I was introduced to the Queen and had quite a chat with her. She is a woman of 50, not handsome but well enough—quite intelligent and speaking the English language perfectly. There were also present three Princesses, daughters of Lucien Bonaparte, two of whom I was introduced to late in the evening. Rouher, Minister of State, and wife were there, also, and indeed any number of high old dignitaries. The ladies were all very much dressed, low necks and bare arms. But the most agreeable people there were the English, particularly Lord Clarence Page and Lady Clarence. Lord Clarence is a British Ad-

miral, and lately in command of the English Mediterranean
Squadron, who entertained Farragut at Malta. He is a
plain, cordial, frank old fellow. And you might have taken
him for one of our Joe Davy's County Supervisors. Lady
Clarence is very much younger and a most charming person
and was full of praise of the Farraguts. They both invited
me most cordially to visit them in England. At half past
ten the Queen took her departure, and then we all left.
Lord Lyons is a most pleasant gentleman, and he, too, is
very plain and unpretending. The fellows of the least
account had on the most trappings.

There have been great riots and disturbances during the
last week in some parts of Paris. Indeed, many thought we
were on the eve of another revolution. Vast crowds assembled every night on the Boulevards, singing the Mar-
seillaise, raising seditious cries, destroying property, etc.
Friday night I took a voiture and rode down the Boulevards, even to Montmartre where the greatest disturbance
had been. My driver kept on until he saw a regiment of
cavalry sweeping the crowd out of the street, when he
turned around and "put" in the other direction. A vast
number of arrests have been made of the "perturbators"
and also a good many editors have been seized. Two
Americans were arrested, who were in the crowd, and I
have had to intercede officially to get them out of the jug.
I think the trouble is now over and everything seems to be
quiet. . . .

Palace of Campiègne, Saturday morning, Nov. 13, 1869
. . .

Yesterday the "Royal Party" visited the grand old
Chateau of Pierrefonds, on the other side of the forest, some
eight or nine miles, I should think. We started about noon
five large open wagons, four horses each and each carrying
nine persons. The Emperor again invited me to take a seat
with him and M. Le Roux, one of his ministers. I cannot
go into a description of that wonderful old chateau, but
must wait till I return. We remained there an hour or two,
returning to the palace at 4 o'clock. The performances

last evening were diversified by a lottery and they had a heap of fun—There was a big table in a grand old hall, and chairs all around the table, a little ways off, for the ladies to sit in. On the table there were a great many little things suitable for souveniers, of all values, such as cigar cases, glove and handkerchief boxes, photograph frames, match holders, candy boxes, vases, dolls, birds in cages, and all sorts of nice little French jim cracks. All these things had a number. Then each guest drew from a bag a button with a number on it. An old gentleman goes to the table and takes up an article and calls out the number and the person holding that number comes forward. Then the old gentleman carefully unrolls it while the whole crowd is on the qui vive to know what the party has drawn, and then goes up applause and all sorts of exclamations. The Emperor, the Prince and the Princess Matilde all had a button. The Prince drew some little thing and the Princess a cigar case, but the Emperor drew a blank. The most valuable thing was a beautiful little Sevres vase, made for the Prince Imperial, and having his portrait with the letter N. The number of that was called out, the old gentleman unrolled it to the admiring gaze of the company and a great shout went up as I stepped forward with the number and claimed it. The Emperor and the Princess and all hands congratulated me on having drawn such a beautiful prize.

After the drawing was over we went back into the dancing hall. I danced a quadrille with the Princess Matilde, who is really a most charming and pleasant lady, and a graceful dancer. She speaks "English a little." The standing round in company is awful on my back and it aches this morning "fit to kill." I do not know the order for to-day, but I wish I might have quiet. . . . They are going to keep us here over Monday as a ball is to be given in honor of the Empress Monday night. . . .

Legation des Etats Unis
Paris Le 29 Apl. 1870, Friday morning
I dined last night with Papa and Mamma le Lien, some 17 covers, mostly French. The women were covered with

diamonds, but hideous to look upon. There was there a most celebrated woman whom I did not suppose was alive. It was La Marquise de Boissy, the widow of Le Marquis de Boissy, a Senator and a distinguished man. La Marquise was the *friend* of Lord Byron in her early days, and was then the Countess of Guechioli. She wrote the life of Byron and is going to send it to me. She is a most interesting person, and is the best preserved person of her age I ever saw—I shall go and see her some Wednesday. She is very rich and has a sort of palace. The dinner was very pleasant. After dinner I went into the Erlanger's party for an hour. It was the most brilliant private party of the season. I did not see many persons whom I knew and came off very soon. I am going with Baron Erlanger today to see the Postmaster General about the postal treaty business.

On July 3, 1870, Washburne had left Paris for Carlsbad to take the cure. On July 15 he received notice that France had declared war on Prussia. There was no railway at Carlsbad, so he took the diligence from that place to Eger, rode all night and caught a train for Paris where he arrived on July 18.

To Mrs. Washburne

Paris July 19, 1870, Tuesday Morning
You will see I am back again at Paris. I telegraphed you yesterday from Belgium that I was on my way. I heard of the declaration of war on Saturday and left that night and arrived here at 10 o'clock last night after a terribly hard and continuous trip of 52 hours, the first night being in the stage. I was sorry to have to give up my cure, but it was inevitable. This is my place where duty calls me and here I must remain. I have no time to write particulars this morning. I am feeling better than I thought I should after my hard trip. . . .

To Mrs. Washburne

Paris, Sunday, Oct. 16, 1870, evening

. . .
I am going to try and get the Americans, who want to go, out of Paris. Bismarck has agreed to let them go. As soon as I can get all out who want to go and get the rest cared for, then I will begin to think of getting out myself. But I can't think of going as long as it is my duty to stay here. We are ·very comfortable at Mr. Huffer's. Dr. Johnston dines here today. The weather is rainy and cold and fall has evidently set in. . . .

Things look more and more unpromising here and I can see no glimmer of light. No one can tell what there is in the future for poor France, or how long we will stay here. During these terrible times and the great responsibility thrust upon me, I have sighed for home more than ever. I would be delighted to bid a final adieu to public life and settle down with our children around us and spend the remainder of our days in quiet. . . .

In a speech which he made in 1875 when he was home on leave of absence, he said of his mission to France:

"The position that I was some part of the time called upon to occupy, was a novel one, and almost without precedent. At the time of the unlooked-for declaration of war, there were large numbers of Americans in Paris and in France, with large interests at stake. There were also some forty thousand Germans in France, the most of them settled in Paris, where they had made their homes for years, and where centered all their interests. The breaking out of the war suddenly ruptured the diplomatic relations between the two countries, and it then became necessary in respect of these interests, as well as in the interest of humanity, that the Germans should have other protection for their persons and their affairs. And

it was then that the government of the North German
Confederation, and the governments of Darmstadt,
Saxony, and Saxe Coburg-Gotha, applied to the government of the Great Republic to have the American Minister
at Paris charged with the protection of their people in
France during the continuance of the war between the
countries. You know how readily and cheerfully our
government acceded to the request upon the condition
that France would acquiesce. That acquiescence was
promptly granted, but in accepting the charge of the
Germans then in France, I was only the organ of my own
government, and carrying out its instructions and wishes.
I could have accomplished but little, however, had it not
been for the great interest taken by the German government in its subjects, suddenly expelled by the Empire,
and its unbounded liberality in furnishing me with all the
pecuniary means necessary to aid them, and the ever-
ready support accorded to me by the French government, and which enabled me to accomplish the mission
with which I was charged. Therefore, but little credit
is due to me personally in this regard, for if I succeeded in
accomplishing anything it was due mainly to circumstances, independent of my own action. With no experience in such matters, and with no pretension of having
been initiated in what are called the mysteries of diplo-
macy, with no precedents laid down in the books to govern
such an emergency, I had simply to do the best I could
under the circumstances, and I took a sort of town-
meeting view of the whole subject and made precedents
to suit the occasion. I could claim nothing more, if I
could claim anything, than the practical sense I had
picked up among the fir-clad hills of my native New
England, and in the proud state of my adoption. Situated

as I was, in the midst of events that were convulsing France and Europe and the world, I deemed it a high privilege to do anything in my power to aid and assist, not only our own people, but all peoples and all nationalities, whenever and wherever I could properly do so. Alas! could such efforts at all times have been successful, the world might not have been called upon to witness one of the most tragic and fearful events in history, the foul murder of the Archbishop of Paris—that eminent man who in his life illustrated all the Christian virtues, honored by the rich and the exalted, and loved by the poor and the humble, and who alike in the gloom of the prison cell and under the fire of assassins, rose above the things of this earth, and who bore his faculties so meekly and was so clear in his great office, that his virtues plead like angels, trumpet-tongued, against

"The deep damnation of his taking off."

This tells in part the story of a remarkable diplomatic mission. In reality Washburne had had an exceptionally good training for the duties which he was called upon to perform. His long public career had accustomed him to responsibility. As a leader of the House he was skilled in controversy and his mind was alert and well exercised. As the head of the great *budget* committee of government he was habituated to dealing with large subjects and to giving a negative reply to improper requests. Having stood with Lincoln and Grant during the Civil War, and visited the front and seen real battles, he heard the bombardments of Paris and saw the soldiers and the fighting in the streets without trepidation. His equipment for his mission was a great deal better than it would have been, if he had spent his life in the brain-sapping duties of writing polite diplomatic notes about trifles and attending punctiliously to the formal, unimportant affairs which constitute the business of a diplomatic officer in normal times.

Yet he went to France in the hope of enjoying himself. He wanted to go in order to please his wife and to be in proximity of the springs and baths which he believed were beneficial to his health. On his visit to Europe in 1867 he had taken the Carlsbad cure and he went there annually for eight years afterward. His fondness for all things French, which had come as a part of his fondness for Mrs. Washburne, made the post of Minister to France peculiarly desirable to him. Because he was a representative from the West and had not been on the Foreign Affairs Committee, the public in the East assumed that he was ignorant of foreign life and that he knew nothing of France.

He was commissioned Envoy Extraordinary and Minister Plenipotentiary to the French Empire in 1869, and he presented his credentials to the Emperor Napoleon III. It was a brilliant court. Fêtes, dinner-parties and other entertainments succeeded one another at short intervals. They were carefully planned and carried out with beautiful effect. As Mr. Washburne reported, the Emperor Napoleon III was especially desirous of cultivating the American envoy, in order that he might overcome the unfavorable impression which existed against him in America, because of his efforts to control the destiny of Mexico. Moreover, our Civil War had revealed to Europe the great power of our government, and the French Emperor, as Mr. Washburne knew, had favored the recognition of the Confederate government. The Emperor wished to make amends and cause these things to be forgotten. Mr. Washburne himself made a favorable impression at the French court. On one occasion when he introduced a large number of Americans to the Empress and called each one by name she was astounded at the power of his memory. He did not tell her that he had cultivated the faculty of remembering names and faces because it was a valuable possession to an American public man who had to get votes. His personality was striking in the throng of uniformed courtiers. He was out of the common run and suggested the vigor and simplicity of the country he represented. He had no personal affectations or pretensions. Among the public men of France he was recognized as an equal and he was received on terms of intimacy by those with whom he came in contact.

As the war progressed it was not only Americans and Germans whom the American minister had under his protection, but citizens of Santo Domingo, Uruguay, Costa Rica, Ecuador, Chile, Paraguay, and Venezuela. Those countries had no diplomatic representation in France and their consuls asked Washburne to take charge of their interests which he did without special instructions from his government. He was successfully appealed to also by the Roumanians in Paris. Indeed the disposition to appeal to him was general and he interested himself in all meritorious cases which came before him. Many scoundrels, crazy people, frauds and meddlesome busy-bodies invoked his aid for their wild or nefarious schemes, but he was too experienced in judging men to be deceived by them. Complicated and novel questions of international law arose and he met

them with common sense, but, in these matters it was
his good fortune to have the counsel of George Bemis, an
international lawyer of note then living in Paris, who had
attended the Harvard Law School at the same time with
Washburne.

The amount of relief work which Washburne managed
was enormous. By December, 1870, he was feeding more
than 1000 Germans; by March, 1871, the number had
increased to 3000. He had a large amount of American
property to guard.

The war went on and Paris was besieged. Great
admiration for the French arose in him and he saw and
recorded many instances of their patriotism and bravery.
He took intense interest in the drama which was enacted
before him. He attended the debates of the legislative
assembly; he drove out to the environs of Paris near the
fighting; he visited the public offices and made friends
with men who were managing the destiny of France.
After the siege began the isolation, the suspense, the
repetition each day of the scenes of sadness and suffering
of the day before. The whole became extremely irk-
some to Mr. Washburne, but there was no suggestion of
his abandoning the scene of his great usefulness and unselfish devotion. When there was nothing new to record
he would sometimes amuse himself by writing in his
diary a remembrance of the early days of his political
life in Illinois. His mind went back to these experiences
while all around him was ruin and distress.

On the great day of the siege the bombardment of Paris
began and continued for twenty-two days, and on March
1, 1871, Mr. Washburne saw the German troops enter the
city. Peace had come for France was conquered. The
protection of the Germans in Paris now became even a

more difficult task than it had been while war lasted, for the hatred for the conquerors was now aflame. The war being over it might reasonably have been expected that the American Minister might be relieved of his extraneous and abnormal functions and might enjoy the experience of representing only his own country's interests at a peaceful capital. On the contrary new duties were presented to him more trying than those of the war had been, involving greater responsibility and graver danger. During the war he was resident near a responsible government managed by responsible men, and during the supremacy of the Commune he lived near a band of enemies of society who had seized upon the government and were administering it in hideous caricature.

Lord Lyons, the British Ambassador, reported to his government that when the regular government fled from the Paris mob to Versailles Mr. Washburne was the only minister representing a foreign government who remained in Paris. Lord Lyons indicated what was the truth, that Washburne being charged with German interests which centered in Paris had duties which his colleagues did not have and that he could correspond with his government without exciting the suspicion of the Commune, as his country was not only neutral but had no interest in the politics of Europe. It may well be doubted whether the Commune would have permitted the representatives of European powers to remain in Paris. At any rate, from the time that the Commune obtained control until the government troops took possession Elihu Washburne was the only foreign minister in Paris. He guarded American and German interests with sleepless vigilance. To effect this purpose he did not hesitate to communicate with officers of the Commune. He was told afterwards that

Jules Favre at Versailles criticized him for this, but he was convinced that it was the proper course to pursue. Washburne was having a strange experience. The Frenchmen with whom he had thus far been brought in contact were men of the highest type—such as Duc de Gramont, Jules Favre, Thiers, Casemir, Perier and Gambetta; now he met Pascal Grousset, Charles Lullier and the leader of the Commune, Raoul Regault, whom he described as "an architect of murder, pillage and incendiarism, a cruel and blood-thirsty villain, not even having one virtue to a thousand crimes." One incident of this period must be given because it shows how Mr. Washburne performed his duties and because he himself looked upon it as one of the most interesting experiences of his diplomatic career.

George Darboy, Archbishop of Paris, was arrested by the Commune on April 4, 1871, and put in prison as a hostage for the safety of several Communards who had been seized by the regular forces, the chief of them being the leader Blanquin. Mr. Washburne did not know the archbishop except by reputation, but he made inquiry into the circumstances of the arrest as soon as he heard of it. The Papal Nuncio in Paris applied to the British Ambassador at Versailles for his intercession in the archbishop's behalf, but the British Ambassador declined to intervene. Application was then made to Mr. Washburne by the Papal Nuncio and other Catholic dignitaries in Paris and he agreed to act without waiting for instructions from the government at Washington. He obtained permits to visit the archbishop and was the first person from outside the prison who was permitted to see him after his arrest. Washburne sent a confidential message to Bismarck informing him of the archbishop's danger. He acted as intermediary between the archbishop and the outside world and delivered letters for the archbishop. He sent a memorandum drawn up by the archbishop to Thiers at the head of the regular government stating that Blanquin be released or permitted to escape. The American minister would act as intermediary in effecting the exchange. Thiers was unwilling, however, to make any concessions to the Commune; he insisted, moreover, that the archbishop's life was not in danger. The government troops entered Paris, May 22, and were stationed between the legation and the prison where the archbishop was confined which was held by the Communards, so Mr. Washburne was cut off from communication with the archbishop. On May 24, 1871, he was shot in the courtyard of the prison of La Roquette. A few days later, the government troops being in possession, Mr. Washburne went to see his cell, and then joined the great throng of people who visited his palace and viewed his body lying in state. On June 7, by special invitation he attended his funeral at Notre Dame. The whole incident made a deep impression on Mr. Washburne. His admiration for the archbishop arose from the high reputation he bore and his personal intercourse with him when stood face to face with an ignominious death. When Washburne was at home on leave of absence in the autumn of 1872 the Catholic Union (Circle of New York) addressed him a letter of thanks for what he had done for Archbishop Darboy in the course of which they said:

"You beheld around you God's temples desecrated, and the ministers of His holy religion hunted down like wild beasts, by an infuriated rabble.

"Eminent among the victims was the venerable Archbishop of Paris. He was 'sick and in prison,' and, in obedience to the divine commandment, you visited him;

sympathized with him in his sufferings, consoled him in his affliction and distress, and endeavored, at no small risk to yourself, to save his precious life." Probably the thanks showered upon Mr. Washburne for his efforts to save Father Darboy were as highly prized by him as any he received in the course of his long career.

In the middle of June, 1871, the German envoy to France arrived in Paris and Washburne surrendered his charge as German Minister, and in July he went back to Carlsbad to complete the cure which had been interrupted by the gravest crisis he had ever been called upon to deal with.

Mr. Washburne performed the ordinary functions of a minister without fault. He did not favor a large salary nor a princely establishment. He wrote to a friend:

"Matters are well as they are. The salary is ample for all practical purposes, and ought not to be increased. If a man have a big fortune, and wants to make a splurge on his own account, he can do so. But if with little fortune, like myself, let him attend to the business with which his government has entrusted him, treat his compatriots with invariable courtesy and politeness, protect them in all their rights, and there can be no reasonable grounds of complaint."

After the inauguration of President Hayes Mr. Washburne resigned his mission but actually served until the autumn of 1877, eight and a half years, longer than any American envoy has ever served in France.

Of course Washburne's services for Germany deserved recognition from that government. During the war with France he had corresponded as much with Prince Bismarck as he had with Secretary Fish. A rumor was started in Berlin that he was to have conferred on him the order of the Black Eagle and that the Emperor was selecting the precious stones which were to ornament the decoration. George Bancroft, the Minister at Berlin, reported the circumstance to Washburne in January, 1872, and Washburne replied promptly that he would accept no title or decoration and was amply repaid for his services by the thanks he had received. Bancroft said it was a good letter and he informed the German Foreign Office of its purport. But when Washburne was about to return to private life he consented to receive a testimonial of the obligation of the German government, expressing his preference for a portrait of the Emperor. The Emperor sat for the portrait and sent it to Mr. Washburne with this letter:

To Mr. E. B. Washburne, till now Envoy Extraordinary, etc., of the United States to the French Republic.

Beurath, Sept. 7, 1877.
My dear Mr. Washburne: After you have been recalled from your post as Ambassador of the United States at Paris, and as you are about to return to your native country, I take occasion to renew my acknowledgments, already personally expressed, of the zeal and devotion with which you, under difficult circumstances, protected the German interests during the German-French war. As a testimony of my gratitude I send you herewith my portrait executed in oil. You will please to receive the same as a remembrance of the eventful times during which you have been in a position to render beneficial and efficient services to my Government, and at the same time as a sign of my regard and kind wishes with which I accompany your return to private life. I remain, my dear Mr. Washburne, your affectionate—WILHELM.

262 Israel, Elihu and Cadwallader Washburn

This was sent to Mr. Washburne by the Chancellor Von Bulow.

Foreign Office, Berlin, Sept. 8, 1877

The undersigned discharges an agreeable duty in sending to the former Envoy Extraordinary and Minister Plenipotentiary of the United States of America to the French Republic, Mr. E. B. Washburne, a letter of his Majesty the Emperor and King, our most gracious master, which has just been received from the imperial court at Castle Beurath, near Dusseldorf, and with which his Majesty has been pleased to send his portrait. Hoping that the portrait, which has been sent to Bremen, may have come into the possession of Mr. Washburne, and that the inclosed most gracious letter may reach its destination before Mr. Washburne leaves the European Continent, the undersigned at the same time wishes Mr. Washburne a happy journey to his native land, and that after the full discharge of his arduous duties he may enjoy a long and blessed repose in his native country. With these wishes, in which all Germans, in grateful remembrance of the debt which they owe to Mr. Washburne, heartily unite, the undersigned begs Mr. Washburne again to receive the assurance of his . high esteem.

The Secretary of State of the Foreign Office.

V. Bulow.

More prized than either of these, however, was the letter Mr. Washburne had received from his own government.

Your Government has sympathized deeply with you in the trials and privations and annoyances to which you were subjected during the long continued siege of the capital to which you were officially accredited, and where a high sense of duty, which is appreciated and commended, induced you to remain in the efficient and heroic discharge of the most difficult and delicate responsibilities that fall within the power of diplomatic service. The President recognizes that your continuance within the besieged capital after the discretionary permission given you in my dispatch of the 24th January last, has been from the promptings of your own conviction that the interests committed to you required the very great sacrifice of comfort of the separation from your family, isolation from the intercourse of friends, personal discomforts, and risk of health and life. This sacrifice and these trials you have endured, and I desire officially to record the high appreciation and warm approval of your Government. You have done your duty faithfully and ably, and the President tenders you his thanks for the manner in which you have discharged the delicate duties devolving upon you, and have on all occasions maintained the dignity of your position and the rights of your Government.

PRESIDENTIAL CANDIDACY OF GRANT AND WASHBURNE

On November 22, 1875, the *Post and Mail* of Chicago published a notable article in which it was argued that Elihu Washburne was the most available candidate that the Republican party could nominate for the Presidency. The paper spoke of him as a friend of the farmers, as a friend of the Germans, as a man of long and tried experience. Other Illinois papers joined the *Post and Mail* and he was formally presented as the favorite candidate of the West. These publications were a natural result of what many men were saying. He, himself, did not take the matter seriously. The Rock Island *Union* of January 11, 1876, quoted from a letter of his: "I am not vain enough," he said, "to suppose that my name can ever figure seriously in that direction. . . . While I receive many letters of the same kind, I am so impressed with what I have written, that I decline all action in the way of candidature, and in the end, when the convention comes off and my name is never mentioned, you and other friends will say that I have been wise." To this his friends replied: "He does not know how, in the era of the unmasking of extravagance and corruption, his career in Congress shines like an oasis in a desert." He was strong, they said, because he had "been out of the country and done nothing indiscreet." Suggestions were made that he would make a good candidate for the Vice Presidency, with Blaine the candidate for President. It was brought out in his favor that he had been the first man in Congress to warn the people against the aggressions of the great railways. It was insisted that he was a granger in sentiment. His candidacy was favored by the reform element in the Republican party. An article on May 31, 1876, in the Chicago *Staats-Zeitung* shows where much of his strength lay:

"No German can or ever will forget that, at a time when all the other representatives of foreign nations fled from Paris in cowardly manner, Washburne remained at his post during the siege and the fighting to stand by the German citizens who had been confided to his protection; that he brought himself frequently in conflict with the existing Powers in Paris on this account, and that the German Emperor and Parliament have expressed their thanks to him for this service in the heartiest and warmest words."

To nominate a man towards whom many thousands of voters felt as the former Germans felt towards Washburne would be a sensible thing to do. Outside of Illinois there was a leaning towards Washburne in many quarters. The *Evening Express* at Rochester, New York, put him next to Roscoe Conkling as its choice. All agreed in praising his integrity and rigid honesty in Congress. But there was yet another point in his favor; he was the friend of Grant; he had brought the conqueror upon the scene; he had stood by him and saved him from his enemies in civil life; he had obtained for him his command and his honors.

This year, 1876, a number of Illinois newspapers proposed that Mr. Washburne be made the governor of Illinois. Shelby M. Cullom and John L. Beveridge were the candidates, but Washburne was stronger than either of them. It is highly probable that if he had sanctioned it he would have been nominated; but he telegraphed his

friend, J. Russell Jones, collector of customs at the port
of Chicago, that he would "decline absolutely" the nomination. The reason for declining was that his nomination would have been effected only after a bitter struggle
which he wished to avoid. Already one newspaper, the
Aledo (Illinois) *Record*, had placed at the head of its
editorial columns the words: "For President, 1876,
Elihu B. Washburne of Illinois." No one surveyed the
field of presidential candidates without seeing his figure.
The Anglo-American *Times* in London under date of
February 4, 1876, put the leaders with reference to the
probability of nomination in this order: Blaine, Bristow,
Washburne, Morton, Fish and Hayes. Calculators who
had no personal bias narrowed the contest to Hayes,
Bristow and Washburne. Voices in Washburne's favor
were heard as far west as California. A point urged by
some of his admirers was that his friendship for General
Grant made it probable that Grant would like to see him
nominated. If such was the case, however, no direct
sign to that effect came from Grant. The feeling grew
within the party that he would combine its strength and
smooth its dissensions. His New England birth predis-
posed New England for him. Governor Rice of Massachusetts, as late as May 25, 1876 (*New York Herald*,
May 26) said he should be nominated and spoke of him
as the original reformer. Those who favored Bristow
were believed to be for Washburne as their second choice.
The Paris and English papers always found him on the
lists sent to them by their correspondents in America.
The New York *Herald* worked for him steadily. Charles
Francis Adams, an Independent, himself proposed as an
Independent candidate, said Washburne was "a kind of
Lincoln," and added: "More than that he is firmer and

more settled in purpose than Lincoln. I am not intimate with Mr. Washburne. I met him personally two or three times in Paris and was in Congress with him some fifteen years ago, so that I know him tolerably well, and regard him very favorably."

The event showed that Washburne had been wise to treat his candidacy as improbable. His name was mentioned by the members of the convention but was not formally placed before it and he received no votes.

Almost immediately after the nomination of 1876 had been made the movement for his nomination in 1880 began. The same arguments were brought forward, one of the strongest being that he was the "constant and unsparing foe of corporations and especially of the land grant railroads."

In 1877 what appeared to be a favorable opportunity for advancing his political fortunes arose in the contest over the election of a senator from Illinois. The legislature stood one hundred Republican members, ninety-nine Democrats and five Independents. It was plain that no Republican could be chosen unless he received a few Democratic votes. The Republican candidate was General John A. Logan and for him no Democrat would vote. An agreement was reached by certain Republicans and Democrats that they would vote for Washburne, if Logan would allow the Republicans to do so, but Logan refused.[1] The result was that David Davis, an Independent, was elected.

Before the sentiment in the Republican party had had opportunity to form definitely with reference to a candidate for the Presidency General Grant returned to America after his trip around the world. No American had

[1] James L. D. Morrison in the St. Louis *Globe Democrat,* January, 1879.

been as much honored as he had been. He was the embodiment of the international prestige which had come to the country in consequence of the success of the Union cause in the Civil War. His friends, who were opposed to Blaine for one reason or another, thought that it would now be an easy task to put General Grant back in the Presidency and restore their own influence and power. It does not appear that Washburne was one of the "original Grant men" and he was not an anti-Blaine man. He had been out of the country during the whole of Grant's administration, when the circle of men who enjoyed his confidence and profited by it had formed around him. He had kept himself informed of the moves which were being made in the game of politics but he was not in the game itself. He was never enthusiastic over the Grant candidacy. He saw its weak points clearly. It was largely an artificial "boom" manufactured and launched by powerful party leaders who were thinking of themselves, the advantages they would derive from Grant's return to power and their enmities towards Blaine; for unless Blaine's enemies should agree upon a candidate Blaine's nomination was probable and they could expect no countenance from him. They were not thinking of the effect that a disputed candidacy and possible defeat would have on Grant's reputation. There was a considerable amount of popular support to his candidacy, however. General Grant continued to stand well with a great many people who overlooked the scandals of his administration because of his services in the field. But there were others who did not overlook the scandals, and the reformers were many. There was a still larger element composed of people who regarded the idea of a President serving for three terms with serious apprehension. They thought it a menace to our form of government.

As soon as Grant's candidacy was announced Washburne gave his adherence to it. As Grant's best friend there was nothing else for him to do. To all suggestions that he should avow himself a candidate he replied with a firm refusal. In fact, an avowed candidacy on his part would have failed, for all other elements would have combined against him in Illinois and the state was more strongly for Grant than it was for anyone else and next to Grant was for Blaine. If Washburne was to be nominated at all it must be as a "dark horse." One of General Grant's friends, an enemy of Blaine, who was as much responsible as anyone else for Grant's candidacy and who was determined to carry it through by easy or rough methods, was General John A. Logan, now a senator, wielding much power in Illinois politics and ambitious to wield more. The following extracts of letters from him to Washburne show something of the methods of the Grant campaign and the suspicion which arose in Logan's mind and doubtless in the minds of others that Washburne was not as heartily engaged in furthering Grant's interests as he might have been.

Washington, Dec. 18, 1879

Of course you have seen the result of the action of the National Rep. Com. on the chairman; it was a square fight against Cameron because he was a Grant man, but I write for another purpose, that is to give you a point that must be looked to very soon. There is work, very active, commenced here within a clique who are working up Sherman and the program is to have as many Sherman papers as possible come out against Grant or take the stand that they will not support him. Schurz is the medium for that work. Sherman pretends to like Grant but he is cold and subtle. He goes to Philadelphia to the reception and some people here say that the Grant people of Philadelphia are somewhat inclined to S. I give you all the points, and the Chicago German papers ought to come out and say that they will support G. if nominated and it ought to be translated and published in the English papers.

Washington, Jany. 15, '80

I had a talk today with "Don" Cameron; he says the Penn. convention will instruct for Grant. The whole talk here among all the small fry and scribblers is that the "boom" is dying out. This is kept up persistently, and the Bureau of Correspondence is kept hot sending out squibs south and east for Blaine, or Sherman, and also a story is being quietly circulated that some of the Chicago people are preparing to back down at the proper time for them. . . .

I understand Snider is not quite enthusiastic for G. and has made some suggestions on the subject, by way of substituting another name. This is very foolish talk, as any idea that G. was being used to work up matters for anyone else would end his prospects everywhere. . . .

Washington, Jany. 18, '80

There seems to be such a great desire to have some one of the various Ills. men now in the Treasury Dept. nominated for Gov. that it looks like there may be some underground work in the direction of delegates to the Natl. Convention. The Treasury Dept. is now commencing to move in much earnest and all the power of patronage and everything else will be used. I see quite a number of papers are speaking of you for Governor. How is it?

Your friend.

Washington, Jany. 21, 1880

You ask me about the statement that the "boom" is increasing. I can see no difference here, except that the enemies are at work and raising every means possible to get things in mixed shape. . . .

The papers in Penn. are now using the Chicago stories about your candidacy to some effect as I am told, that is to say that Grant is merely covering you as a candidate, of course I understand that this is being done by G's enemies, but some of the Chicago fiends give some ground for the story. I send you inclosed a copy of part of a letter containing a conversation with one of your friends and I am told that W. H. S. is writing a great deal on this subject, to his master and co. "Sam" Medill is here and has talked considerable. I understand he is against Grant and says that the "Concern" is not for Grant but for Blaine, but that Ills. is not to support Grant but to give you the delegation. Of course I have not seen him, as the Medill family do not "hanker" after me. . . .

Before our last Convention some of your friends in Chicago wanted you to be a candidate for Gov. but they told others that they thought were with them in this move that you could be nominated for Gov. and have the delegation also to the National Convention, and if nominated all right, if not, then be elected Gov. and then go to the Senate. This of course you knew nothing about, but it was too large a mouthful, and provoked opposition at once. All whose scalp was under the knife came together in solid opposition. I would then have been glad to have seen you Gov. and told one of your friends, or was willing that you should have the delegation to the Natl. Convention, but I saw my own head under the axe, which was not so pleasant and so it was with others.

Now some of the same men are talking in the same foolish manner; seem to be trying to travel over the same road. This cannot be accomplished as you well know, and shall not be attempted. If you wish to run for Gov. or in other words if you are willing to be run for Gov., that is one thing, and might be successful, but the two could not go together in my district. Grant for Pres. and yourself for Gov. might help both along with a certain element, but the moment you are by your friends put forward for Pres., unless G. had positively declined it, leaves you both out, and we are all defeated. Let this once be believed, and Blaine will be nominated without much of an effort. Men will not be guided by reason, but will, in such a case, act from a different cause—disappointment and anger at being deceived.

The fight in Penn. is waxing hot, but Cameron says he will carry instructions for Grant. It is not long however to wait for the result, and I hope all will come out as we want it, and it *will*, unless some of our own "fool friends" spoil it. . . .

Washington, Feby. 22, 1880

Now my dear friend, we must win this fight. Grant must not let us drop after staking our future on him. I would have been willing to support others, he out of the way, to beat this crowd of jobbers and gamblers in N. Y. that are backing Blaine, but it is too late; it is now Grant or Blaine, no one else will be thought of in two weeks more, as you will see. You have a great many friends all over the West and East, and you will pardon me for suggesting it, but I am of the opinion that should you write a good strong letter giving reasons for Grant's nomination, and make it public, it would do great good just at this time. I am in favor of using all the ammunition we have on this occasion, as this is our fight and our time to win. Such a thing will bring back many in your old district as well as elsewhere, and would do more to stop this German clamor than anything else. With Sherman's pretensions, and Blaine's impudence, with Gould and all his R. R. influence, in Kansas, Nebraska and Iowa, we have work and much work before us. A great many honest republicans are covertly for you. However they fight Grant thinking him out of the way, you would come in, and in this way they become antagonistic to Grant. Others are duped into the idea by the Tribune that you would perhaps be willing to be a tail to Blaine's kite, by being V. P. They argue this would give Ills. a candidate and make a very strong ticket. They start on this line and grow against Grant as things proceed with their accounts to others. I have had several letters on this line, all of which I have answered that we do not want any tails in Ills. We want first or nothing. . . .

Washington, Mar. 31, '80

The Kane Co. Convention was 8 G., 6 Blaine. Farwell intends to bring up enough in Chicago to make some division in our delegation, we must bring Ills. solid, and that will settle the matter.

As the matter stands now, if Grant should weaken, Blaine would be nominated, and he would put power as much as possible in the hands of Farwell and co. in Ills.

I hope you will return home with Grant, let him go from Cairo to Chicago, and then home—let the people know along the line and stop only a short time at each station. Let him bow and shake hands with a few, and let the boys whoop a few times and all will be right, if some sharp fellow would come to Cairo and go up with you. . . .

Your friend.

. . . (*Undated*)

Your old district in many parts of it is out loud for Blaine. Mr. Carrol, I understand, is against Grant. I see Hawks letter from them saying so. If we are to have Ills. anyways solid, we must go to work and those that you can have influence with must go to work. . . . The constant row on me in the Tribune and Times about my wanting to pack the delegation is making all the Elements combine to have the delegation against us, all the office holders in Chicago except the P. O. is into it. Jim Root is here to fix up with B's friends about the patronage. If they carry Ills. Farwell, Root, Charley Reed and Co. are to carry and put up Chicago in the Convention, and are to commence getting up Blaine Clubs at once. You may think that I am alarmed, but I tell you there will have to be plain straightforward work from this on, or B's friends will get part of our delegation, and perhaps prevent instructions. This in Ills. would be fatal. Look the ground over, and write me. Old Bross of Tribune is here running Blaine and Washburne and many readily fall into it. This will carry many of your friends in Ills. over to B. not thinking of the design of the matter.

I am sick of this infernal duplicity of the papers in Chicago.

Write me

Your Friend.

Logan quotes somebody unnamed:

He stated, "It is clear that Grant can not get the nomination; now Washburne and Logan can make the next nomination and save the party. If Logan will help give this State to Washburne, he, Washburne, can be nominated. Washburne must see Logan and his friends and fix up with them. That the programme was for Washburne to run for Governor, that is for the nomination for Governor, and then he would be in a position for President and the State Central Committee could select another man for Governor."

Washington, April 4, '80

Since writing you the other day, I have recd. some news from our state that is very strange. Knox Co. and Champlain have held conventions, and altho the conventions were seemingly Grant, they have appointed Blaine delegates. Hurlburt and other of Bs. paid emissaries are traveling all over the state setting up conventions. This is being done by sending delegates professedly Grant until appointed—I also learn that Carroll, Whiteside Lee and perhaps Stephenson are likely to be Blaine. No man can correct this in those counties unless you can do it.

Can you not write your friends there and ask them to work? I hope you are in health and that you can return soon and set some of your friends in Chicago to work. The Boom is running wrong just now, and it must be counteracted some way. I can not be at home or I think I could head it off, but were I to go home it would be a text for all the opposition. G. ought to be in Ills. very soon. If we should be divided in Ills. I fear the result. This is the game now.

The dirtiest race that can be conceived is now being made on Grant.

. . .   *Washington, May 7, 1880*
I write merely to say to you in the most emphatic manner, that the article from Chicago, in the Globe Democrat, reflecting on yourself with others, and especially making me out a fool, tho pretending to praise me, was in no sense inspired, or known to myself or any one connected with the Grant Headquarters here, we all felt indignant at the article, and regarded it as having been inspired by some enemy of all parties mentioned in it.

I must emphatically repudiate the whole article, as the work of no friend of any of us, however he may pretend.
                                        Your Friend.

The star of the piece has no part in all these preliminary arrangements behind the scenes, but Washburne, of course, as his most trusted friend, knew his position. General Grant wrote to him February 2, 1880, from Havana. "On that subject, (candidacy for the Presidency) I stand just as I told you in Chicago. I shall not gratify my enemies by declining what has not been offered. I am not a candidate for anything, but if the Chicago convention nominates a candidate who can be elected it will gratify me, and the gratification will be greater if it should be some one other than myself."

It was plain that he would accept the nomination. He wrote to Washburne from Galveston March 25, 1880:

"In regard to your suggestion that I should authorize some one to say that in no event would I consent to ever being a candidate after 1880 I think any statement from me would be misconstrued and would only serve as a handle for my enemies. Such a statement might well be made after nomination if I am nominated in such a

way as to accept. . . . There are many persons I would
prefer should have the office to myself."

In the Washburne papers is a rough draft of the statement which Washburne had in mind as proper for General
Grant to make to him:

> "It could be properly said that you have seen in the
> press of the United States the progress of the campaign
> which seems to have been opened for the Republican
> nomination for President and had observed that your
> name has been used, and that in Penn. the delegates had
> been instructed to support you. It might be added that
> I am aware of the position which you have always held
> in relation to the subject and that you have in no wise
> changed that position, that you have never, directly or
> indirectly, had part nor lot in any movement tending
> towards *your* nomination by the Republican party. Noth-
> ing could be more admirable than what you say in your
> letter to me: That all your interest centres in this, that
> the Government should remain in the hands of those who
> saved it until all the questions growing out of the war are
> forever settled—that you would much prefer to see many
> whom you can mention President, for the coming term,
> than to be President yourself, that no one knows better
> than I that you have never sought position for yourself,
> either in the military or civil service, and were never a
> candidate for anything. If the Chicago Convention shall
> nominate a candidate, as it unquestionably will, who can
> be elected, it would be far more gratifying to you, than
> if the nomination should fall upon yourself. And I should
> also add, that whatever services you may have been able
> to render your country were not rendered in the hope of
> office but in vindication of a Holy cause, involving the
> Union, and the happiness, glory and prosperity of a great
> people for all time; that your services have received the
> highest reward which a free people could bestow, and that
> all suggestions that you are seeking anything more are
> unjust to yourself.

"Now as to the third term business, the most important of all, I hardly know how to properly reach it. But I venture to submit something like the following for your consideration:

'Much discussion is being had in our country in regard to what is called the "third term" and my candidacy in connection therewith. That is also unjust as I have never been a candidate for any term. But I cannot misapprehend what it is endeavored to be made understood, that after a President has served for two terms, and though the preceding term should be filled by another person, if the preceding President, who had served two terms, should then again become a candidate, it would be for a third term, the same as it would have been if he had been elected three consecutive times. This view of the question seems not to have taken into account that the outgoing President stands in the position of every other citizen, who is out of office with no patronage to bestow, without power and no influence to exercise.'

"You may have seen the views I expressed on the third term question in a letter addressed to Genl. White of Pa. in May, 1875. I could never see the dangers of a third term so vividly depicted by many good citizens and patriotic men. I said that 'the idea that any man could re-elect himself President or even re-nominate himself is preposterous. It is a reflection upon the intelligence and patriotism to suppose such a thing possible.' But whatever may be the argument or the reason on the subject of a third consecutive term, the disposition of the people is to hold to the example of Washington and the traditions of the Country. There might be a fear, nevertheless, that by being too long in power and so strengthening himself by the use of the vast patronage of the Government, and controlling political organizations, a President might perpetuate himself in office. While such a state of things might seem impossible in a country so free, enlightened and intelligent as ours, such a sentiment, inspired by a feeling of true patriotism, wants to be heeded. And if in the future of our country it should so happen, as it probably never will, that after a man had twice served as President and should after the intervention of one term, be elected a third time, he should in deference to a sentiment of the people inspired by a feeling of true patriotism, have it understood that he would under no circumstances or conditions whatever be a candidate for re-election,"

As the weeks passed on and the time for the convention grew nearer Washburne's position became very embarrassing. He had given his adhesion to the movement to nominate Grant, and he had absolutely refused to become a candidate himself. He became convinced, however, that the anti-third term sentiment was so strong that Grant's nomination could only be accomplished, if at all, after bitter struggle. The opposition was strong among his own friends and especially among his ever-faithful voters of German birth. It was a sentiment over which he had no control whatsoever. He did not falter in his own refusal to be a candidate. When a Washburne club was organized at Mt. Carroll, Illinois, in March, 1880, to advance his candidacy he sent word to the members that it must disband,—that he was for Grant. He met all other overtures with the same declaration. Preliminary to the national convention at Chicago was the state convention at Springfield on May 19 to choose delegates to the national convention. General Logan and several lesser lights led the Grant forces and the fight between them and the followers of Blaine was savage. It had been the custom up to that time for the delegates to the state convention from each congressional district to choose the delegates to the national convention. Several districts in Illinois being opposed to Grant, this meant that the Illinois delegation would not be a unit for Grant. So the convention changed the method of choosing the delegates and they were named by a committee appointed by the chairman of the convention. Thus Grant delegates were named to represent anti-Grant districts. When the national convention met, an appeal from this action of the state convention was made and the system of election of delegates by the districts was upheld. The contestants from Illinois were seated. General Logan and his followers found themselves less powerful at Chicago than they had been at Springfield. The Illinois delegation was not a unit for General Grant.

Five years after the convention the Illinois *Staats-Zeitung* (March 2, 1886) through Herman Raster gave this account of the Washburne candidacy. It is correct, except that it gives to the former Germans the whole responsibility for the candidacy, whereas in reality it came from many other sources as well.

"Grant and Washburne

"Adam Badeau, formerly body-servant and body-scribe of Gen. Grant, has recently published reminiscences wherein he speaks of the year 1880 and, in connection therewith, of the fact that Elihu B. Washburne had been urged as presidential candidate by Republicans who regarded a third term of Grant as imprudent and inadmissible. We learn on this occasion from Badeau that Grant never forgave any one who he thought betrayed him at that time, and that he never afterward spoke except with bitterness of his life-long friend Washburne who he believed—I know not how rightly—played him false. . . .

"The truth of the matter is—and in this we call the entire German-American press to witness—that Washburne's candidacy in 1880 emanated *solely* and *entirely* from *German* (not exclusively Republican) papers; that

the *boom* for Washburne had been under full headway in
German (Republican and Independent papers) six months
before the *Evening Journal* (Shuman) even thought of it
and that the *Evening Journal* entered into it, like the
laborers into the vineyard of the Lord, at the eleventh
hour. The Chicago elections to the Republican State
Convention were, within four days, turned into a brilliant
triumph for Washburne but *not* through the *Evening
Journal* or through Andrew Shuman who now claims the
credit for it.

"Under different circumstances it might be quite interesting to recall the memory of those proceedings at
Springfield when the late Gen. Logan achieved his greatest
victory, only to suffer two weeks later in the National
Convention of the Republican party an ignominious
defeat. But let us pass that. Logan's grave is yet too
fresh and those against whom the *Politician* Logan was
then in bitter feud have too good a memory of the *man*
Logan to re-vamp now those old stories. Enough—he
failed in his effort to make his friend Grant President for
a third time. And he failed because those who preferred
Washburne had succeeded in breaking down the unit-
rule, i. e. the usage that the *majority* of the representatives
of a State should cast the vote of *all* representatives of the
State.

"When that was done Elihu B. Washburne, as sure as
twice two is four, *would* have become President in place of
Garfield if—he had held his tongue, *i.e.* if he had not on
every proper and improper occasion, by speech and writing, declared that *Grant* was his candidate first and last.
But that, unfortunately, he did. Like a true Eckardt he
remained to the last faithful to his 'friend' Grant and
thereby the chance to make him President was lost. For,

when the National Convention had been in session five days and was tired out, he who would first attain fifty votes was sure to be nominated. These fifty votes *Garfield* got and that settled it, but Washburne would have had more than fifty (he reached 44) if every solicitation for a vote in his favor had not been met with the reply: Why should I vote for that man who declares that *Grant* is his only candidate?

"In that way Garfield (having the first 50 votes, afterwards everything was done by whoop and shout) was nominated and elected after Elihu B. Washburne, *through exaggerated friendship for Grant*, had committed *harikari i.e.* political suicide. Washburne would have been President of the United States from March 4, 1881 to March 4, 1885 if *Grant* had been just as honest, just as sincere a friend *to him* as *he* was to *Grant*.

"That is the darkest spot in Grant's life. Grant had a thousand good qualities of head and heart, among them gratitude for unworthy frauds and nobodies whose character he had not enough knowledge of human nature to discern. But the ability to understand in 1880 that it was his duty for once to help his true, real and genuine friend, Washburne, with the same loyalty and sincerity with which Washburne had helped him, that ability he did, unfortunately, not possess.

"The body-scribes left by him may say and write what they like, it remains nevertheless true (and, as said before, it is a very dark spot in the life of Grant) that in 1880 he was a *bad friend* of his friend Washburne, of the same friend who, (foolishly enough) sacrificed himself for a man who never was able to appreciate the sacrifice."

One thing, however, must be said in extenuation for General Grant: in his letters to Washburne before the convention, while he said that there were several men whom he would rather see nominated than himself, he never said that Washburne was one of them. It cannot be charged that he ever led Washburne to believe that he would throw his strength to him. But, for the matter of that, there was no question of his throwing his strength to anybody, for his strength was managed for him without any consultation with him. It was Logan, Conkling and others who had proposed his candidacy, who had persuaded him that his nomination would be easily effected, who had taken possession of him body and soul. During the sitting of the convention he was at his house at Galena. He was notified by his friends at the convention that he would be nominated at one o'clock on the afternoon of June 8, but at that hour he received word that General Garfield had been nominated. He was deeply disappointed. The whole story was told in the remark he made to his neighbor, General Rowley, the next day—that his friends had not treated him fairly. "They assured me," he said, "that there would be no serious opposition to me in the convention. I could not afford to go before that convention and be defeated," and so he visited his displeasure upon Washburne who had not urged him to be a candidate, whose advice with reference to an announcement that he would never be a candidate again he had refused to follow, who had realized the strength of the opposition to him and who had, nevertheless, stood by him when he knew that he was standing by defeat. Forty votes were cast for Washburne in the convention in spite of his own repeated declaration that he was not a candidate. They were cast by anti-Grant men and Washburne had no control over them or over the constituencies which they represented.

General Grant and Elihu Washburne never met again after the Chicago convention of 1880. The very name of each was hateful to the ears of the other. In February, 1885, when General Grant was lying so ill in New York City that it was believed his death was near, Washburne went to that city. The newspapers announced his arrival and Grant knew he was there, but he sent no invitation to his old friend to come to see him.

HISTORICAL WRITINGS

The retired statesman did not have anything that he must do. Politics furnished him with much to think about but did not fill his time. Abraham Lincoln once wrote to him that he should write ten letters to Lincoln's one, because he wrote ten times as fast as Lincoln did. It was true that he wrote rapidly and easily and his pen was a busy one, although it was often a careless one. After the war in Europe he had much leisure and he employed it in studying and writing. It was then that he composed his lectures on the French Revolution and the Siege and Commune of Paris. These he delivered, chiefly in the winter of 1878–79, by invitation in many places,—in Toronto, San Antonio, Boston, New Bedford, Philadelphia, San Francisco and other cities. He made original research in the Archives of Paris and gathered the material concerning Thomas Paine which appeared in *Scribners'* magazine under the title "Thomas Paine and the French Revolution." Later it was printed separately. From the standpoint of national American history this was the most valuable of his writings. In the same magazine appeared his "Reminiscences of Thiers," an interesting account of his intercourse with that statesman and a graphic description of the sitting of the Corps Legislatif August 9, 1870, when the ministry which had carried the country into the war went down. The article has the freshness and vividness of a picture from life written by one who was steeped in his subject. Following these came his series of articles in *Scribners'* running in the issues for January, February, March and April of 1887. These were entitled: "The Downfall of the Empire," "The Siege," "The Commune" and "The Downfall of the Commune." They appeared with additions in his two volume work *Recollections of a Minister to France 1809–1877*, published by Scribners' in 1887. He had seen the book through the press and the handsome volumes were in his hands, but he died before they had really circulated. This was the most important of Washburne's publications and holds permanent rank in the literature of the Franco-German War and the Commune of Paris. It was written from his diaries, despatches and letters contemporaneous with the events described. Mr. Washburne also printed several letters and addresses written in consequence of his European experiences, notably his efforts in behalf of Archbishop Darboy, and in 1878 the government published in separate form his despatches to his government on the subject of the war and the commune. These despatches were well written, and have been accepted as part of the history of that period. They were republished in 1905 in St. Louis, under the title *America's Aid to Germany in 1870-71; An Abstract from the Official Correspondence of E. B. Washburne*, the English text being accompanied by a German translation and the whole with a preface by Adolph Hefner. The speech on Abraham Lincoln delivered in 1860 and then distributed was reprinted in 1915 in Tarrytown. Mr. Washburne contributed the article on Illinois for the 9th edition of the *Encyclopedia Britannica*. It was an admirable presentation of the history and resources of the state, and well deserved the separate publication which it received in Philadelphia in 1881. Mr. Washburne's historical sketch of Edward Coles, a governor of Illinois, published in

Chicago in 1882 under the auspices of the Chicago
Historical Society ranks very high. He was attracted to
Coles' career especially because he was an Emancipationist
and had prevented the introduction of slavery in Illinois.
In 1884 appeared in Chicago *The Edwards Papers*, being
a portion of the collection of letters, papers and man-
uscripts of Ninian Edwards, presented to the Chicago
Historical Society, October 16, 1883, by his son William
Wirt Edwards, edited by Elihu B. Washburne, an histor-
ical contribution of solid value. He also edited in 1882
(Chicago) the *History of the English settlement in Edwards
County, Illinois*, by Morris Berbeck and George Flower.

His further contributions to western history were:
In 1884, Chicago, his eulogy delivered before the Chicago
Historical Society on Isaac N. Arnold. He and Arnold
had been colleagues in the House of Representatives from
1861 to 1865, both were of New England revolutionary
stock, both had been friends of Lincoln, both had worked
to build up the Chicago Historical Society. Mr. Washburne's eulogy was one of his best sketches and is a
good example of the literature of eulogy. Washburne's
experiences with Lincoln took the shape of two excellent
articles in the *North American Review* for November, 1885,
under the title "Lincoln in Illinois," in which he told of
Lincoln's early career in Illinois and his own experiences
with him there and when he arrived in Washington to be
inaugurated as President.

While he was in Europe in 1875, he printed at Galena
his *Historical Sketch of Charles S. Hempstead* to which is
appended a *Memoir of Edward Hempstead, First Delegate
to Congress from the Western side of the Mississippi River,
Representing Missouri Territory from 1811–14 by Hon.
Thomas H. Benton*. It was in the form of a letter from

Washburne to Captain Daniel Smith Harris, president of the Early Settlers Association at Galena. The occasion for the letter was the death of Edward Hempstead on December 10, 1874. Beside the sketches of the Hempsteads there were interesting reminiscences by Washburne of the lawyers of Galena. In 1881 (Jefferson City, Mo.) was published the address on Edward Hempstead. He delivered it before the legislature of Missouri when he presented Hempstead's portrait acting for Hempstead's nephew Edward Hempstead of Chicago. The address followed lines similar to those of the previous publication and quoted liberally from Benton's sketch. In 1884 (Chicago) was published *Henry Gratiot a Pioneer of Wisconsin; an address on the occasion of the Presentation of his portrait to the State Historical Society of Wisconsin Delivered before the Society at Madison, Wis., Thursday evening, Nov. 13, 1884.* Of his historical publications relating to his wife's relatives this was the best, having been carefully prepared and showing familiarity with his subject. The portrait, it should be remarked, was given to the society by Mrs. Washburne.

In 1885 (Chicago) his address at the dedicatory exercises of the Washburne Memorial Library at Livermore was printed. It was in large manner a family history for it dealt with the history of the town of Livermore, the founder, Deacon Elijah Livermore, and the Hamlins, Washburns, Benjamins, all of whom were more or less closely related to him. His family publications have, of course, a local interest chiefly, but they are all creditable works and show an amiable and attractive side of Washburne's character.

Mr. Washburne's writings about members of his own and his wife's family began at an early period. He printed a letter to Governor Emory Washburne under date of June 24, 1859, in which he gave the lineage of the Washburns from 1631. About this time he printed (Washington, Buell and Blanchard) a *Brief Notice of Lieutenant Samuel Benjamin, an officer of the Revolutionary War, with extracts from a Diary kept by him during the War*, Lieutenant Benjamin having been his mother's father. Thus his writings fall into three catalogues,—those relating to his own and his wife's ancestors, those relating to Illinois history, and those relating to his diplomatic experiences. Of these the last named are the most valuable but the other two have high value also. He contributed from time to time fugitive pieces to the newspapers,—notably to the Galena *Gazette*, but they have not been identified. They served their purpose for a day and he made no effort to preserve them.

The interest which he took in Illinois history attracted Washburne to the Chicago Historical Society, and he took an active part in its affairs. He contemplated making it the permanent depository of his valuable collection of books, papers, and pictures. The papers were his correspondence during his eventful career at home and abroad, which he partially arranged during the last ten years of his life; and his pictures were those of famous European characters and had been acquired by him from time to time, many of them as gifts from the originals. He hesitated, however, to turn his collection over to the society because it had not built a fireproof building but he confidently expected to make a permanent disposition of it for the benefit of the public before he died. He failed to do so and by his will it went to his son Hempstead. His papers now constitute a monumental collection in the library of Congress at Washington.

END OF LIFE

When Washburne came back to America from his mission to France he was sixty-one years old. From the medicinal waters in Europe his health derived temporary benefit but there was no cure. Ripe age had made his appearance more impressive. The hair was still thick but almost white, the eyes glowed under heavy eyebrows which were white, the lines from the nose to the mouth were deeper. The straight, determined mouth was the same. In photographs it gives the impression of a mouth that has just spoken. There was no look of contemplative repose in the face and his movements were as quick as ever.

He was now in private life after twenty-six years of uninterrupted public service. He settled in Chicago but did not resume the practice of the law. That profession he had, of course, completely abandoned when he went to Paris, but before that his practice had been intermittent. He had, at one time or another, made a good income from his law cases before the local courts and occasionally before the federal courts. He did a general law business but he was not connected with any cases which reached historical proportions. In the House he had not been known as a lawyer member. He had not served on the Judiciary Committee and had not made lawyers' arguments instead of political speeches as some of his colleagues did. In fact, Washburne the lawyer was only known to Galena.

He had acquired an independent fortune. The severe poverty of his youth and early manhood had taught him lessons of thrift which he did not forget, and in the rapidly growing Western country he availed himself of the opportunities for profitable investments. Probably his income when he retired to private life was more than fourteen thousand dollars a year and less than eighteen thousand. He and his brothers and sisters were legatees of Cadwallader Washburn in 1882 and for the last five years of his life Elihu's income was doubled. When he died he left an estate valued at about $850,000.

He bought a handsome house at the corner of Dearborn Avenue and Maple Street on the north side in Chicago and henceforth it was his home, but like his other houses, it was rather his headquarters, a place to which he returned from time to time from his frequent journeys. His children were grown up and had settled in life. His eldest son, Hempstead, was a lawyer of high rank in Chicago. His father saw him elected city attorney, and fairly started on the career which carried him into the high office of mayor of Chicago. His daughters were happily married, one in Bridgeport, the other in Denver. After his wife's death he gave up the Dearborn Avenue house and lived the last seven months of his life with his son, Hempstead.

During the trying days in Paris, Mr. Washburne was frequently ill. In December, 1870, he had a severe attack of the grippe, in February, 1871, he was ill again. The intervals of good health were never long.

Soon after his return from France, in May, 1878, he went to the Hot Springs of Arkansas in search of health and then on to the Pacific Coast. In November of the same year he was obliged to postpone an engagement to lecture at Toronto, because he was seriously ill. The following year, 1879, he tried the climate of southern Texas and Mexico.

In 1879 his brother, Algernon Sidney Washburn, died at Hallowell. There was no one to whom he felt under greater obligation. Sidney had remained in Maine and had made an honorable if inconspicuous career for himself as a banker. When Elihu made his will he left a sum to be expended for gold watches for each of Sidney's sons, "in remembrance," he said, "of all their father's unbounded kindness to me in my younger days."

In 1882 Cadwallader Washburn was taken sick, and it was apparent that his days were numbered. In the spring of that year he went to the Eureka Springs in Arkansas in the vain hope that the waters might benefit him. Thither the brothers Elihu and Israel repaired to bear him company in his sickness. On May 5, when his disease took a turn for the worse, Elihu wrote to his wife: "I am prostrated with grief and anxiety today." Israel slept in the same room with Cadwallader to watch over him, and when Elihu entered the morning of the fifth the patient said, "I feel the end is near." Later in the day his mind was clouded. He wanted to speak but could only say "I am going soon to die." "My heart is heavier than I can express," wrote the stricken brother, "but it seems now that we must soon confront an appalling affliction and that the inevitable hour must soon arrive and that a great light is soon to go out and that a great and noble heart will soon cease to beat. May God in his infinite mercy support and comfort us." Cadwallader Washburn died on May 14. He had preceded Elihu to the West, he had advised his going to Galena, and they had supported each other through every vicissitude and success of life. Cadwallader was only two years younger than Elihu, and they had been companions, contemporaries and friends. The death of this younger brother not only left a void in Elihu's heart, but served to remind him that his own hold upon life was weakening.

In the following year Israel Washburn died. Next to his father, Elihu honored him. The tribe was diminishing. On March 20, 1887, Mrs. Washburne died in Chicago. This supreme affliction left Elihu Washburne in a deplorable condition. He had no surcease from pain and weakness and mental distress. Seven months after his wife's death he had an attack of congestion of the brain complicated with heart disease of long standing. On Saturday morning, October 23, 1887, he rose feeling rather better than usual and had seated himself in his barber's chair to be shaved when he was seized with a severe pain in the region of the heart. He was assisted to his bed where he lay speechless, but in a few hours he rallied. At four o'clock in the afternoon feeling stronger he left his bed to get a glass of water when he had another severe seizure, and died a few minutes afterwards without speaking.

As his will was made April 16, only eight months before his death, it shows the kindly thoughts that were in his mind when his race was nearly run. He left a small sum, having already made a more substantial provision, for the support of the little Universalist church at The Norlands, "being the same church," the will said, "in which my revered parents worshipped from the time it was erected in 1828 until the time of their death." He directed that a memorial window be put up to his wife's memory in the South Presbyterian Church at Galena. His farm in Maine he left to his son William Pitt and upon his death it was to remain in the family. He remembered by tokens of affection his wife's nephews and nieces, the children of Colonel E. H. Gratiot. He directed his executors to provide for the education at college either at Madison or

Beloit, Wisconsin, of "Master Bertie Hagar, the son of my old friend and associate in the Chicago Historical Society, A. D. Hagar."

To satisfy the demand of the people of Illinois there was a public funeral. Mr. Washburne's body was taken from his son's house to the Unity Church where he had worshipped, the procession included honorary and active pall-bearers, a platoon of police, the Chicago Turngemeinde, and last the German guard of honor.

> *Imperial German Consulate, Chicago, October 25th, 1887*
> Hempstead Washburne, Esq.,
> 73 Maple Street,
> City.
> Dear Sir: Baron Zedtwitz, the German Chargé d'Affaires at Washington, acting for the absent German minister to the United States, directs me to express to you and your family his profound sympathy and sincerest condolences on the death of your father.
> In order to give full expression to these feelings I have begged of the gentlemen in charge of the arrangements for the funeral services to be allowed to lay the German colors as shown by the flag of this Consulate before the catafalque and will participate in the services as the delegate of the representative of the German Empire in this country. It will be gratifying for me to think that you will accept these symbolic acts as the tribute of gratitude of the German nation to the blessed memory of the illustrious dead.
> Sincerely yours,
> BARON NORDENFLYCHT
> Imperial German Consul

The honorary pall-bearers were the governor of the state, Mr. Oglesby, the federal judge, Walter Gresham, the German Consul, Baron Nordenflycht, Lyman Trumbull lately the senator from Illinois, his intimate friends and political coadjutors, General A. L. Cheltain, J.

Russell Jones, Leonard Swett, Joseph Medill and twenty-four others representing the life of Illinois. At their own earnest request representatives of the German societies in Chicago were the active pall-bearers. The city offices were closed, the church was crowded with people and Dr. Swing preached an eloquent sermon. The funeral ceremonies were held at three o'clock in the afternoon and after they were over, the body lay in state while crowds passed before it. At eight o'clock in the evening it was taken to Galena.

Arriving in that town the following morning it was taken to Turner Hall, the largest building in the city, which had been elaborately decorated to receive it. Here it lay in state again, and, as in Chicago, the American and German colors rested together at the foot of the bier. Fifteen hundred people crowded into the hall at two o'clock in the afternoon to attend the funeral. The Reverend Dr. A. C. Smith, Pastor of the South Presbyterian Church, which Elihu and Adèle Washburne had always attended when they were at home delivered the funeral sermon, and the Reverend H. D. Schmidt, the German Lutheran minister, made a brief address in German. The funeral procession from Turner Hall to the cemetery was the longest that had ever passed through the streets of Galena including military guards, civil dignitaries and a long line of friends. The public schools were closed on that day and while the funeral was in progress all business ceased.

And so the curtain fell and the drama was over. The newspapers throughout the country and in Paris and London eulogized him. So did many political and other organizations with which he had had connection of one kind or another. All of them praised his upright character, industry and ability in public service, and most of them saw in his career a shining example of the opportunity which the free institutions of America afforded to the deserving man to rise to great heights through his own exertions and by his own merits.

His life had been a success. He himself considered that he had succeeded. He had been an agent in building up his adopted state and he had reflected honor upon the state of his birth. He had been an agent in extending civilization in the West. He had been a factor in destroying human slavery and in making the American nation strong. He had guarded the national treasury from the thieves. He had served humanity in the crisis of the French and German war and had brought credit on his country by his intrepid and intelligent conduct as its representative. He had contributed to the history of the past and was a part of the history of his generation.

Major General Cadwallader C. Washburn

CADWALLADER COLDEN WASHBURN

THE PUSH TO THE WESTWARD AND SETTLEMENT
AT MINERAL POINT

The brothers had their own standards and when they voted Cadwallader the greatest among them, it was not with any lack of appreciation for the respective powers of the others. Their opinions were based on knowledge to be gained only in the family, something which an outsider could not possess.

Cadwallader's boyhood was spent, as was Elihu's, in a contest with necessities. He worked and studied, alternating between laboring on the farm and attending schools in the neighborhood.

He was born April 22, 1818. His education did not pass beyond that which the common schools afforded, nor does it appear that he made an effort to go to college. If he had desired it earnestly, a way would have been found to gratify his wish. Boys of Washburn's class could get a college education by one means or another. His desires seem to have set in other directions. When he was approaching manhood he wanted to go into the army and to receive an assignment to West Point. His failure to do so caused a severe disappointment. Probably this was the first real disappointment of his life.

As his brothers, he came under the influence of his uncle, Reuel Washburn. While he never regularly read law in Reuel Washburn's office he was directed in his law studies by this Mr. Washburn and when he decided to go West, received advice from him. Reuel Washburn impressed himself on the young man. The advice he gave him must have been of strong influence upon his career, for in his will, made a few years before his death, when he could look back on his life and measure his obligations he said: "To the three daughters of Alonzo Washburn, son of my uncle, Reuel Washburn, I give one thousand dollars each, $3,000, in token of my respect for the memory of my excellent uncle, their grandfather, who was one of the most honest and conscientious men I ever knew, and whose advice to me when I left home I have never forgotten."

Cadwallader Washburn's contemporaries who remembered him when he was a boy said that he was studious and popular with a remarkably good memory, quiet, persistent, and fond of reading.

He had a more patient disposition than his brothers Elihu and William Drew and had no aversion to teaching boys as had Elihu. He was a school teacher in Maine when he was twenty-one. He became wholly self-supporting when he was eighteen and a clerk in a store at Hallowell. After that he had become principal of the chief school in Wiscasset. Until he arrived at man's estate Hallowell was the largest place he had ever seen. It contained about 3000 people. Wiscasset contained not more than 2000. Both places were on the water;— Hallowell on the bank of the Kennebec River and Vaughn's Brook; this latter having cascades once used to run mills. Wiscasset had a fine harbor from its situation on the Montsweag stream where there had been eight water power plants and where was an old mill with a dam. Hallowell was a conservative old community, living rather in the past than in the future, and Wiscasset had once been a busy seaport, but had lost its prosperity when it lost its shipping in consequence of the War of 1812. There was nothing in either place to attract an ambitious boy.

When Cadwallader Washburn was of age the vast domain of Louisiana had been a part of the United States for only one generation. The curiosity to know what it was like had stimulated emigration to it. At first the emigration had taken the direction of the lower part of the territory above and around the city of New Orleans. This region was supposed to be very rich in resources and both Cadwallader and Elihu Washburn at one time contemplated going to the Mississippi territory. When Cadwallader went West he had no definite idea where he would stop, but he held in his mind the advisability of going to the banks of the Mississippi River—that much of his original predilection carried.

Here was the young man when he set out to conquer the world; of light complexion with light brown, straight hair, the blue eyes of an Englishman, a straight, prominent nose, a broad mouth with compressed lips, broad shoulders, deep chest, a large body, rather below the average height, about five feet eight inches, sound in body and mind, not a handsome young man perhaps, but certainly not an ugly one. His manner was retiring, but frank when others chose to be friendly.

The influences which had shaped his character were simple; he lived in a community of hard-working people who were all equal, all American, born of English descent, most of them descended from soldiers of the Revolution, all of pilgrim, Puritan stock, disposed to discourage gayety and pleasure; he had never been a hundred miles from the place where he was born; he was accustomed to long, hard winters,—indeed, he did not know hardships were hardships, because he had never experienced soft luxury. Of individuals who had molded him were the lawyer Uncle, wise, industrious, learned, scrupulous; the elder brothers, Israel and Sidney and especially father and mother with their unselfish, patriotic, conscientious intelligence. His character was formed when he left Maine. In all of the rest of his life nobody ever spoke of him without speaking of his honesty and firm common sense—these were his strongest characteristics. His brother, Sidney, loaned him the money to pay his way to the West. He never forgot the obligation even after he had repaid the money. He liked to harbor the feeling of gratitude. He felt kindly towards people in distress,— towards the Southerners when he had fought and conquered them, towards the Indians whom he saw cheated and despoiled. He was naturally a philanthropist. Much that happened to him in after life which would have embittered a weaker nature, only mellowed him.

On May 20, 1839, Cadwallader Washburn and his brother, Samuel, went to Hallowell together and there Cadwallader embarked on the steamer, *The Huntress* for Boston, the first stopping place on his way to the West. He would go to Iowa, Illinois or Wisconsin,—he had no more definite idea in mind.

On May 25, he wrote to his brother, Algernon Sidney Washburn. This was sent from the Erie Canal somewhere between Schenectady and Utica. He described the fortifications in New York harbor, mentioning that as he passed West Point many bitter recollections and unavailing regrets crowded into his mind.

Then on June 16, he wrote his first letter to his father. This was sent from Galena.

Dear Father: I have been postponing writing till my arrival here, from the fact that before I left Chicago, I had seen scarcely anything of the country and of course from observation was able to say nothing concerning it. But before I speak of the country or how I like it, I will give you a slight account of my journey. You are aware that at Hallowell I went on board the Steamer *Huntress* for Boston. We had a fine passage up, arriving in Boston about five o'clock the next morning and quartered at the Franklin House, a house by the way that I do not think much of. After breakfast I sallied forth and found Sidney, who was on hand. With him I went round to see the City. Made a visit to the dome of the State House, etc. In the P. M. we got into an omnibus and rode out to Cambridge to see Elihu. Found him well and wide awake, in one of the most pleasant places upon the face of the earth. Sidney returned to Boston the same night but I remained with E. B. Next morning walked into the city, where I remained till afternoon, when I took the cars for Providence. But before going farther, I would say, that at Boston I went into the office of the American Transportation Co. and contracted to go to Green Bay or Chicago as I might see fit, for $28. in the first style, with board from Albany. Well this was tremendous cheap you will say, and so it was. I paid him $16. to Buffalo and the balance I was to pay there at Buffalo.

At Providence I took the Stonington cars, where we arrived in the evening and went immediately on board the Steamer R. Island. Had a fine passage and next morning between six and seven arrived in the big City. While there stopped at the City Hotel which is equal to any they have. The passage up to the city is very interesting. The passage through Hell Gate, from associations, is famous. I looked for the place where Van Courtland, the dreamer, was whirled round in his tub and shipwrecked, in vain. While in the City I was most of the time upon my feet, but notwithstanding which I did not begin to see it scarcely. While there called at Woodman's office, but he was not at home. At five o'clock, went on board the fine Steam Boat

Swallow for Albany. She had a host of passengers, but the way she went ahead was a caution.—I should have been very glad to have gone up the Hudson in the day time as I wished very much to see the scenery upon its banks, of which so much has been said and sung. As it was, I did not go to bed till all the best scenery was passed and so far as I could judge, all that has been said about it comes far short of the reality. The passage through the Highlands is the most sublime of anything I ever saw. As it was quite dark when we got to West Point, and as the Military Works are situated high above the River, I could see but little of it. Could I have seen ever so much it would not have given me much satisfaction. At three o'clock in the morning the boat arrived in Albany. Remained till nine and took the cars for Schenectady. Albany, from what I saw of it, appeared to be a fine place. Its situation on the side of a hill is very much like Hallowell. After taking seats in the cars at Albany, an inclined plane of nearly a mile and a half in length has to be overcome, for which horse power is used, and then the locomotive is hitched on and we are at Schenectady in a trice. Schenectady is most delightfully situated in the valley of the Mohawk, and is a place about as large as Hallowell or Augusta. Here found a canal boat belonging to our Company about ready to start for Buffalo, which I went aboard of and which proved to be a very good boat with a good Captain. We got along at the rate of about 60 miles a day, travelling day and night. Travelling on the canal would be very pleasant, could we go a little faster and not be quite so much crowded at night. With us (I say we and us because I got in company with some persons from N. H. that came clear through to Chicago with me) the weather was very pleasant but we were a good deal crowded, we had however a very good company, and I enjoyed myself very much. We had about 30 passengers besides the crew, which made pretty close packing at night, I assure you. The canal follows up the Mohawk to its source which is a very fine stream, winding through a most delightful, tho' in many places very narrow valley. At a place called Little Falls, about 60 miles from Schenectady, there is some most imposing scenery, and here it was necessary to blast a good deal to get the canal through, here too are several locks. There are numerous villages along the canal but none that are anything to brag till we get to Utica and this is as fair a village as I ever saw. Syracuse is also a fine place. Here they make vast quantities of salt; the evaporating works here cover something like a hundred acres. But the greatest place between Albany and Buffalo is Rochester. Here perhaps are the most extensive flour mills in the U. S. Here the canal crosses the Genesee River in a vast aqueduct with 11 arches. . . . Before leaving Rochester I ought to have said that I went to see the famous Genesee falls. They are situated about ¼ of a mile below the village and are well worth going to see; saw the place where Sam Patch made his last leap. The fall is something like a 100 feet perpendicular. Found ourselves in Buffalo Friday morning after having been a week on the canal, and here we had to remain till Monday morning for a boat. A few days before my arrival at Buffalo, the Steam Boats all combined not to carry passengers to Chicago or Green Bay for less than $20. Well, my agreement was that I was to go on from here if I chose for $12. I shewed my agreement to the Agent here, but he backed out. Said he wouldn't do any such thing, and by a mere quibble contrived to shirk off from the agreement. Had he been up to the agreement which I made in Boston I should have got to Chicago some $8. cheaper. He offered to compromise with me by giving me $2. to say no more about it, which when I found I could do no better, I concluded to do. On the whole I got through some three or four dollars cheaper than I should had I not paid anything in Boston. At Buffalo we went on Board the Steam Ship *Great Western*, which is a new boat and the largest on the lakes. She is a splendid boat though not so fast as some others. We had a rather long passage but a very smooth and pleasant one and good company on board. Gov. Mason of Michigan came with us from Buffalo to Detroit.—In the appearance of Detroit, I was disappointed, as it appeared much better than I expected. It was a very fine day when we were there; in a wet day it would not appear near so well I presume;—it is said to be a very muddy place. At Detroit we took on board several new passengers, among others the Hon. H. R. Schoolcraft, Indian Agent who resides at Mackinaw. We made two stops to wood, one upon St. Clair River, the other at Presque Isle on the west shore of Lake Huron. The country upon the St. Clair River is very low and uninviting. In fact after leaving Detroit, we see no good country before we get to G. Bay and then nothing to brag of. At Presque Isle are two or three log huts where fishermen and wood-cutters live; they have no neighbors within a hundred miles or more. The passengers, ladies and gentlemen, manifested a good deal of curiosity by going in and examining all the cabins. In the best looking one, we found a lady from Ohio who said she had been there about a week and was calculating to spend the summer there with her husband who was carrying on the fishing business. At Mackinaw we made a short stop, enough however to give me a chance to look round a little. The village is situated upon the south shore of the island and overlooked by a high rocky bluff some 300 feet high, and here the fort is. I went up into it and reconnoitered. The situation I should judge to be a very strong one. There are no soldiers here now, save one orderly sergeant who takes care of the buildings. Mackinaw is a great place for fish and the Mackinaw trout are famous. I saw some there that I should judge to weigh nearly fifty pounds. Leaving Mackinaw, we next morning found ourselves within sight of G. Bay. And here we got aground, so that it was nearly noon before we got up to town. Here we had to stop five or six hours to discharge freight and take on wood. Green Bay is very prettily situated and is said to be remarkably healthy, but on the whole I did not exactly like the 'looks of 'em.' I heard of one fellow there from Maine who had lately arrived, who was trying to get up a school and was likely to succeed very well. His name was Lufkin from N. Yarmouth. Probably Mrs. Quimby knows him.· Here are generally a large number of Indians. While we were there a later number of the Menomonies were in town, who, to all appearances, are the most degraded set of beings on earth. Most of them were most hideously painted. Before we left, they came down upon the wharf and gave us a dance, cutting up some of the most fantastic tricks imaginable. After leaving G. Bay we made no stop till we got to Chicago, save off Milwaukee in the night to land passengers and take on wood. I was disappointed in not being able to see the place. Did not get to Chicago till Monday night, too late to look round and see much. Next morning had a chance to see a little. Was not very much taken on the whole with the place, its situation is very low and flat and it is very muddy. At Chicago I found a chance to ride on horseback as far as Rockford, half way to this place, which (as riding in the stage is very dear business) I accepted, and put my trunk on board the stage. The ride from Chicago to this place is very pleasant. We passed over some of the finest lands between Fox and Rock rivers that I ever laid my eyes on. I think I may say that I was not disappointed in the country between this and Chicago. The accommodations for travellers are generally better than they look. Every house I stopped at between here and Chicago, with one or two exceptions, was a log house, but they know how to charge notwithstanding! . . .

We got here last night, just on the edge of the evening, and too late for me to see anybody. Today is Sunday so of course I can tell nothing about what I can do until tomorrow. Business here is said to be very good and I have no doubt that I shall find something to do to advantage. I shall call on Mr. Melville tomorrow morning. I should not send this till I have looked round some, but the mail does not go again under two or three days and, as I suppose you are rather anxious to hear, I will delay no longer. I shall write again shortly, I have a great deal more to say about the country which I have not room to say now. There is a young fellow here from Albion, Me., by the name of Farnham, who stops at the same house where I am; he came to town Friday.

Love to all.

Yrs. aff'tely and truly.

On July 11 he wrote again to his father. This was from Davenport, Iowa Territory.

> . . . At Galena I found business contrary to my expectations most horrid dull. I called on Major Melville and found him to be a first rate old gentleman. He interested himself a good deal in my behalf, but to little purpose. I finally, through his aid, got an opportunity of going out on survey as Assistant, which, had it been a different season of the year, would have been just what I wanted. The contractor was waiting for orders from Washington when I was there, and had been for several weeks. Had he been ready, I should have accepted his proposal; but, taking into consideration that I might have to wait several weeks, and the season of the year, July and August, the most unhealthy part, I concluded to abandon the proposition. I spent a little more than a week in Galena, and while there got a very little acquainted. Took tea with Maj. Melville who has a very fine family. Also spent one evening at the meeting of the sewing Society. Galena itself is the roughest place you ever saw or heard of, and there are also a good many rough chaps about it, but there is notwithstanding a good deal of good society there. Well, after I found I could do nothing to advantage at Galena, I concluded I would just drop down the river a piece to Quincy. I had a letter to C. Gilman, Esq. and Maj. Melville gave me one to a gentleman of his acquaintance there. Well, I got on board a boat for Quincy, got as far down as Stephenson which is directly opposite this on the Illinois side, where the boat stopped a moment. I thought I would run up and say how-de-do to an old friend, T. B. Wells, Esq. Found him without difficulty. He insisted upon my stopping a day or two with him at least; said he thought I could get up a school over here if I chose. Accordingly I concluded I would stop to see what could be done. I was most favorably struck with the appearance of Davenport at first sight, which favorable impression has lost nothing by seeing more of it. Wells came over with me, and found out what could be done. They have a school here now which has been

for sometime in operation, but the teacher is very unpopular with the body of the people, and has but a small
school. After enquiring, I concluded that I would get up a
school that would pay my expenses at least, if nothing
more. Some of the people were very anxious to have me go
ahead and themselves knocked round to get scholars for me.
Encouraged I made some little arrangements about a room
and then dropped down to Quincy. Here I found business
about as dull as anywhere else. I had a letter from Major
Melville to a merchant of the name of Artemus Ward
formerly from Massachusetts. Called at his store but he
had gone to Boston. Called on C. Gilman, found him a
very pleasant, clever fellow. He interested himself a good
deal in my behalf. 'Tis through his influence that I can
have a large and good school sixteen miles from Quincy, in
the town of Columbus, if I want it. As they are not
ready to have it commence under eight weeks, I decided to
come back and keep a quarter here anyhow and see what
could be done, and if anything, remain here; if not nego-
ciate for that school. With Quincy I was quite well pleased,
and I should liked to have stopped there, if I could have
brought things to their proper bearing. 'Tis quite a pretty
place and has more the appearance of an Eastern town than
any that I have seen in the West. 'Tis not near as healthy
a place as this is, 'tis quite sickly there now, this place is
perfectly healthy. I spent the 4th of July at Quincy. The
day was celebrated very handsomely. They have one of
the finest hotels to be found in the Western country. A
good hotel is a scarce article here I assure you. I have
stopped at some public houses since I have been in the
country that would be a caution to you Eastern folk.

Got into Quincy on Tuesday. Monday P. M. walked
out into the country to see if I could find I. Leverett or
the Thompsons. Found Uncle Bill Thompson without
much difficulty. Leverett has moved up north some
twenty-five miles. Uncle Bill appears to be about the
same old "Jacknife" that he used to be. . . . Left Q.
Thursday night expecting to be at this place by Saturday
morning, but got stuck upon the Rapids and did not get

here till Tuesday morning. However, I notified them that
I was on hand and commenced school same day. Had
sixteen that first day. This is the evening of the third
day, have had twenty-two. Think there can not be much
doubt that I shall get thirty. My terms you will see by a
paper I shall send you. I keep five days per week. Either
next Saturday or a week from Saturday, I intend to ride
out back into the country and see how it looks. Wells
will probably go with me. Davenport is situated right upon
the banks of the Mississippi at the foot of Rock Island, and
is allowed by all to be the most delightful spot upon the
river. There is a strip of timber runs along back of the
village; about half a mile from the river, which is, I am told,
about the same in breadth; there you come upon a most
beautiful prairie twelve or fifteen miles across. They are
settling in here with a rapidity almost without parallel.
The lands are all claimed within six or seven miles. Some
of them are very valuable. I think it not unlikely that I
shall make a claim when I go out. There can be no doubt
but what all the lands within ten miles of here must before
long advance a good deal upon the government price.
When these lands will be in market is more than I know.
It is generally thought, I believe, not before a year from
this fall. You can have no idea without seeing it of the
richness of the soil or the ease with which it is cultivated.
I wish you could see some of the corn that I have seen
growing, 'twould do your eyes good. They say there is now
plenty of prairie of the finest kind within seven miles of here.
The great trouble with prairie is the difficulty of getting
material for fence. . . . Here a person who has money
can make money. I have neither money nor credit.
Whether I shall ever make anything here remains to be
seen. I think, however, if I don't get homesick and continue to enjoy good health there may be a chance to do
something by and by. Never in my life have I enjoyed
better health than since I left home. My spirits have been
equally good. I have not heard one word from Maine,
save that the Kennebec Dam is gone. I feel very anxious
to hear from you all. I should like to have you send me now

and then a *Ken. Journal.* They have a paper here but it is small fry. You will see that the Editor gives me a slight puff.

I have before told you that Davenport is situated upon the noble Mississippi. My boarding house looks right out upon the water and is within thirty yards of the river. I am situated nearly opposite the south end of Rock Island. Right on the south point of the Island is Fort Anthony. 'Tis a beautiful spot. A short distance above, is the seat of Mr. Davenport, one of the fathers of the town. He has one of the most splendid situations you ever laid your eyes upon. Opposite Davenport's place, and right above the village, is the seat of Antoine Leclaire, a great, fat, rich half-breed. He owns a section of land, the finest you ever saw, which he has enclosed with a white fence. He has, too, a fine house and other buildings. It makes decidedly a splendid appearance. I suppose Leclaire and Davenport both to be worth two or three hundred thousand dollars each. I intended to have told you something more about my journey, particularly my ride on horseback from Chicago to Rockford, for I thought that it was decidedly romantick, but I shall not have room. I need say nothing more about the country to convince you that I am pleased with it. But this I will say, that all other things being equal, I had rather live at the East than here. Yet Eastern people are pouring in very fast, and society will soon be as good as at the East. The man that is well off at the East, to him I would not say come here; but to him that is not, I would say come, if you can get here. There is no young man, if he has got any kind of spunk, but what can get here. This making a mountain out of a mole hill is all folly. It has seemed a dream to me, I can't realize any way I can fix it that I am 2000 miles from home. . . .

I conclude that Sidney will be at home making you a visit about the time you get this and perhaps Elihu. I can not see much of a chance for Elihu here at this place. They have three or four lawyers here now. I think if he comes to the West, he will find St. Louis the best place. There is no place in the West that is growing so rapidly.

"Tis destined to be the largest place this side of the Alleghanies. . . .
Monday, July 15th: Have had today several new scholars, now have about thirty. Think I may average at least that number.

What is not related above but which Cadwallader wrote to his brother, Sidney, on July 13 is that upon his arrival in Davenport he possessed but five dollars which should have been expended in the purchase of a pair of shoes. Little wonder he believed "money begets money." He felt, though, had he had more, he would have travelled farther.

Davenport had been a wilderness until a settler located a claim on the land of the city in 1833. When Washburn came the population was not more than a few hundred people, yet he considered the country, for farming purposes, as far ahead of Maine as Maine of Patagonia.

He wrote again to his brother Algernon Sidney Washburn.

Rock Island, July 27th, 1841.

. . .

Since I last wrote you, I have been to the great City of St. Louis from whence I returned last Friday. The object of my visit was to secure a government contract of Surveying in which I succeeded.[1] I shall have something like three townships to survey this fall, probably shall not commence till the first of October. This will be a small contract, but better than nothing and will serve I doubt not to make me square with the world. We get for surveying $3. per mile. There are 60 miles of surveying in a township, and it requires from one to two weeks to survey a township. I had to employ five hands to assist me. These

---

[1] He kept his school for three months when he became an assistant under David D. Owen and made a geological survey of the territory for the federal government. This occupied him till late in the autumn.

take off part of the profits of the job, but it will be pretty profitable for all that.

If I am fortunate I can make at least $100. a township. I am in hopes this contract will be but a prelude to more. If I could get enough Government Surveying to employ me half the time, I would not sigh for the best office in John Tyler's gift. But the facts are, there is not much surveying to do at present; the Government not having made any recent purchases of the Indians and most of the old cessions having been surveyed; my office of County Surveyor just about pays my expenses; I am not employed much of the time, but when I am, I am tolerably well paid.

St. Louis is a great place and will be much greater. Fifteen hundred houses are going up this season. While there I stopped at the Planters' House, which is second to no House in the Union. It could swallow up the Tremont House at a mouthful and is as large as the Astor House at N. Y. I think a great deal of St. Louis. It must be the greatest place in the Mississippi Valley except New Orleans. No person can stand upon the levee and see the immense number of Steam Boats lying in port, with others constantly arriving or departing, without being penetrated with the immensity of the West and its destiny to mighty greatness. . . .

Write immediately and believe in truly and sincerely thine

C. C. Washburne [1]

To Algernon Sidney Washburn

Rock Island, Nov. 17th, 1841

When I wrote you last was after my return from St. Louis where I had been to receive a contract for surveying. . . . Since then the whole has been kicked over in consequence of the rejection by the Senate of the nomination of Dr. Silas Reed who was appointed Surveyor General. Another man has been put in his place with whom I have

---

[1] In this letter, it will be observed, he signs his surname with the final *e*, which after about five years he abandoned.

Israel, Elihu and Cadwallader Washburn

been trying to negotiate for a contract. Whether I shall be successful, I can't say. I am not without my fears and doubts.

I don't get much to do in connection with my office, and when I am not otherwise employed I study law and read some other books occasionally. On the whole get along tolerable pleasantly, live in the pleasantest town in the world in which are many pleasant fellows, yet everything is now very dull in the way of business, never more so and times are the very hardest. But we are looking forward to a great and glorious day when this shall be what nature made it for, the Manchester of this union. Gen. Armitage, Col. Long and Surgeon General Lawson left here this morning. They have been stopping several days, and are on the lookout for a site for a National Armory. They were highly pleased with this location and did not hesitate to say that we had eveything requisite for the establishment and carrying on an Armory. We feel confident of getting it here. Col. Long who is known from one end of the Union to the other as one of our most scientific men, predicted that we were to become a great manufacturing community and that soon, as soon as Eastern capitalists can be made acquainted with the superior advantages of this point.

We had a little set down last night over a glass of champagne when Col. Long gave for a sentiment "Rock Island, the hospitality of whose citizens and her water power, both equally abundant and overflowing." I tell you what, we have got the elements here. All we want is capital. We are all poor together now, and times are hard so that we are at present making slow advances. But when we do take a start we shall go it with a perfect rush.

· · · · · · · · · · ·

Yours Sincerely
C. C. Washburne

The winter was a problem. There were the possibilities of living on a farm eighteen miles from Davenport at a place called Round Cove. (The owner was to sell him half the land for the price he had paid for it and it was sure to appreciate in value.) He inclined more favorably toward opening a store in the spring if he could borrow the capital. (This would amount to some two or three hundred dollars of freightage from Boston.) And he wished to print a book with a good map giving information about Iowa.

At length, he went over to Stephenson and started a school again. "What in heaven's name," he wrote Sidney, "can a fellow do, who is bound down by the iron hand of poverty as I am?"

Stephenson was the county seat of Rock Island County and in a few years changed its name to Rock Island. At this time, 1840, it was about five years old.

During the summer and fall of 1840 Cadwallader Washburn was clerk in a store. When his employer died he had difficulty in collecting his wages and finally by winter was reading law under Joseph B. Wells, many years later lieutenant governor of the state.

Washburn wrote his brother in December, 1840, of his appointment to the office of surveyor of the county. "'Tis an office of no great importance," he said, "but may be worth having." His interest in politics was increasing. The Whigs were not in power in Illinois but they rejoiced at what the rest of the country had done. "What do you think old Tip will do?" he wrote. "Will he give us better times do you think? Will he make a clean sweep among the office holders? I hope he may rout every mother's son of 'em'." He believed the future of Rock Island was assured and was resolved to bide his time and await a change of fortune. In February, 1841, he communicated the following to his brother.

Stephenson

You ask what I am up to and what my prospects are. To tell you the truth my prospects are not so bright as the brightest, neither are they so desperate. . . . I have a claim against the estate of the store keeper for whom I worked of something like $150.—one cent of which I have not received and fear I shall not within a year. The estate will not be settled up before that time, if it is then. This failure to recover my dues leaves me somewhat minus. When I was chosen County Surveyor last fall my election was contested, which cost me $40. right out of pocket tho' I succeeded in the contest. I received my commission so late in the fall that I have not been able to do any surveying of any consequence as yet. I think there will be a good deal to do upon the opening of spring. I think I may make something out of it one of these days, so I live in hope. A fellow who comes to a new country, penniless and an entire stranger, can not jump into a fortune at once. He has many things to contend against which are not to be over-come in a moment. But if he holds out, minds his own business, does not become dissipated, as at least one half of the young men here do, he will generally come out right side up.

Truly and Sincerely Yrs.

In another six weeks he wrote.

Mineral Point, Wiskonsan T. March 31, 1842
Dear Brother: What the devil does this mean, methinks I hear you say as you open this letter and see the heading. What in the name of the "ten muses" has brought me here you will undoubtedly ask. I will tell you, sir, how and why I am here. I have come to hang out as Attorney and Counselor at law and am hung out accordingly. But why did you leave Rock Island you ask? I will tell you that too. R. I. is no place for law, nor at present for any other business. I staid there as long as I did, because it was a good enough place to study my profession, but always intending to go elsewhere to practice, when I was admitted.

Thinking myself sufficiently advanced in legal lore, I thought I might as well get admitted this spring as ever, so about three weeks ago, in accordance with the advice of Elihu and others, I left R. I. and came up the river to Galena, where I stopped a few days and from thence came here. I immediately engaged an office in which I now write. This week I have been to Lancaster, Grant County, to court, where I was examined and admitted. I now expect to stop here permanently and have strong hopes that I may be able to do something. Mineral Point is the Seat of the County, and here all the lawyers live.[1] There is a great deal of litigation in the country and I do not think we are so much thronged with lawyers as most places. The town is a rough place, containing about seven hundred inhabitants. I have very strong hopes that I shall make it go here, and be able soon to do you justice.

I must ask of you to be yet patient a little longer. Since I have been studying my profession I have had as much as I could do to keep along, but I have got along. I think I shall come out straight as a shingle by and by.

As I before said I stopped a few days with Elihu. He is doing a first rate business not less than $2000. a year and his business is still increasing. I consider that he was very fortunate in his vocation, if I am half as much so, I will be satisfied. From Galena I came on out to Platteville, and stopped two days, visiting Ben. Eastman and his wife Charlotte, my friend Fillibrown who lives near upon a farm, and G. W. Lakin who has a law shop there. . . .

Mineral Point, Wiskonsan T., October 16, 1842.
Touching myself I have a few words to say, and then I will pass to more interesting matters. 'Tis most true, I am here in Mineral Point, as I have been for seven months past. I have a good comfortable office, good boarding house, a little business and large expectations. I like it here well and think I have every inducement to remain and

[1] The town was hardly larger than Stephenson. It had not even a newspaper. It was the *Galena News* announced that Mr. Washburn was ready to receive clients.

shall remain. Most of the business which I have obtained
has not yet matured and consequently I have got hold of
very little money and am kept hard up. But I think with
the knowledge of my prospect of doing something by and
by, Elihu and myself can make a dicker, by which I shall
be able to do what, God knows should have been done long
ago, i. e. cancel that affair of yours. I brought suit in
four courts this fall, but have yet realized nothing from
any of them. I go to Madison in a short time to attend to
three or four cases which I have there. I do not flatter
myself that I am going to make a fortune in a hurry in the
law, but I do that I shall make a living of it, and pay what
I owe. I saw E. B. a couple of weeks ago at the Grant
County Court. . . .

By the last mail we got Webster's Faneuil Hall
speech. . . . The old envious jealous "cuss" would
sooner see the country d—nd than he would see Harry exalted over him. I don't hear a single voice lifted up in
his defence, but the universal cry now is Harry of the West.
No Whig in this quarter of the Union thinks of any one
else. Will the Whigs of N. England do their duty? Captain Tyler is execrated by all, as well as all his infamous
clan, from Webster, Cushing etc. downwards.

During the two years following, his law practice
commenced its growth. In August, 1844, he formed a
partnership in the law with Cyrus Woodman who combined with his law practice the agency of the New England
Land Company. In time practically the whole law business
concerned the work of land grants. The profits were large.

The law gave lands to all who enlisted in the war with
Mexico, and in many cases, the rights to these lands were
sold by the soldiers. Of course Washburn and Woodman
stood in a splendid way to study the country and take
over the more valuable land tracts. These they chose with
special reference to mineral and timber wealth.

This was the basis of Cadwallader Washburn's wealth.

On January first, 1849, Cadwallader Colden Washburn married at Mineral Point Jeannette Garr of New York City. She was born in New York City, June 9, 1818, and was the daughter of Andrew Sheffield Garr who in 1805 had married Elizabeth Morell Sinclair (1788–1855). Mr. Garr was born in Auchencairn, Gallowayshire, Scotland, in 1745.

After the death of his mother he came to this country with his father, Andrew Garr; the elder was a shipbuilder and owned a lumberyard in addition to shipyards on the East River at the foot of Catherine Slip and in Rutgers Street. The son graduated from Columbia College (where he had Martin Van Buren as a classmate) in 1796. He became a lawyer and in connection with an obituary notice of his partner, Richard Wells, in the *New York Times* of March 22, 1863, is referred to as "One of the most astute lawyers because of being preëminently the most skillful special pleader of his day."

Andrew Sheffield Garr had fourteen children. Of these Catherine married Mortimer Jackson in 1838. He was a New York lawyer who settled at Mineral Point and ultimately became an important judge of the state. It was while visiting her sister, Mrs. Jackson, here that Jeannette met her future husband.

Mr. and Mrs. Cadwallader Washburn after their wedding established themselves in Mineral Point. Two daughters were born to them, Jeannette, April 25, 1850, and Fanny in 1852. Because of an attack of puerperal fever following the birth of the second child, Mrs. Washburn's health was permanently impaired. This necessitated the breaking up of her home and the sending of the children to Cadwallader's parents in South Livermore, Maine.

Mrs. Washburn died at Brookline, Mass., March 12, 1909. She was buried in Walnut Hills Cemetery, Brookline.

In 1852 Washburn and Woodman started the Mineral Point Bank. It stood solvent through all panics and never suspended specie payments.

On March 1, 1855, the partnership was dissolved when the bank became the sole property of Washburn. In breaking with Woodman, Washburn formally recorded the act saying, "Whereas they had been doing business as partners for upwards of ten years their intercourse had not been interrupted by any untoward circumstances and had been marked by a constant feeling of kindness and good will coupled with an unusual degree of unanimity of sentiment." Washburn and Cyrus Woodman were friends to the end of Washburn's life. The latter held no man in higher esteem than Woodman.

Before Cadwallader was thirty-five years old he was the chief man of business in his part of Wisconsin.

FIRST CONGRESSIONAL SERVICE

Wisconsin became a state in 1848 and in 1854 Cadwallader Washburn was elected a representative in Congress from the second district, there being only two members from the state. He took his seat December 3, 1855, and served for three terms, six years, until March 3, 1861. His residence during four of those years was at Mineral Point, but the last two years he resided at La Crosse, the Prairie City to which he was much attached. His district embraced two-thirds of the territory of the state from Rock and Dane counties in the east to Lake Superior on the north. The idea of nominating Washburn originated in Rock County and several citizens of the small town of Janesville wrote to ask him to become a candidate. On August 9, 1854, he replied that he could not promise to accept the nomination because of his business engagements, but if he should be nominated by a unanimous vote of the delegates of his party he would consider the invitation. His nomination and acceptance followed. As an opponent, the Democrats offered the nomination to Cyrus Woodman, but he declined it. They then put up Dr. Otis Hoyd, of Hudson. At the subsequent elections Mr. Washburn's opponents were Judge Samuel Crawford for the second election and Judge Charles Duncan for the third. All of them were men of good standing and strong candidates, but Washburn easily beat each one.

When he entered Congress his brother Israel had been there four years and in 1861 he and Cadwallader left together. Elihu was serving his second term and when

Cadwallader returned to the House in 1867 after an absence of six years Elihu was still there. Cadwallader was 36 years old when he was elected, the same age as Elihu and Israel when they were elected to Congress. The effect of three brothers being in Congress at the same time was more important than was generally realized. Illinois, Wisconsin and Maine could help each other when they chose to do so. The brothers were, in fact, in full agreement on the more important measures coming before Congress, but in minor debates sometimes spoke in opposition to each other. Thus, in February, 1859, Israel defended the Coast Survey from the attacks which Cadwallader levelled against it. When he came to Congress Cadwallader lived with his brothers at 29 Indiana Avenue (as mentioned in connection with Israel Washburn), but afterwards they separated and during his last term Cadwallader had rooms at the Clarendon Hotel at the corner of sixth Street and Pennsylvania Avenue. When he entered Congress he was placed on the Committee on Military Affairs. Israel was chairman of the Committee on Elections and Elihu chairman of the Committee on Commerce. Finally, in his last session, Cadwallader became chairman of the Committee on Private Land Claims. He was not a frequent speaker, but he became known as a useful member who attended carefully to the interests of his constituents. On December 3, 1858, he debated earnestly the claim of Georgia and Alabama for compensation for losses incurred in the Creek Indian outbreak in 1836 and 1837. The burden of his argument was that fraud had been perpetrated against the Indians by their removal from rich lands in Georgia to inferior lands in Alabama. He disclosed a knowledge of the subject and a keen sympathy with the Indians. It was only one of the numerous examples of his sympathetic nature.

Passing over the details of legislation in which Washburn showed an interest in so far as they affected his state, and which had no permanent concern, we come to the most important act of his congressional service,— that in which with only one member to stand with him, he opposed and checked the progress of the slave power in Congress.

When he came to Congress the Union was, apparently, approaching collapse. The Missouri Compromise had been repealed, and slavery was free to spread itself wherever it could find a foothold. The federal government was subservient to the slave-holders of the South. The bitterness of the sections against each other became stronger every day, and, finally, when the country elected Abraham Lincoln to be President, many Southerners declared that they would not remain a part of a Union over which a Republican opposed to slavery presided. As the tide swept on towards secession frantic efforts were made to stop it. Peace meetings, conventions and proposals of compromise followed one another at short intervals. It was after South Carolina had seceded that a final effort at accommodation was made by the House of Representatives. By an overwhelming majority it was agreed that a committee composed of a representative from each state should be appointed to take the critical situation into consideration and suggest a remedy for it. Corwin of Ohio was appointed the chairman and Cadwallader Washburn was the member from Wisconsin. The meetings of the committee must have been acrimonious for hardly any two members agreed upon what ought to be done. Finally it made a report on January 14, 1861, three days after Alabama, Florida, and Mississippi had joined South Carolina in secession. The most important feature of this report was a recommendation that the Constitution should be amended so that no alteration of it with respect to slavery could ever be made, unless it was proposed by a state in which slavery existed and should be agreed to by every state in the Union. This was the recommendation of a majority of the Committee of Thirty-three, as it was called. A minority report was submitted by Mason W. Tappan, a member from New Hampshire, and Cadwallader Washburn. It had been drawn up by Washburn. They offered this resolution:

"That the provisions of the Constitution are ample for the preservation of the Union, and the protection of all the interests of the country; that it needs to be obeyed rather than amended, and our extrication from present difficulties is to be looked for in efforts to preserve and protect the public property and enforce the laws, rather than in new guaranties for particular interests, or compromises or concessions to unreasonable demands." On January 24, 1861, he made a long speech on the issue.

"This resolution," he said, "expresses the conclusion of the small minority of the committee to which I belong. The majority of the committee have reported various propositions, but only four of them contemplate definite action. All of these propositions, Mr. Speaker, although not sanctioned at the final adoption of the report, were adopted singly during the sessions of the committee. I do not wish to place any one in a false position by saying that these propositions are the opinion of the majority of the select committee. They were adopted, as I have already stated, one by one, by a majority then present, as they came up for consideration.

Now, sir, the propositions looking to definite action reported from the select committee are; a joint resolution to amend the Constitution of the United States; an act for the admission of New Mexico into the Union as a state; and an amendment to the fugitive slave law and the law relating to fugitives from justice. These propositions have been reported with sundry resolutions expressive merely of the opinions of members. Having been unable to concur in any one of these propositions, and not wishing to be regarded as an ultra or unreasonable man, I wish at this time to state the reasons why I could not concur with the measures here proposed for the consideration of the House. I will take the propositions in their order; and if I shall succeed in showing that all of the complaints which the propositions now offered are intended to remedy, are groundless, and that their adoption will only subject the people of the North to further derision and contempt, then, sir, I shall have accomplished all that I desire. I think I shall be enabled to show very clearly to the members of this house that the measures now submitted are wholly powerless for good, even if they were all to be adopted.

"I have been a patient attendant on all the sittings of this committee; and it has been my desire to learn what were the troubles, what the difficulties, what the grievances which were complained of, and which required the remedial action of Congress. Although no two members could concur exactly in regard to the grievances complained of, yet upon being grouped together they amount to about this: first, it is complained that the North does not faithfully execute the fugitive slave law; second, it is complained that some of the non-slaveholding states have passed personal liberty bills; third, it is complained on the part of the South that the people of the Southern States are deprived of equal rights with the people of the North in the territories of the United States; and it is alleged also, as a complaint against the North that fugitives from justice are not delivered up in accordance with our obligations under the Constitution of the United States. These constitute the principal causes of complaint, except the further one that we have elected a President, who, it is claimed, is hostile to slavery. This last is believed to be the occasion for existing treason and impending civil war; and as the committee propose no remedy whereby the minority shall rule the majority, I am justified in saying that the measures that they do propose will have no effect towards restoring peace to the country.

"Sir, it is not pretended, it has never been pretended, that the Federal Government has legislated to the prejudice of the people of the South. It has never been said, and with truth it cannot be said, that they have not had all their rights in this Government. Never, in a single instance, can it be maintained that Congress has refused to pass laws necessary for the security of their rights. For sixty out of seventy-two years since the Government was formed, they have controlled the Federal Government in all its departments,—legislative, executive, and judicial. They have so long been accustomed to regard themselves as specially appointed to rule this country, that they have forgotten how to obey, claiming to be exclusively the ruling class; and, grown haughty, proud, insolent, from the possession of power, they cannot brook the idea that a man who is peculiarly the representative of the great laboring classes should be at the head of the executive department of the Government.

"We know full well, Mr. Speaker, what will restore peace. If we will yield up for all time to come the control of the Government to those who, with small exceptions, have ruled it heretofore; give them the Executive; allow them to retain the legislative and judicial departments, and dictate our foreign and domestic policy, they will no doubt return to their allegiance and save the Union. Sir, their terms of salvage are enormous, and cannot be acceded to. To show that they mean to control the Government or destroy it, I beg to read the following extract from a letter from a United States Senator from the State of Alabama, (Mr. Clay) to friends in South Carolina, written a short time since. He says, speaking of the people of the North:

"'They are the most bitter, relentless, and vindictive enemies we have on earth. . . . Of course, we cannot live under the same Government with these people, unless we could control it.'

"There, sir, you have the conclusion of the whole matter expressed in concise language. The whole thing is in a nutshell. We must control the Government, or we will not live under it. The question, then, stares the people of the North full in the face. Will they pass their too obedient necks beneath the southern yoke, or will they assert their manhood, and refuse to purchase either continued union or peace at any such price? No, sir; let us have disunion, and, if need be, civil war, rather than dishonor."

Passing to the specific complaints of the South he insisted that, odious as it was, the northern states had executed the fugitive slave law. The proposition of the committee that another and more drastic law be enacted was insulting to the North.

"If you will give us no amendment which is an improvement on the old law, then let that stand as a memorial of the barbarous age that passed it.

"But, Mr. Speaker, it is said that the North has passed personal liberty bills, which give cause to the Southern States to secede. The committee do not propose any legislative action in regard to these bills any further than to request the States that have passed them to repeal them. I am opposed to the resolution reported on this subject. I regard it as an unwarrantable interference with the rights of the States. I have been pleased to notice that the southern gentlemen on this committee who have joined in making reports are very careful to say nothing about these personal liberty bills. They are too smart to put themselves on paper as advocating that Congress should interfere with what strictly belongs to a State. They do not even speak of them as grounds of complaint. I do not oppose this resolution because I would recommend to any State to pass unconstitutional laws, or laws which will in effect impair the rights of any State in this Union, or the citizens of any State; but because it is the province of the States themselves to judge, and that without any outside interference, as to what they owe to their own citizens, and what to other States of the Confederacy. I am willing that it should be left to the States themselves to determine what laws it is necessary to pass, and what they ought to forbear to pass. If they pass unconstitutional laws, they are merely as so much blank paper, and can harm no one. If they pass unconstitutional laws, the Constitution itself provides a way to determine that question; and it does not confer upon Congress the right to decide what laws are constitutional and what are not. When the constitutional tribunal shall decide what laws are unconstitutional, I have no doubt that any State in the Union which has passed such laws will repeal them, or make them conform to the Constitution.

"But, sir, these gentlemen of the South have been so long in the habit of controlling the Federal Government, that they now desire to go into the States, and indicate to them what laws they must pass and what they must not pass. And though they are careful in their reports to say nothing in advocacy of this idea, yet such is shown to be their desire by the resolution they report. Sir, it is an interference which the States may very properly resent.

"The committee have also recommended the passage of a resolution requesting the southern States to revise their laws, and if necessary to pass laws to protect northern citizens from mobs. I am opposed to this resolution for the same reason that I refuse to vote for the resolution relating to the personal liberty bills. I will do no Southern State the injustice to suppose that they have not passed all the laws necessary to protect our citizens from the action of mobs. If the laws are not executed, it is because the public sentiment there overrides the law; and it is in vain to pass laws, or recommend their passage, unless there is a public sentiment to sustain them."

Concerning the proposed amendment to the Constitution he said:

". . . There is no gentleman upon the committee from the seceding States who will say that this amendment will have any effect towards allaying our unfortunate difficulties. What is the proposed amendment? It proposes that we shall never interfere with the institution of slavery in the States; never until a certain contingency arises, which never can arise until all the States shall sanction such a proposition. Now, sir, I listened to the argument of the gentleman from Ohio (Mr. Corwin) yesterday upon that proposition; and his argument demonstrated to my mind most conclusively that such an amendment ought not to pass. He demonstrated that there was no necessity whatever for any such provision in the Constitution.

"It is well known that neither the Republican party, nor any party at the North, proposes to interfere with the institution of slavery in the States. They do not claim to have any such power. Under the Constitution, as it now is, the people of the North have no right to interfere with the institution of slavery in the States, and they have no desire to do it. But southern gentlemen say that we shall acquire the power and alter the Constitution in that regard. The argument of the gentleman from Ohio (Mr. Corwin) was conclusive that that time cannot arrive for fifty years, and, perhaps, never. He showed that we could not take the first step towards amending the Constitution, on the subject of slavery, until we had forty-five States in the Union,—an event which can hardly be anticipated. I say, then that he demonstrated conclusively that there is no necessity for this amendment of the Constitution; and every gentleman who listened to him must be satisfied that there is no such necessity even though any party desired to interfere with slavery in the States. It is useless to submit such an amendment to the people, not only because it is unnecessary, but because it is a humiliating proposition to the people of the North. It is equivalent to declaring that you do not believe what they say, and that you think they do design to interfere with the question of slavery in the States, although you know full well the time is far distant when they could do it even had they the disposition.

"The people of the North will not accept such an amendment. Why, then, do you want to agitate the question further, when you know no good can come of it? In my judgment, such an amendment of the Constitution will not be adopted by the people of the North,—not because they have any desire, or claim that they have any right to interfere with the institution of slavery in the States,—but because they believe you have no right to demand from them any such bonds for their good behavior; and for that reason they will vote it down. They feel in regard to it, no doubt, as I do. I certainly shall vote against any such amendment here or elsewhere, and yet I have not the slightest design or desire to interfere with slavery in the States. I protest against the possession of any such power by the people of the North. Why, then, do you wish to keep the country in an angry discussion for the next one or two years over this amendment, when no possible good can grow out of it, only absolute evil?"

After disposing of the proposition to admit New Mexico as a state, which he said was simply designed to introduce additional slave representation in the Senate and thus strengthen the slave power, he took up, incidentally, the so-called Crittenden Compromise which had been offered a few months before and which in effect divided the country between slavery and freedom and said:

"Mr. Speaker, we are invited to adopt the proposition of Mr. Crittenden, or of the border-State, self-constituted committee,—which I regard as virtually the same thing, and equally objectionable. We are invited to abandon the Republican platform, to abandon all our principles, and take our position on a platform which shall guaranty that we will protect slavery in all the territory south of the line 36–30'. I do not know that I fully understand your border-State proposition. I think it does not apply to territory to be acquired in the future. I care not. Adopt that proposition; and if you acquire territory hereafter, it will be contended and maintained, and truthfully, that the intention was that all the country south of the Missouri line should be given up to slavery. (A Voice on the Democratic side. 'Certainly.') We are approached very plausibly in this regard. Gentlemen say that, under the decision of the Supreme Court of the United States, they have not the right to go with their slaves into all the Territories of the United States, whether north or south of the Missouri line. The Supreme Court has decided that they have that right. But they say that we of the Republican party dispute that right; and that, therefore, they want it put in the Constitution. They say that, although it is their right to go with their slaves into the territory north of the Missouri line, yet they are willing to be magnanimous, and to give up to freedom the country north of that line. We do not thank them for their liberality. We have vindicated our right to the country north of the Missouri line; so that, in conceding that to us, they really concede us nothing. I will say to these gentlemen, *Timeo Danaos et dona ferentes.* I fear you when bearing gifts.

"I have, then, sir, I think, examined all the projects and propositions of the majority of the committee that propose definite action, and I believe they are powerless for good. Southern gentlemen say they are powerless except one, and that is the proposition to amend the Constitution. That proposition, as I have endeavored to show, is unnecessary, as the Constitution cannot be changed in that particular until we have at least sixty states admitted into the Union. I see, therefore, no reason for it, nor can I give my sanction to turning the North upside down in discussing this amendment of the Constitution.

"Sir, nothing will do any good that does not allow these gentlemen of the South to control the Government. You can make up your minds to that point. If you are willing to concede that, you will have peace at once, and South Carolina, which has gone out of the Union never to return, will come right straight back again. It is not claimed by these southern States,—by those cotton States,—that they are compelled to contribute an undue proportion for the support of the General Government. The truth is, they have been so long in the habit of believing that Cotton is king that they have come to entertain the idea that the world could not get along without them; that they control the destinies of the world. . . .

"Sir, I have no special dread in regard to the future of this Republic. Civil war may come, disunion and dissolution may come, but I pray God to deliver us from both; but, sir, whatever may come, I have an abiding faith in a kind Providence that has ever watched over us, that passing events will be all overruled for good and for the welfare of mankind in this and other lands. Gentlemen may talk about reconstructing this Government after it shall have been broken up and destroyed—I tell them no. If this Government is destroyed, it will not be reconstructed on the basis on which it now stands. Gentlemen may as well understand right here that if the Government is to be reconstructed, the people of the North will have a word to say as to the basis of that reconstruction, and no new union wil lbe formed that does not give them terms of perfect equality. If this Union must be dissolved, whether by peaceable secession or through fire and blood and civil war, we shall have the consolation of knowing that when the conflict is over, those who survive it will be, what they never have been, inhabitants of a free country."

PART IN CIVIL WAR

The story of Cadwallader Washburn's military career cannot be told here except in outline; to enter upon a detailed account would involve writing a history of military operations extending over a vast area. He declined a renomination to Congress and early in December, 1861, began recruiting the second regiment of Wisconsin cavalry, having been commissioned a colonel on October 10, 1861. He had no military training, but in this respect was as well equipped as his brother officers. As we know he had had military aspirations when a boy and these were now satisfied. He threw himself into the work of making his regiment ready for service with characteristic energy. His brother, Elihu, was a tower of strength in helping him. Elihu in Washington, the center of military administration, assigned to the Wisconsin colonel all that was necessary for his regiment. Cadwallader wrote to Elihu, December 27, 1861, that he would have the finest regiment in the West so long as he was not interfered with. As his work went on he grew very impatient and thought of going on General Grant's staff in order to see active warfare. "I feel anxious to participate in a battle," he wrote January 22, 1862. "This holiday soldiering I do not fancy. It is pleasant enough but not profitable to the country. I must demonstrate that my patriotism is not all put on." He joined General Grant at Fort Donaldson and found him "very cordial." He wrote his brother Elihu from there March 3, 1862:

. . .

The public cannot over estimate the importance of the victory here. It is in my judgment of more practical importance than all other battles that have been won by our army. The capture of this point was the capture virtually of Nashville, and settled the rebellion throughout the valley of the Mississippi. . . .

He became a staunch adherent of Grant. As time went on the mismanagement and dishonesty he saw, filled him with savage disgust and he expressed his opinions with usual violence. He gave Elihu all the information he could convey and Elihu must have been one of the best informed men in Congress on the subject of the army in the West. Thus, from Fort Henry, March 7, 1862, he wrote:

> . . .
> To-day Genl. Grant received a dispatch from Genl. Halleck saying that his course here was strongly censured by Genl. McClellan and the authorities at Washington, and that he was advised to place him under arrest. The last he did not do, he relieved him from the command of the Expedition, and he will remain for the present in command here, with one or two Regts. The pretense was that he had no business to have gone up to Nashville, and that he had not furnished daily reports of the strength of his command. The pretense is frivolous and contemptible, and the last I am assured is destitute of truth. The idea of a man commanding and directing here who is a thousand miles away is simply absurd. The truth, I have no doubt, is that they wanted an opportunity to prevent Genl. Grant from winning any more victories. Their excuse is far-fetched. I have seen the credit of planning the capture of Henry and Donaldson claimed both for McClellan and Halleck. I have seen the correspondence which shows that Genl. Grant called Halleck's attention especially to both points and desired to be allowed to take them. I much doubt if McClellan knew of the existence of either Fort.

The Second Wisconsin Cavalry left the state for active service on March 24, 1862, and went to Benton Barracks near St. Louis for final equipment. Washburn desired the appointment to brigadier general in hope that he might serve under General Grant and "have a show," as he expressed it. After he had been at Benton Barracks a few weeks a report reached him that his regiment might be ordered to New Mexico. This filled him with alarm. It would offer "no field for distinction," he said.

To ELIHU B. WASHBURNE

Benton Barracks, April 9, 1862

Dear Brother: Yours of the 6th is recd. On reflection after I last wrote you and seeing Brigadierships so cheap and that it was a badge of dishonor rather than honor I told Harvey that I would not be an applicant. To-day we have news of the great battle in Tennessee. It makes Grant the man of the war, and will put out Halleck's pipe. He did not mean that this battle should be fought until he got there. I have been praying for some days to have Beauregard attack, as I was satisfied that Grant had orders not to, but the intent was not to allow him to win any more laurels. You say that I ought to have remained with him. That I could not do after my Regt. was ordered to move. Besides I had rather have a command of a Regt. than be on anybody's staff. If this battle in Tennessee is as decisive as we suppose, I guess that the rebellion has about gone up. I don't see now much prospect of my Regt. getting beyond here and shall not be surprised if we are disbanded in 60 days. . . .

Perhaps Colonel Washburn did not really expect the war to end immediately. He wrote to his brothers recklessly, saying anything that passed in his mind when he had his pen in hand and criticizing freely. Sometimes the criticisms represented his judgment but more frequently showed the unrestrained mood of the writer.

The pride he took in his regiment was a genuine conviction. On June 6, 1862, he said:
"Thus far campaigning has gone well with me. My health is excellent and my command I am proud of. I have good men and good horses and I am certain that I have the best swordsmen in the service."

Washburn was commissioned a brigadier general July 16, 1862, but before that he was doing brigadier's duty. He began active fighting in the summer of that year.

To ELIHU B. WASHBURNE

Post Head Quarters, Helena Ark. July 15, 1862

Dear Brother: I write to say that I am here tho. not in the best of health, tho. better than when I arrived. I had a very hard march from Springfield Mo. the details of which I cannot give you until I feel better. When I overtook Genl. Curtis he was on the move and had heard that a large fleet of transports with one or two gun boats was waiting for us at Clarendon on White River. We were nearly out of supplies and on short allowance and hastened our march to reach our boats, fighting a battle and dispersing a rebel force of five thousand who disputed our passage. When we got to Clarendon what was our consternation to find that the boats had mysteriously abandoned us to our fate and left the day before. It only remained for us to starve or cut our way to the Miss. Gen. Curtis decided to strike for the Miss. He gave me an advance guard of 2,500 Cavalry and six Mountain Howitzers, and I left at 4 o'clock A. M. and forced my way through some sixty miles in 24 hours. I hailed the first Boat and sent to Memphis for supplies, and started another for the lost fleet. The Army has now safely come up, and supplies are now arriving. The faux pas made by the Boats changes all our plans. Had we but our supplies we should have been in Little Rock by this time, and Hindman would have been a fugitive. When I came here I took up my headquarters at the splendid residence of Genl. Hind-

man, but gave it up to Genl. Curtis on his arrival, and I
now have fine quarters in a more central part of the town.
I have command of the post here. I am not advised as to
my confirmation as a brigadier. How is it? I have been
doing the hardest kind of a brigadier's duty ever since I
left Springfield. Write me here. While at Clarendon we
heard fearful rumors about the reverses of McClellan, and
as our boat had left without leaving any word for us we
did not know what to think—I have stood the fatigues of
the Campaign well until the last few days, when with
forced marches, sleeping in swamps and nothing but
putrid water, I was getting badly run down. I think I
shall recruit now, tho my place is not an easy one. For a
month we were entirely cut off from news, and very meager
is what we have got since we came here.

On July 20 he wrote in a little different vein to his
children.

Post Headquarters, Helena Ark.

. . . If you wish to know where I have marched you
must take the map of Arkansas and Missouri which you
will find in Uncle Sylvester's office. Look on the map of
Missouri and find Springfield. From there I marched to
Ozark and had a little battle. From there to Forsyth on
White River to Jacksonport. Here I crossed Rock River
on a Pontoon Bridge and met Gen. Curtis' Army. From
here the army meandered down to Clarendon, meeting and
clearing out the enemy on the way; when we got to Claren-
endon we were greatly disappointed at not finding Steam
Boats with provisions as we were nearly out. I then had
to take 2500 cavalry and six small cannon to come through
to here, sixty miles, in double quick time. Arrangements
for something for the army to eat had to be made. We
are all right now.

When shall I see you again? I don't know. It seems
as though this war would never end. I pray to get home
once more.

I hope that you will improve your time well and shall
expect that you will have become quite accomplished by the

time I return. You must apply yourselves well to your music and be able to sing and play well. Write me when the next term will begin. I shall direct this to La Crosse as I expect that you are at home by this time. You must write me every week and tell me all the news.

With much love,

Your affectionate father.

And on September 14 from the same place to Elihu B. Washburne.

. . .

Our condition here is gloomy as elsewhere. Our army is in unclothed condition, and in most incompetent hands. It has lost much by the absence of Gen. Curtis. You can judge by that of the material of our Generals. . . .

If the management of the war could be given to the volunteers exclusively, we would soon end the war.

Grant *is* the only regular Army Genl. worth a cuss— He will fight and is not intent on preventing the war from being ended unless the regular Army officers can have the honor of it. . . .

On the same day he wrote another letter to Elihu.

I go to-morrow in Command of a Division on an important and dangerous expedition. In case I should not return alive, I have placed $1,000 in the hands of a gentleman to send you to be paid over to Young. If I return alive I shall be able to pay Dean as I proposed.

The name of the gentleman I have left the money with is A. Bascom, a friend of J. B. Worrick. I hope you will hear a good acct. of us.

To ELIHU B. WASHBURNE

Helena, Nov. 25, 1862

On the 27th we shall leave here with about 7,000 men to cooperate with Grant. Shall land about 10 miles below here in Miss., and shall move the whole force about 40 miles into Miss. to the crossing of Tallahatchie River and from there I propose to make a sudden dash with about 2,000 cavalry on Grenada. The principal object will be to break up the rail roads north of Grenada and in the rear of Price and Pemberton's Army. The country I have got to cross I have but little information in regard to. What I have leads to the belief that it will be attended with great difficulty and danger, but I think the object will justify a good deal of risk. Much of the route is over low swampy land, and I expect I shall find many obstacles in the way, but hazzards must be incurred if we expect to accomplish anything. The expeditions to White River the other day proved a failure as we found an impassable bar in the river, to the ascent of our boats, and it was not possible for us to reach the "Port of Arkansas," a fortified port on Arkansas River, without our boats. We retraced our steps with great reluctance. . . .

This expedition was a success. Washburn dislodged the Confederate force and opened the Yazoo Pass.

By December 7 he had returned from his Mississippi raid. He wrote to Elihu December 9: "I stampeded the entire rebel army. Was in many a tight place, but got out well."

From Memphis he wrote to Elihu on December 13:

I came here this morning from Helena, my object being to find out what move Grant and Sherman had in view, and how rapidly they would probably move down through Miss. I found that Sherman had moved back here with one division of his army, and is going to move down the Miss. Part of the Army at Helena will go with him and we shall take Vicksburgh. While the Army menaces Vicksburgh, I expect to land 100 miles above with 5,000 men and make for the Yazoo and capture and destroy the rebel Gun Boats there. The move is a hard one but of great importance and I hope to carry it through successfully. If I do and can see Vicksburgh fall, the hard work in the west is done, and I shall be willing to retire. I see by a paper that a Genl. Washburn's name is mentioned for Sec. of Interior. Should the Reps. from Minnesota, Iowa, Wis. and Ills. favor that, it might win. I don't know why they will not favor it. Gen. Sherman is vastly pleased with the success of my Miss. expedition. He admits that it saved them a big fight and large loss of life. Their fortifications at Abbeville were very extensive and strong. The moment they heard of me in their rear, they broke on a double quick. The march made by me exceeds anything in the war, and such results as have followed, are a thousand times in excess of the force I had employed. All the work was done with less than 2,000 men.

To Elihu B. Washburne

Head Quarters 3rd Div. D. E. A. Helena Jan. 28, 1863
Gen. Grant was here last night on his way to Vicksburgh. I saw him for a short time. He looks well and feels pretty well, but feels that he has got a heavy job on his hands. The high water and overflowed country render it very difficult to operate now on land, and Vicksburgh can only be taken by a great sacrifice, except by a land force in the rear.

Gen. Grant proposes to give me a command at Vicksburgh as soon as anything can be done there. In the mean time I shall remain with my Cavalry division here. . . .

As I do the duties of a Maj. Genl. and as our State has none (unless Schurz has been apptd.) I don't see why I may not as well be promoted as any body. The State has furnished 45,000 troops, and has only five Brigadiers. Why should not Wisconsin be as well used as any other State? If I did not feel as competent for that position as Carl Schurz, or most other Maj. Genls. that have been apptd., I wouldn't say it. That I can say with a very moderate estimate of my ability. I will say further that had I had the command of the Arkansas army for the past six months there would not now be an enemy west of the

Miss. River. Such trifling as I have witnessed has been most discouraging to all men of common sense. . . .

As Wisconsin was entitled to several brigadier generals, it was natural Washburn should have been one of them. As a matter of fact he had been commissioned (November 29, 1862) a Major General of Volunteers.

The General who was fighting the enemy so hard and devising means to conquer was not unmindful of the miseries the war was inflicting upon the enemy. To his daughter, Nettie (Jeannette) he wrote March 8, 1863:

. . .
You, my dear, who are living so pleasantly and quietly at home have little idea of the misery and unhappiness that war brings. Just imagine ten or twenty thousand rude men coming into La Crosse some morning and taking possession of the town, going into houses of the people and helping themselves to whatever they want, burning houses, killing cattle, hogs, sheep, chickens, and almost everything they see, destroying furniture,—and you will have a pretty good idea of the march of an army through a country. The people here are paying dearly for their wickedness in trying to destroy our government.

From Memphis in the spring of 1863 Washburn watched the course of events with increasing impatience and anxiety. He wrote to Elihu April 11, 1863 (Memphis):

. . .
This campaign is being badly managed. I am sure of it. I fear a calamity before Vicksburgh. All Grant's schemes have failed. He knows that he has got to do something or off goes his head. My impression is that he intends to attack in front. If he does it may succeed but it is the act of a desperate man and nine chances out of ten are that our Army will be slaughtered. The past six months has been worse than thrown away, as I could show you. I make no

pretensions to military Science, but I claim to have some Common Sense. I say that Grant with the means he has had should have taken V. long ago. There is but one way to take it. I could show you how it can be speedily taken. Grant is a good fighter. . . . I say to you that I am distressed at our prospects and cannot sleep nights for thinking of these things. Time seems to be no object here. I have been here four days and yet have not been able to get a list of the troops to compose my command. You are responsible for Grant. You must go to see him and talk with him. He can do no less than tell you what his plans are. As one after another of the schemes fail, I hear that he says he has a plan of his own which is yet to be tried in which he has great confidence. Vicksburgh is now the strongest point in the Southern Confed. by all odds. The fleet has backed out of the Yazoo Pass. That should have been an overwhelming success, and I am mortified and humiliated at its miscarriage—Come down I pray you.

To Elihu B. Washburne

Headquarters, 13th Army Corps Carrollton, La. Sept. 5, 1863

. . .
Gen. Grant reviewed this Corps yesterday accompanied by Gen. Banks and Thomas. We had a fine review and all passed off well until the review was over. The soldiers received Gen. Grant very enthusiastically. After the review was over and Gen. Grant was returning to the city his horse fell and injured him severely. I saw him last night. He was suffering a good deal, but the surgeons think that the injury is not of a serious character and that he may be around shortly.

. . .
I have yours making some remarks in regard to a Presidential Candidate. I take no large amount of stock in your Company at present, and I regret to say that in looking the field over I can see no one that fills the bill properly. It seems to be a necessity that we should take up a military man. Grant has the prestige of success and so far is the

very man, but he is anything but a statesman to say nothing about some other points. I reserve my judgment at present hoping that some man may yet tower up along and above the steep. . . .

Again on the subject of General Grant he wrote September 11, 1862, from Carrollton, La: "I have already told you that I take no stock in him as a Presidential candidate. I can tell you why another time."

In the Battle of Grand Coteau Washburn distinguished himself when he saved the 4th Division under General Stephen G. Beerbridge from destruction. When Vicksburg surrendered he was put in command of the 13th Corps and sent to the Department of the Gulf. On November 29, 1863, he landed on the coast of Texas with 2800 men and compelled the evacuation of Fort Esperanza, an armoured fort garrisoned by 1000 men and supposed to be a most difficult point to capture. He hardly spoke of these exploits in his letters. Towards the close of the war he became extremely anxious concerning the Presidency.

In January, 1864, Washburn went home for sixty days. Then he went to Annapolis to help reorganize the 9th Corps to which he was assigned.

To ELIHU B. WASHBURNE

La Crosse, Wis. Feb. 21, 1864

Useless must be carefull. Abe has the people with him, and if Grant allows himself to be fooled by the Copperhead Democracy, he is ruined. No man however loyal, can live with such friends. . . . I am getting my affairs in good shape, so as to swing entirely clear this summer. I have cleared out all my lands on Chippewa waters, and Mill at Waumbeck to Knapp Stout & Co. I gave the thing away, but there was no help.

To Elihu B. Washburne

La Crosse, Feb. 26, 1864

Touching Ulysses S. Grant I think you have crowded him about as hard as he will bear and anything more looks fulsome.

He's a good man, and we all know it now, and we don't want to be told many times what we know already. He should be cautioned how he allows himself to be seen in company with such dogs as get round him in St. Louis. Abe has got the people, there's no doubt of it. Is Chase a fool? . . .

After this he was ordered to take command at Memphis to relieve Stephen A. Hurlburt and wrote:

Elihu B. Washburne

Head Quarters Dist. of W. Tenn. Memphis, Tenn. Apl. 23, 1864

I arrived this morning. Found that Gen. Hurlburt had left before I got here. Persons report to me the existence of a very bad state of things, and my arrival has been greeted with a good deal of satisfaction. The amount of contraband trade that has been carried on through this point is enormous. I suppose that there is hardly any article that the rebels need that they could not get here. The policy of allowing any trade to go beyond our lines I have always fought against, and believe that it has been most mischievous. For every dollar's benefit that the treasury will derive from allowing trade, we shall have to pay thousands of dollars additional expense in crushing the rebellion. The people who come here to trade are all rebels. We have hardly a true union friend outside of Memphis in West Tenn. The policy of fighting rebels, and furnishing them with food, clothing, and munitions of war at the same time I do not understand. If I had my way there should not a pound of cotton come into our lines, or a dollar's worth of goods go out so long as the war lasts. . . .

I find matters tolerably quiet here, but there is something in the wind. I have reliable information, that Forrest, after running his prisoners and plunder down into Miss. has returned to West Tenn. with all his force, about 8,000, and is now at or near Jackson. I am very weak, only about 2,000 very poor Cavalry, 2500 White Infantry, and 3,500 Colored troops. I am nearly too weak to do anything but act on the defensive, but I think that as soon as I can get some horses shod, I shall make a dash. Jackson is 100 miles from here. I shall take what Cavalry I can raise, and shall put 2000 White and 500 Colored Infantry into wagons and start in pursuit. Gen. Sturgis has been ordered here to command the Cavalry and I look for him hourly. I lament that I have not more means at my disposal. . . .

To Elihu B. Washburne

Head-Quarters District of West Tennessee,
Memphis, Tenn., May 8, 1864

Dear Brother: Forrest is retreating as rapidly as his horses will carry him. My forces pursued him as far as Ripley, when from utter want of forage further pursuit was useless.

The day after my forces left him, viz., on Sunday the 1st, Forrest left Jackson for the South. Look at the map. You will see that by reason of the flood in the Hatchie, his only retreat was via Pardy. I foresaw this position, and asked Gen. Sherman to send an infantry force which he had at Cairo to land at Crumps Landing and move to Pardy the same time I moved from here. I was led to believe that the force would be sent, but it was not, tho. it might have been as well as not. In consequence Forrest was able to get South of Hatchie and escape. Forrest with four or five thousand men was at Pardy Monday night retreating South. The Infantry force which I requested, should have been there 24 hours before, thus effectually shutting him in between the Tenn. and Miss. with Hatchie south of him and so swollen that to cross any where below Bolivar was impossible. I have driven him out of the State, but

346 Israel, Elihu and Cadwallader Washburn

that does not satisfy me. I meant to have destroyed him. There is now no enemy in my District, and is not likely to be soon. In two days I shall issue an order stopping all trade.

Who is to command the 16th Corps? I should have it, unless the Dept. of the Gulf is given me. I know that I can handle that Dept. better than any man who is likely to be sent there. I should like to clean out that nest of corruption. . . . If I could have command of those troops on their arrival at N. O. I would guarantee that it should not be ten days before I had the Army before Mobile, with safe Communications opened with the Gulf at Pascagoula. With the miserable slow loading there, if any such move is desired, they will be a month making it. I will send you my trade order as soon as issued. Ben Wade said he would back me. I told him what I was going to do. I shall hear a howl that will rend the welkin when the order comes out. Get Wade to offer a resolution if you can, approving it as the true policy to be pursued.

To Elihu B. Washburne

Head Quarters District of West Tennessee
Memphis, Tenn., May 16, 1864

. . .

I regret to say that my health is not good. I get out of bed to write this. I have chills and fever. I thought ten days ago that I had broken them up, but they have come back and I feel pretty miserable. I have had a world of work to do since I came here. I send you a copy of my last order issued this morning. This course I have taken has pleased the few loyal men here, but the Army of Jews, speculators and smugglers, are down on me, as I expected they would be, but I shall trot them right strait through unless I am overruled by higher authority. The amount of money involved is immense and they will die hard. I have taken pains to ascertain the probable amount of trade from here, that goes into rebel lines, and I am satisfied that it will reach $36,000,000 a year.

General Slocum, who has lately taken command at Vicksburgh, and who I learn will cooperate with me and Gen. Buford at Helena, is all right and will do all he can to help break up the rascality that is being practiced on the Miss. Chase has got the biggest lot of Scallawags employed that the world affords. . . .

To Elihu B. Washburn

Head-Quarters District of West Tennessee,
Memphis, Tenn., Aug. 25, 1864

. . .

I suppose Govt. intends to go into the business of buying Cotton and paying the "Secesh" Scoundrels $1.50 per lb. under gun law. To that I must consent. My plan will give Govt. at least $100,000,000 in the next year clear profit, while the voucher given the seller for ½ the purchase money will act as a bond for his good behavior. I have considered this matter well, and believe my plan will commend itself to the good sense of the people of the country, as it does to all to whom I have submitted it. Talk with Fessenden. We had a big thing here on Sunday morning and ran a very narrow escape, indeed it was almost a miracle that I was not either killed or captured. One main drive of the Expedition was to catch me. Forrest fooled A. J. Smith very badly, leaving his immediate front at Oxford and making a dash at Memphis without Smith knowing it, tho. he had 4500 Cavalry with him. Had not Smith disregarded my orders he would have caught Forrest on his retreat. The whole Expedition was barren of fruits. They were in so great a hurry to get away that they carried off hardly anything. I lost two fine horses, which is about the biggest loss of anybody. . . .

In December, 1864, he was ordered to take command of the district of Vicksburg and it was from there he wrote to his daughter.

Headquarters, District of Vicksburg,
Vicksburg, Miss., Dec. 20, 1864

My dear Nettie: . . . The officers and soldiers here, as well as the people, appear to be quite as merry as they ought to be, and are having many grand balls and parties, one of which I attended the other night. It was gay and festive yet I did not much enjoy it. While there is mourning throughout the land, and nearly every fireside has its vacant chair, it seems almost wicked to be dancing and rejoicing. But I think on the whole it is better to laugh than cry. I reckon that we had better be as happy as we can. But dear Nettie, I feel much of the time very sad. My position as Commander at Memphis, and now here, brings me in contact with all the people who have grievances to complain of, and I am thus made acquainted with all their sorrows, and every day has its tale of woe. You have no idea of the terrible punishment these people have brought upon themselves, nor can I give you any adequate idea of it. The people of Vicksburg, before the war, were rich and happy, they had fine houses, fine grounds, elegant furniture and plenty of money, with servants without number. All the country around was occupied by rich plantations, and everybody was, as he supposed rich and powerful. Now all is changed. Most of the fine houses are occupied by federal officers, their grounds have been devasted and destroyed, many of the inmates are wandering about the country without money to buy a loaf of bread, thousands have perished in the war, and many that remain at their once happy homes, are living on the bounty of our fort. Now while their punishment is just, the sight of so much suffering and unhappiness can not but make me sad. But away with melancholy, and wishing you and Fanny a very Happy New Year and hoping that you will be able to say that you are much wiser and better than you were twelve months ago, so also I want you to resolve that the coming year shall be one of even greater improvement than the last.

Good bye Dear Nettie.

Your affectionate father.

In March Washburn returned to Memphis where he remained till the end of the war. A public dinner was given him at the Gayoso House. He was announced as

> The guest of the evening, Major General
> C. C. Washburn. No less distinguished in
> the field and in the Hall of Legislation
> than in the walks of private life. By an
> impartial, just and liberal course in his
> high official capacity, he has endeared
> himself to all classes and condition of
> our citizens.

· · · · · · · · ·

In response he said:

"Mr. President and Gentlemen:

"I lack words to give expression to the emotions that overwhelm me. To be the recipient of such an ovation as this, on my return to the scene of my former duties may well embarrass me and render it difficult to know what to say. It is always so hard for me to say sensible things, and particularly so now that I have been so long out of the habit of speaking, that I hardly dare trust myself to speak at all, for fear that I should say something that my deliberate judgment would not approve, and I am almost tempted to ask you to excuse me with a simple expression of my most profound and grateful thanks. But I know that you expect something more, therefore begging your kind indulgence for the ill-expressed and disjointed remarks that I may make, I will endeavor to comply as well as I may with your expectations.

"The position of commander in a large commercial city like this, governed by martial law, is, at the best, most embarrassing. Unfortunately, so it is that the

pecuniary interests of most of the inhabitants, however
loyal, are in antagonism, with the interest of the Government.   To repress that antagonism and control conflicting interests and to settle unpleasant troubles that
may arise among citizens is one of his most disagreeable
duties, and if he shall succeed, in the discharge of that
class of duties, in retaining the good will of the citizens,
and retain at the same time, the confidence of the Government he serves, he is indeed fortunate.

"In the discharge of my responsible and often delicate
duties, here, I believe there is no one that will say of me
that my first duty was not always to my Government,
and that no private interest was ever permitted to stand
in the way of the public welfare.   Duty to my Government being discharged, it was always my study to do as
little harm and as much good to the citizen as was consistent with my position and obligations resting upon me.
I have never hesitated to do any act that I thought proper
to be done because it might raise a clamor, or might be
prejudicial to private interests.   Nor will it be said that
I ever made use of the almost absolute power that I
possessed, to oppress any one.   Military law is to be
dreaded under even the most favorable circumstances,
and particularly so when it is entrusted either to weak,
wicked or unjust hands; and I can conceive of no condition more deplorable than that of a community whose
lives, whose fortunes and whose sacred honor are placed
in the power of such a man.   Military power is not to be
wielded for purposes of oppression.   A magnanimous
mind scorns such a use of power, nor will a brave man
exult over a fallen and prostrate foe, or unnecessarily add
affliction to the afflicted.   If, while I was before in command here, it became necessary for me to adopt some

measures which seemed harsh or unusual, I believe that they were all fully vindicated by their success. The occasion which called them forth passed away. They served their end in their day, let them now be forgotten.

"If the position which I occupied when here before was difficult, I fear it will be equally so now. The new regulations in regard to trade from the Treasury Department, are very embarrassing to the military, but I shall endeavor to execute the general policy of the Government on the subject, so far as I understand it, and I deem it not improper here to say, that the time has come when we may treat the people of West Tennessee and North Mississippi in a spirit of kindness and forbearance. I do not suppose that there is an intelligent man in West Tennessee, or even in all rebeldom, who does not know that the Southern Confederacy 'is played out,' and is an utter failure, and that such a thing as any other Government than the Government of the United States is simply impossible.

"Such being the fact, we can afford to be magnanimous and forgiving towards the mass, who have been by wicked, cruel and ambitious men, seduced from the paths of duty and involved in ruin. I wish that I could speak to every disloyal man in West Tennessee, and even that my voice might be heard beyond these narrow limits, and entreat the disloyal everywhere no longer to strive with his government, but accept as inevitable the present condition of things, and prepare to make the best of it. To this conclusion they must come at last, and I would beg of them by every consideration tending to their own welfare and the welfare of those near and dear to them, to no longer delay, but to return to their first love, and again take shelter under the glorious Stars and Stripes.

"To those who have the disposition to return home to their families and friends, I say that I shall

'Make no deep scrutiny
Into their mutiny,
Rash and undutiful.'

The spring time of the year has come again, the plow rusts in the furrow, and without the labor of the husband-man famine must overspread this land, so long desolated by the tramp of armies. But peace and quiet will soon remedy all this, and so elastic is the character of the American people that the traces of this bloody struggle will soon be obliterated, and with a new order of things, with liberty crowning our efforts in this mighty conflict, the advance in wealth, population and refinement will be such as the world never saw. You have a country and a climate which 'paragons the world,' and, as in admiration and sorrow we look upon it, we have been forced to exclaim:

'Oh Christ! it is a goodly sight to see
What heaven has done for this delicious land;
What fruits of fragrance blush on every tree,
What glorious prospects o'er its hills expand,
But man mars it with an impious hand.'

"I predict that ten years will not elapse before those who 'bless the tyrant, and who hug the chain' will sing Glory Hallelujah over its redemption, and find it fifty years in advance of what it was at the beginning of the war, and will wonder how it was possible that their eyes could ever be so dimmed by the scales of injustice and error.

"Let then these veterans from the 'climes of the sun, all war-worn and weary,' who have fought as only Americans can fight, and worthy of a nobler and better cause, accept what is inevitable, and returning to their homes, beat their swords into plough-shares and their spears into pruning-hooks, and practice war no more.

"I know that it is a question which troubles some as to what should be done with the people who have been guilty of this great sin, and some there, perhaps we, who would delight to see this carnival of blood go on until the last rebel fills a dishonored and a traitor's grave. With them there is no styptic to staunch the wounds of crushed and bleeding humanity, short of annihilation. With them there is 'no balm in Gilead—no physician there.' With these men (and thank God, I believe they are few) I have no sympathy.

"No punishment that we can inflict can restore life to the hundreds of thousands that have fallen in this struggle, or wipe away the widows' tears or soothe the orphans' cries, and I hesitate not to declare as my opinion, that we should inflict no greater and further punishment than is demanded by national safety. Great God! Have they not been punished as no other people were ever punished since Christ wept over Jerusalem—aye, since 'God said let there be light'? Look at their desolate hearthstones, their ruined towns, their blasted fields, and tell me then if you will that they have not been adequately punished. Their crime was great and their punishment has indeed been great, and they may well exclaim with Cain, 'Our punishment is greater than we can bear.'

"I pretend to speak for no one but myself. I do not regard it as becoming for military men to be making speeches, and this is the first time, since the war began, that I have been guilty of such imprudence, but in view of the utterly prostrate and helpless condition of this people, I declare that, in my judgment, our great and good

Government can afford to be merciful, magnanimous, and more than just.

> 'The quality of mercy is not strained;
> It droppeth as the gentle rain from Heaven
> Upon the earth beneath. It is twice blessed,
> It blesseth him that gives and him that takes,
> 'Tis mightiest in the mightiest; it becomes
> The throned monarch better than his crown.
> His sceptre shows the force of temporal power,
> The attribute of awe, and majesty
> Whereon doth sit the dread and fear of kings.
> But mercy is above his sceptered sway;
> It is enthroned in the heart of kings;
> It is an attribute of God himself,
> And earthly power doth then show likest God
> When mercy seasons justice.'

"Every consideration of Christian charity, and every consideration of public policy requires that we should be most forbearing, and should pray that all remembrance of this unhappy struggle should be buried in the waters of oblivion, deeper than plummet sounds. As illustrative of this spirit of brotherly kindness, I call to mind an instance in English and French history, a story, which I remember to have read in an old school book when I was a boy, so long ago that I hardly dare to think how long, lest I should be reminded that I am older than I once was, but I may safely say, that it is at least thirty years since I read it, and my memory may not enable me to relate the story with historical accuracy, but as near as I can I will do so:

"Edward the III, of England, after the Battle of Cressy, laid siege to Calais. The city was beleaguered by a large force, but was defended with great bravery and determination. But after many months of siege it became apparent that what the army of Edward could not accomplish would be accomplished by famine, and the besieged were finally reduced to the last extremity, and it was certain that they must capitulate. Their resistance had been heavy and stubborn, and much apprehension was felt in regard to obtaining terms. Negotiations, however, were opened, and Edward sent a noble knight, Sir Walter Manny, to inform the Governor of the city, that he would accept its surrender on condition that he would deliver up six of the first citizens of Calais for execution, who were to be led to his presence barefooted, and with halters around their necks. When the terms were made known, there was for a time wailing in Calais, but not long, for almost immediately a prominent citizen by the name of Eustace St. Pierre, volunteered as one of the six who were to appease the wrath of Edward, and save the doomed city, and soon the whole number had volunteered, when struck with admiration at the conduct of those noble men, Sir Walter exclaimed, 'Alas! why was I not a citizen of Calais.'

"The victims were led to Edward's presence, barefooted and with halters around their necks, according to the terms, and as they passed between the long lines of English soldiers, the spectacle was one of such tender sublimity, that the whole army was moved to tears. As they reached the headquarters of the King, he rudely accosted Sir Walter, and demanded to know if he was certain that they were the first citizens of Calais? 'Yes,' responded the Knight,—'they are not only the first citizens of Calais, but they are the first citizens of France,' and he volunteered some words to show why their lives should be spared. But he was rudely repulsed, and told to go and lead them to instant execution. At this moment the Queen Phillippa, whose beauty was said to be equalled only by her virtue and goodness, learning what was transpiring, appeared before her husband and besought him to spare the lives of those devoted men. She reminded the King of the glory of his reign and the splendor of his achievements which the whole world then acknowledged, and begged him by every consideration to spare their lives, and finally by the use of those arts of persuasion which women so well know how to use, caused him not only to relent from his purpose, but to dismiss them, loaded with presents. Then it was that the noble St. Pierre, who was willing to give up his life, a martyr to his country, burst into tears and exclaimed: 'Alas, my country, it is now that I for the first time fear for thee. Edward only wins our cities; Phillippa conquers hearts.'

"The accursed cause of this rebellion is wiped out, and forever, and we may safely proclaim an amnesty to the most of the participants of the rebellion. There are a few that should be sent into exile or imprisoned in some penal colony, for the national safety would be endangered were they to remain in the country. Those who left our halls of Congress, and those who deserted from our army and navy might safely be included in that class. I fear that we do not always make the allowance we ought for many who have been engaged in this strife; at least one-half have been drawn into it against their will and judgment by 'stern oppression's iron grip, and mad ambition's gory hand.'

"Perhaps they did not resist as they ought, for while they had actually the numbers, the traitors had the noise and clamor. I think that it is Æsop who tells us that a single frog croaking in a pond will make more noise than a dozen fat bullocks grazing upon its margin. The noise and clamor being with the enemies of the Union, they were able finally to sweep all before them, and to resist the current was impossible. The truth is, the whole people finally became afflicted with a species of moral insanity and were incapable of rational action. As the acute mania gives way to calmer moods we should avail ourselves of every opportunity to dispel the fatal delusions that have nearly worked their ruin.

"The expressions to which I have just given utterance may surprise some. That I, who have always been known, when known at all, as an anti-slavery man, (which with many is the synonym of the enemy of the South), should after all our sacrifices, after all the rebel atrocities, and after starving so many thousands of our brave defenders in Southern prisons, have this feeling, may be unexpected. It may seem strange. This war has developed many strange things, and not the least so, is to find men who were always in opposition to me, and who, by their actions, greatly contributed to mislead the people of the South, by a single bound placing themselves so far in advance of me that I almost lose my identity. These are the men who are most inexorable and unforgiving.

"It is no time to discuss the questions involved in this war. They have been settled not by discussions but by sword;—but as I scorn to acquire the good opinion of any man by concealing my own, and as it might be supposed that here in this strong pro-slavery community I had a set of opinions for this latitude, I beg your momentary indulgence to set everybody right. You have been pleased to allude to my services in the councils of the nation. They were not distinguished, but such as they were, I am not ashamed of them. You all have some recollection of the last session of Congress under Mr. Buchanan's administration, and the many efforts to save the Union by legislative nostrums. Among the devices was raised a committee, consisting of thirty-three members, one from each State, to devise ways and means by which the Union could be kept together.

"I had the honor of being a member of that committee, which was in session quite a long time. A majority of the committee was composed of members of the party to which I belonged, which party was opposed to the extension of slavery. The committee was in session for many weeks, and many were the plans discussed by which the Union was to be saved; and so great was the disposition to yield to southern domination and degrading exactions, that a majority of the committee actually agreed upon a set of measures which passed Congress, of which I presume some gentlemen will not thank me for reviving the recollection. Among the measures was one which proposed a constitutional amendment, under which slavery was to be made perpetual, or at least putting it out of the power of the people of any free State ever to propose a constitutional amendment affecting slavery; and no proposition on that subject could ever be made, unless it came from a slave State. As we had then fifteen slave States, and as no constitutional. amendment could be ratified without a majority of three-fourths of the States; it was thus evident that it would require sixty States in the Union before a change in the Constitution could be affected. Yet our friends were swift to give them the constitutional guarantee which I have named, and it was reported by the committee and passed Congress.

"I have not time to dwell on this subject as I would

like, if I had not already troubled you so long, but I wish
to say that I did not concur in the action of a majority
of the committee, but made a minority report. . . . I
stand by that report today, . . . and I will ask the
newspapers to publish it, that no one may have any excuse
of misunderstanding my position.

"Principles cannot be compromised, and the man who
attempts it, prevaricates with God and his own conscience.
I am the same kind of anti-slavery man that I have ever
been. My *beau ideal* of a statesman was glorious old
Harry Clay, and as he said during the compromise discussion of 1850, that no earthly power could induce him
'to ever vote for the extension of slavery over territory
then free'; I, following him with unequal steps, echoed
the sentiment. I never sought to interfere with slavery
where it existed, regarding it as no affair of mine, and for
which I was not responsible, but was content to leave the
evil with those who had it, and for them to manage as in
their judgment they thought best. I did not believe
that I had the right so to interfere with it, and I may say,
that this was almost the unanimous opinion of the people
of the North, but believing it to be a great moral, social,
and political evil and the greatest curse that ever befell
any nation or people, I felt bound to do all I constitutionally could do to prevent its extension into free territories. Our offence hath this extent, no more. But before
I close, I doubt not you wish to hear something more
definite on questions of trade, in which this city is so
deeply interested. Presently you will know all that
through the medium of military orders, which I hope will
be satisfactory. I say to the honorable merchants and
business men that you will find me ready to extend to
you all the privileges consistent with my duty to the

Government to grant, and I know that you want no more. To such as are not disposed to do a legitimate business or conform to necessary orders (and here let me say that I do not intend to vex the people with frivolous or oppressive orders, or to unnecessarily remind them that they are under military rule), but endeavor to carry on contraband or dishonest traffic, let me say that they will find me, as they have ever found me their bitter and unrelenting foe.

"To see Civil Government restored, and peace reigning throughout all our borders, is the ardent desire of my heart; and happy will be the day to me when I can return to the walks of civil life, with a hand unstained by any act of cruelty or plunder, and engage once more in the pursuits of peace. I am neither by instinct or education, a soldier; but I am a soldier solely from a solemn sense of duty to a Government under which, in common with others, I have enjoyed a degree of prosperity and honor greater than I could have enjoyed under any other Government on earth. Of our Government and people I am now more proud than ever, and the title of American citizen is a prouder title than other Governments can bestow. But, as the war approaches to a conclusion, there are new duties and obligations that will be forced upon you, which, if you neglect, God will not hold you guiltless. The cry of the widow and the orphan must not go unheeded; nor may you forget the down-trodden and despised race, who, by this war, have been endowed with the priceless boon of liberty, and I trust that you will read your duty not more in your inclinations, than in the language of Him who declared that 'inasmuch as ye did it not to the least of my brethren, ye did it not unto me.'

"The condition of affairs in West Tennessee is now such

that a liberal policy, I think, may be tried and I say to the
people that so long as they discourage the armed bands
of the enemy from coming among them, it will give me
pleasure to lend them a helping hand. It affords me no
satisfaction to add one drop to the cup of sorrow which
they have been compelled to drink even to the very dregs.
I regard the insurgents as at our mercy, and I hope they
will not render necessary the further shedding of blood,
but set themselves earnestly to work to repair damages.
The past is secure and cannot be changed or altered.
The present moment is your own, see that you improve it.

"Sad, indeed, would be our condition if after all our
sacrifices, we had nothing to show for them but the thousands of nameless graves which dot the surface of the
earth from Gettysburg to the Rio Grande. Thank God,
we have a country redeemed, regenerated and disen-
thralled, by the genius of universal emancipation, which
shall live forever. But though no marble marks the place
where sleep our brave defenders, their memories shall long
be kept fresh in our souls. What avail the monuments of
brass or of stone! You raise the statue of marble, it is
cold and lifeless; Time clasps it, and it is dust in his hands;
but their statues are man—living, feeling, adoring man,
bearing the image of his Maker, having the impress of the
Divinity.

"But I have protracted my remarks already to too great
a length, and will close with a reiteration of the confidence
that I have in our dear country, and that the good old
Ship of State will be able to weather every storm, and
be guided safely into port, and

> 'In spite of rocks and tempest's roar,
> In spite of false lights on the shore,
> Sail on; nor fear to breast the sea;

> Our hearts, our hopes, are all with thee,
> Our hearts, our hopes, our prayers, our tears,
> Our faith triumphant o'er our fears,
> Are all with thee! are all with thee!' "

On May 25, 1865, Washburn resigned from the army and returned to his business affairs at La Crosse.

SECOND CONGRESSIONAL SERVICE

Coming home after four years of active service at the front, with a flawless military record Washburn was a man whom his state would delight to honor. From Congress he had stepped into military service and a year after he had put aside his uniform was again elected to Congress. His election in 1867 was by a vote of 13,135 to 6,164 for his Democratic opponent. In 1869 he was reëlected by a vote of 21,164 against 11,477 for the Democrat. His party was not as strong in 1869 as it had been in 1867, but his hold upon his constituents had not weakened.

After his return to civil life his business affairs expanded greatly and he had many plans to carry out. He would have had ample occupation without adding political service to his duties, but he accepted his election to Congress without reluctance. His political ambition was not all-engrossing and he did not over-estimate his political standing. He would have been glad to go into President Lincoln's Cabinet as Secretary of the Interior, (as he intimated in one of his letters to Elihu) but he never became a candidate for the office and afterwards did not think of himself in connection with any appointive office. He wanted to be a senator, but his failure to secure the prize did not prey upon his mind.

When he returned to Washington he lived with Elihu in a house on Capitol Hill, but after his brother went to France he moved to the Arlington Hotel. He accepted the social duties of his position reluctantly. His daughters were not yet old enough to enter society, and his household was without a presiding power.

363

In politics he was a strict party man and accepted his program without misgivings. On January 8, 1868, he introduced a resolution in the House condemning the conduct of "Andrew Johnson, Acting President of the United States," in removing General Sheridan from his command of the Texas district and thanking General Grant for his letter to the President protesting against Edwin M. Stanton's removal as Secretary of War. The resolution was insulting to the President and was in full accord with the temper of the Radical Republicans of the House. He never regretted his action, but in 1869 when he spoke in favor of the repeal of the tenure-of-office act, said it had been passed in order to curb the power of a wicked President. He had a profound respect for public opinion. In advocating any measure he always brought forward as a capital argument in its favor that it was demanded by public sentiment. He considered himself a representative of the sentiments of his constituents. Although he was put on the Committee on Foreign Affairs when he returned to Congress, foreign affairs were not his first interest. He did not debate them and he was often in disagreement with the chairman, General N. P. Banks. He was more in his element when for his second term he went on the Committee on Appropriations. Fraudulent claims against the government, efforts of railroads to secure subsidies from the government, extravagant and corrupt use of public money,—these were the things which excited his interest and which he fought on every occasion. A letter to the Secretary of the Interior, Columbus Delano, from La Crosse, June 7, 1869, illustrates his temper. He said a certain appointment made by Delano was a great mistake and of the appointee: "He was a quartermaster during the war, and the colonel of his regiment assures me that he is a most unmitigated rascal. I have no doubt that he has sought this position for the sake of plunder and you will do well to watch him very closely."

He was an active representative who debated frequently. The three measures in which he was especially interested and in which he may be said to have led the House, were the opposition to the Bouligny claim, the opposition to the purchase of foreign territory, and the establishment of a government-owned telegraph.

The Bouligny claim was an interesting case and showed Washburn at his best. John Edmund Bouligny was a Louisiana Creole who sent to Congress in 1859 by the National American party, a faction which represented the Union sentiment of the state. When Louisiana seceded from the Union two years later, all of the representatives from the state left their seats in Congress except Bouligny. All of the representatives from the south left except Bouligny. He was a dramatic figure seated alone amid the wreck of the shattered nation. He died in Washington in 1864. He had a claim before Congress for an interest in a grant alleged to have been made to his ancestor in Louisiana in 1717 for 75,840 acres of land. The claim had come before Congress during Washburn's service before the war and he had studied it and had become convinced that it had no merit. It was now revived by Bouligny's heirs and during the closing hours of the Congress of 1866 had passed. The committee reported it favorably and it slipped through without notice being taken of it and without knowledge of its merits. A week after Congress had opened, on March 11, 1867, Washburn presented a set of resolutions reciting the facts relative to the passage of the bill, saying that the Supreme Court had once decided that it had no merit and directing the suspension of the law. In his speech he explained that the original grant had been for worthless swamp lands, but that the law permitted the claimants to choose other government lands in the place of the swamp lands. Thus they would locate very valuable lands. He pointed to the decision of the Supreme Court discrediting the claim; he said the members of the committee which recommended the passage of the law had not studied the case which was a most complicated one; he declared it had originated in the Mississippi scheme of John Law, the man who had created the South Sea bubble. Even if a valid grant had been made in 1717, he declared how could the descendants of the first beneficiary now claim, as they did, a sixth part of the land? Rather were there six hundred descendants of the first beneficiary, for he had left four sons. Washburn supported his resolution with remarkable determination. Those who favored the law found him better informed on the case than they were. Man after man who had allowed the claim to go through on the impression that it was meritorious now arose to disclaim advocacy of it. Washburn's resolution was successful; the law never went into operation and a vast area of land was saved to the government.

Washburn's opposition to the acquisition of foreign territory placed him in direct opposition to the policy of Secretary Seward. When the bill to pay for the purchase of Alaska came up on December 11, 1867, he opposed it. The country was utterly worthless and godforsaken, he said, and he quoted at length from books and reports to support his contention. On November 25, 1867, he had introduced this resolution:

"That in the present financial condition of the country any further purchases of territory are inexpedient, and this House will hold itself under no obligation to vote money to pay for any such purpose unless there is greater present necessity for the same than now exists."

The resolution was leveled at the negotiations which Secretary Seward had had with Denmark for the purchase of the Danish West Indies. Washburn said:

"Mr. Speaker: I do not intend that resolution to apply to Walrussia. But it is rumored in the papers—whether it is true or not I cannot say—that the Secretary of State has been making another purchase without consulting anyone, in the absence of any public sentiment requiring it, or of any demand from any quarter. I intend that that action shall be covered by the resolution. I intend to serve notice upon the Kingdom of Denmark that this House will not pay for that purchase; and I mean to serve notice upon the world that we will pay for no purchases that the Secretary of State, on his own motion, may see proper to make,—that no purchase will be sanctioned that is not demanded by the public sentiment and the best interests of the country."

This resolution was promptly passed, and the Danish West Indies were not bought till fifty years later; but soon after Mr. Seward made his treaty to acquire the islands they were devastated by an earthquake. The combination of Washburn's resolution with the earthquake effectually killed the project of annexation for the time being. Washburn never became reconciled to the Alaska purchase, but as late as February 11, 1871, shortly before he left Congress, in the course of a debate on the proposition to extend the land laws over Alaska he remarked that he would willingly vote to give anyone $7,000,000 to take the peninsula off the hands of the United States.

The subject with which Washburn identified himself more thoroughly than any other during his congressional career and which he worked industriously to make successful during the rest of his life, was that of the postal telegraph. He had become convinced by his foreign travel and by his study of conditions at home that the only fair way to manage the telegraph was by government ownership, when the cost of sending messages would be greatly decreased and the use of this means of communication would be within the reach of the people instead of being as it then was, confined to the rich or used by others only in case of emergency. He made many speeches on the subject, conducted many contests before congressional committees and never lost hope that he would eventually succeed. His speech of December 22, 1869, was probably the most comprehensive of those he made on the subject.

He drew an analogy between the post office and the telegraph and showed how Sir Rowland Hill had been ridiculed when he first proposed to reduce the rate of postage in England to one penny; yet the reform had been carried out successfully, and we had followed it here, reducing postage from 25 cents to 3 cents. In telegraphy we were laggards as we had been in postal matters in comparison with Great Britain. She had taken possession of the telegraph and was placing its use within the reach of the people, while we permitted it to be owned by a private corporation whose charges were exorbitant. It was true that the bill to take the telegraph over by the government had been reported unfavorably and arguments against the measure had been offered by the Western Union Telegraph Company. That company, however, monopolized the business and was naturally opposed to it. He determined the foreign rates for telegraphing which were so much lower than ours. His arguments were drawn chiefly from the experience of foreign countries. He showed the value of the telegraph lines in the country and that the amount at which the company appraised them was greatly in excess of their real value. He advocated the purchase of the telegraph lines and the installation of a telegraph office in all the post offices.

He presented a formidable and complete array of facts and figures. It is unnecessary to add that his efforts were unavailing.

Two letters of his belong to this period:

To WILLIAM DREW WASHBURN

House of Representatives
Forty-First Congress U. S.,
Washington, D. C., Feb. 26, 1870

Dear Brother: Yours of the 11th inst. has been rec'd. together with the documents sent by Saner (?), for which thank him, for me. He sent me a bill incorporating Alex. Washburn, Geo. Moore and himself into a company to construct atmospheric telegraphy, etc. Please say to him that to do this now would be unwise. It would look as tho. I had some private scheme to promote in connection with telegraph reform, and would operate against the public bill I have in charge. I must first get that out of the way. I have not yet obtained authority for my committee to send for persons papers, but hope to do it. . . .

Hoar was rejected because of his general discourtesy to Senators. An honest man and good lawyer, his principal happiness is in making others unhappy. When on the bench, he was said to be unhappy because he could not decide against both litigants. He has but little sympathy here. If he was a sensitive man he would resign, but I think he has no intention of doing that. I think that he likes Washington life, and is a good diner out at the expense of other people. I hope that he will hold on. If he resigns God only knows who we shall get in his place. Of course it would be some one never before heard of.

I dined with the President ten days ago. Elijah Program (?) was there. Rather a pleasant time. The President was a good deal put out with Dawes for his attack on the Estimates, but the country praises Dawes without stint. Dawes has gone up to stump N. H. He told me some days ago to give you his love and say that he would write you, but that he could get no time. . . .

To WILLIAM DREW WASHBURN

La Crosse, June 3, 1870

Dear Brother: I left Washington about a week ago, and came home to look, a little, after business. I shall go back soon, but if I had my way I would never set foot again in Washington. The only matter that I care anything about now is my Postal Telegraph. I have got leave to report at any time, and shall report and set the case down for an early day in Dec. . . . If I could stay in Congress and not represent my constituents I might be reconciled to do so perhaps, but certainly not while they make demands on me that do not accord with my judgment. . . .

My affairs are looking pretty fair, and I hope that in a year from now they will be in such shape that I can leave home for an unlimited period. I shall then have finished up my public service for ever. I saw the President a short time before I left Washington. He seemed comfortable and happy. . . .

GOVERNOR OF WISCONSIN

In spite of his desire to be out of public service, Washburn naturally went from the House of Representatives to the governorship of his state. Without serious opposition, he was nominated by the Republicans in 1871. The Democrats nominated James R. Doolittle, probably the strongest candidate they could have found. He had been a leader in the Senate and was a graceful, practiced speaker with oratorical instinct. Washburn, although having experience as a public speaker, failed to rank among the famous.

Simply as a speaker then, the advantage was with the Democratic candidate. Nevertheless, Washburn did not fear him in debate and the two spoke throughout the state from the same platform. They observed the courtesies of debate; created no disorderly audiences; and when the canvass was over could still call themselves gentlemen. The tide flowed with Washburn. Grant was still the hero and those who had acted with him were the people's favorites. The Republican party, and the Union cause were inextricably interwoven. Those who criticized the party which had fomented the war were unpopular with the men who had done the fighting. The state had sent a large contingent to the front, was intensely proud of its military record and for many years was dominated in its political history by its army enthusiasts. It was still an orthodox Republican state, discussing the old war issues, and living on Lincoln and Grant. Washburn was elected governor. He succeeded the popular Lucius

Fairchild, a brigadier general in the Union Army, who had lost his left arm at Gettysburg, a picturesque figure, so popular with the people that he had been elected governor three times, making his term of service six years. Washburn followed in his footsteps,—the same type of man, presiding over the same type of citizen, but not noted for ease in making friends. He was a little distant in his intercourse with men. Self-contained, he had few devoted friends, blunt, to a degree sometimes of giving offence by the plainness of speech. People were a little afraid of him, and those who had plans which were without merit, or were dishonest, sincerely feared him. It was commonly said he was not a politician, but had an understanding of local political forces and knowledge of how to direct them.

The Republican majority in Wisconsin, when he was elected governor, was too large. There were twenty-three Republicans against nine Democrats in the senate, and fifty-four Republicans against thirty-eight Democrats in the assembly. That unwieldy preponderance which usually precedes the breakup of a party had come. Before Washburn's term had expired the attention of the state was distracted from the old political questions and had become absorbed in industrial and social questions which were made political, and which have ever since caused an uncertain quantity in elections and in a measure served as experiment ground for new theories of government. Even before Washburn was elected the "Patrons of Husbandry" or "Grangers" had formed. They were a secret society having for their object to lessen the cost of transportation and to increase the cost of farm products. As a man of wealth with interest in railroads, Washburn was not acceptable to them. It is true that he advocated state control of the railroads, but the farmers would listen only to men who promised everything they desired.

At noon, January 1, 1872, Washburn was installed as governor of Wisconsin. His first message to the legislature was a comprehensive document dealing in detail with the affairs of the state and discussing affairs of the nation. He showed a lively interest in state, educational, charitable, and benevolent institutions. He commended the Historical Society, the state library and the university, to the especial care of the legislature. He dealt frankly with the railroad problems. "The railroads," he said, "represented a cost either actual or fictitious of nearly one hundred millions of dollars. This vast concentration of capital in one interest, alone, affects every other interest in the state, and it may with truth be said, that there is no branch of industry within the state, that is not dependent upon railway facilities, and which unfriendly action on the part of railway managers, may not at any time crush out."

The railway interests, he went on, had grown to their present proportions without any general system and with little responsibility to the people, and their managers seemed to think that their will was law. As they were public corporations and public highways the public was entitled to full benefit from them. Both railroads and public should be protected. He recommended that a board of Railroad Commissioners be constituted to inquire into complaints and abuses and exercise general supervision over railways in the state, to recommend legislation and report annually to the governor.

Passing to national affairs he spoke with familiarity and authority. He favored civil service reform, he wanted a return to specie payment, and he spoke again in favor of a postal telegraph, going over the same ground which he had covered in his speeches to Congress. The legislature, at his request, asked its senators and members in Congress to support a government postal telegraph system.

His second annual message was of the same character as the first,—unpretentious and business-like, showing a grasp of the situation. He renewed the recommendations he had made in his previous message, especially concerning the railway commission and the postal telegraph. He dealt with the question of capital punishment. It had been abolished twenty years before and he showed that the proportion of convictions for capital crimes had been greatly increased in consequence.

During the second year of his term he pardoned fifty-six prisoners from the county jails and state prison. Twenty-four of these pardons were granted to enable the felons to resume their citizenship after discharge, nearly all of the others were granted for humane reasons. One murderer, for instance, was pardoned because he was very ill and his mother and sister, residing in Providence, Rhode Island, who were vouched for as highly respectable people, promised to receive and care for him during the remnant of his existence. Another pardon was "because of the youth of the offender," and another said: "if guilty he had already been severely punished."

The ablest state paper which Washburn issued while he was governor was the veto message which he sent the assembly, March 18, 1873, returning to that body a bill to authorize the Milwaukee and St. Paul Railroad to build a bridge over the Mississippi River at La Crosse. He based his disapproval on constitutional and utilitarian grounds. The Constitution gave Congress the right to regulate commerce between the states, he said, and the United States had control of all navigable waters in the United States which were accessible to more than one state. Congress had assumed absolute control of the navigation of the Mississippi and had spent many millions of dollars in its improvement. This expenditure would be absurd if any other power could obstruct the river and render the improvements valueless. The river was of the utmost importance to the people. "Destroy the navigation of the Mississippi river and you would at once impose a tax of many millions annually upon the people of the adjacent states. The people along and beyond the Mississippi know, that the moment navigation is suspended, rates of freight by rail are instantly largely advanced, as is also the case when it is rendered expensive and difficult by reason of low water." Each bridge across the river was an obstruction, but the railroads had to have bridges. The general government decreed that no bridge should be built across the river unless it was built and located under regulations of the War Department and it must permit safe passage of vessels under or through it. In the case under consideration the War Department had declared that a bridge might be located at a certain point, but the people of La Crosse and the Milwaukee & St. Paul Railroad Co. wanted it somewhere else. Congress refused the request of the railroad company and now the legislature passed an act saying the railroad company could build the bridge where it pleased. This was in effect nullifying an act of Congress and an assertion of state rights far beyond any that had ever been made.

By a two-thirds vote the assembly voted to override the governor's veto, but the senate supported him and the bill failed.

Washburn left the governor's chair more admired by the people than when he had taken office. The Republicans were still with him and the opposition said through one of its leading newspapers: "If Governor Washburn is not a great statesman he is certainly not a small politician." It was the breaking of their power which put him out of office.

His successor was William R. Taylor, nominated by the Liberal Democratic party, commonly designated the "Reformers." His majority over Washburn was 15,000.

THE IMPETUS OF STATESMANSHIP

Statesmanship among the Washburns seemed continually gaining impetus. Cadwallader wrote to Elihu:

> *State of Wisconsin,*
> *Executive Department,*
> *Madison, June 15, 1873.*
>
> . . . I notice what you say about my being "worried" about your correspondence, and that you did not suppose that anybody, not a natural fool, could think of you for the Presidency. I wish you to understand that I agree with you perfectly; having known you as long as I have, it seems rather funny! But you will bear in mind that the majority of people are fools, indeed I may say d—n fools, and hence I suppose it is that a good many are inclined to say, that in the present excited state of the public mind our public robberies, monopolies, etc. you are the only available man. Howe was here two weeks ago and he was inclined to talk that up strong, and others here were fools enough to concur with him. I was rather mortified, as I knew that you would not take the office if offered you, and that your only desire was to get out of public life, and settle down on the banks of Fern River, amid those people whom you love so well, such as Wodly Johnson, Sheehan, Patrick O'Donohue, Michael Murphy, Dennis Doyle, P. Byrne, P. McGinnis *et id omne.*
>
> Last week I was at Chicago and met Tom Hendricks and he said to me that you were the only man the Republicans could elect three years hence. He said that Blaine was out of the question as there was a taint about him that he could not overcome, and that there was no man of any considerable prominence, but what had something pertaining to him that would kill him.

I mention these things simply as a matter of current gossip, not because I believe in them at all, and perhaps I ought not to worry you with them, because they can hardly make you feel otherwise than unpleasantly. . . .

To ELIHU B. WASHBURNE

State of Wisconsin,
Executive Department
(undated) Madison

There is some effort being made to make Howe Chief Justice. I hardly think it will win, but should one of the Associate Judges be made Chief Justice the show would be good to make Howe associate. Miller of Iowa is pressed for Ch. J. and I think that would be the best thing, and appt. Howe in his place. Carpenter is going in strong for Howe and he wanted me to ask you to write Grant. I don't suppose you can, without seeming to be stepping out of your way. Carpenter is very anxious as he thinks it will settle favorably his own case a year from next winter. I suppose I shall have to run again this fall. Indeed it looks as tho. I should be absolutely· "forced" to do so. It looks as tho. if Howe should be apptd. J. that I should be again forced by the people, I hate it, but you know "The lightning hath its pawn, etc."

W. D. is living in mental fear lest he should be also forced. I am sorry for the boy.

What follows is the result of Washburn having been forced to run.

In the candidacy for the United States Senate, he measured swords with Matthew Hale Carpenter, one of the ablest lawyers in national life. The two men were opposite types and each was representative of the political life of the nation. Washburn was essentially a practical man of business instincts. He had gone West in search of his fortune and had grown up with the country. He was one of the makers of the West. The political policies of

the party to which he belonged were accepted by him
and he did not attempt to remodel them, nor lead them.
The will of his party was his will. His Republican constituents were certain of him; he would stand with them.
His Democratic opponents were equally sure that he
would stand against them. In public life his interest
was naturally in business measures—in public land policy,
in highways of commerce, in public expenditures and in
means of communication. Constitutional questions, reconstruction measures, foreign policies he did not discuss
often. These he left to lawyers.

Carpenter was chief among the lawyers. He had no
interest in industrial questions. His reputation in Wisconsin was gained entirely at the bar. He delighted in
celebrated law cases; he was skilled in legal argument.
He went from the law courts into the Senate without
preliminary public service. Until the Civil War came he
had been a Democrat. While the war was in progress he had
refused a nomination to Congress from the Republicans.
When the war should close he thought he might not be
willing to lend himself to the policies of the Republican
party. Afterwards he became a radical Republican.

In 1868, having been put forward for the Senate along
with several other candidates, Washburn made an active
campaign. There can hardly be a doubt, in view of the
final balloting, that he would have been chosen if it had
not been for the unexpected entrance into the contest
of Carpenter who went up and down the state making
speeches and organizing his forces. The legislature met in
January, 1869, and on January 18 there was a mass meeting of members of the legislature and others, at which all
the candidates for the Senate were invited to speak. On
the street it was spoken of as a "prize declamation con-

test." It was organized by Carpenter's friends because his strength lay in his talents as a public speaker. Nevertheless, Washburn approached his audience without trepidation:

"Mr. Chairman and gentlemen of the Legislature— I appear before you in deference to the wishes of a large number of members who have signed a call requesting the candidates for Senator to address them on the political and financial issues of the day, but with no intention of making a speech. From the tenor of my friend Carpenter's speech, it seems that the principal political and financial issues of the day are whether he is a Republican or not. . . . After a residence of over twenty-six years in the State, and after representing for six years immediately preceding the war, so much of the State as now includes three districts, and since the war, a district which elected me by a majority of nearly 10,000, if my position is not understood, I certainly ought not to be here. And I believe that if at this late hour it were necessary for me to make a speech declaring where I stand, I certainly would not be here. So far as I am concerned, my record is made up, and, at this time, I do not care to add to it or take from it. By it I stand or fall, and to it I invite the closest scrutiny. To lay down for myself, at this late day, any new platform, or make new promises and pledges, with the view of influencing your votes I cannot do. High, honorable and desirable as is the position of a United States Senator, it is not so desirable as to tempt me to depart from the determination I have already expressed."

He went on concerning Carpenter, that he had been quoted as saying if he were defeated he would never again appear before the people, whereas he, Washburn, should he meet with defeat, would let it make no difference in his political conduct. He would still do battle for his party. There were cries of dissent and counter cries of approval when he quoted Carpenter and the meeting became disorderly. The next evening the Republican members of the legislature met to choose their candidate for the Senate. On the first ballot Washburn led Carpenter by one vote, on the next vote Carpenter led Washburn by one vote, on the third ballot Washburn led Carpenter by one vote, on the fourth ballot Carpenter led Washburn by seven votes, on the fifth by nine, receiving election.

This was not the end of the contest between Carpenter and Washburn. As Carpenter's term of service drew toward an end, Washburn was found opposing reëlection. Further than that, when the legislature met in January, 1875, a majority of Washburn's followers announced that they would not enter the caucus of Republican members. The result was that for ten days the legislature voted in vain for a senator, Carpenter leading, Washburn coming next, with other votes scattered among lesser candidates.

Then a compromise was effected and Angus Cameron, a Republican, was chosen senator to succeed Carpenter. For this result Carpenter never forgave Washburn. He declared Washburn had said in a letter which was printed, that he would not be a candidate for the Senate against Carpenter. The theory was that this promise was made in return for Carpenter's support of Washburn's candidacy for the governorship. Washburn declared the letter had been garbled,—that he had made no such promise. It is hard to see any reason for his having made it. The governorship was attainable without Carpenter's aid and Washburn was not a man who would have been apt to mortgage his political future.

The La Crosse Republican and Leader, a newspaper

devoted to Washburn's interests, was a persistent enemy of Carpenter, and finally on the 17th of March, 1877, contained a bitter arraignment of him. This brought forth a reply from Carpenter, dated March 23, in the course of which he alluded to Washburn in unfriendly terms. Washburn replied in the *Chicago Tribune* on April 6, 1877, charging that he had been defeated for his second term as governor, because the people were exasperated by Carpenter's course in the Senate. Carpenter replied April 24, 1877, in an open letter to Washburn, a long, abusive, insulting letter, revealing no facts to justify the language in which the writer indulged. The charge that Washburn said he would not be a candidate for the Senate against Carpenter was repeated. It formed, in fact, the only foundation for Carpenter's long letter.

Six years later Carpenter was a candidate again and was elected after ninety ballots had been taken in the legislature. Washburn's friends were still opposing him but Washburn himself was not in the contest and his name was not brought forward as a candidate.

THE FLOUR MILLS

The activities of Cadwallader Washburn in financial and commercial affairs were so numerous that it is out of the question to enumerate them. For investment he was interested in the building of rails and the purchase of land, but the industry, upon which his enterprise had the greatest effect, was the manufacture of wheat flour. As a child at The Norlands he lived close to the Androscoggin River where there were mills, as a youth he lived at Hallowell where again there were mills. Even in Wiscasset, Maine, where he lived last, he could see old, abandoned mills. Throughout his life in the West he clung to the river, at Davenport, Rock Island and La Crosse. When he became governor of Wisconsin he was so taken with the charm and beauty of Madison and the glory of the surrounding lakes, that he built a handsome house at the city's edge; and which he appropriately named Edgewood. But the living here did not make him untrue to La Crosse. That place remained the center of his affections. The prairie lies behind it and the Mississippi River in front of it.

So having crossed the river from Davenport, Iowa, to Stephenson, Illinois, and being familiar with Galena, a little higher up, and having left Mineral Point, to go back to the river still higher up at La Crosse, it was natural instinct and foresight which took him further to the Falls of St. Anthony where Minneapolis now stands.

He had lived in four Western states,—Iowa, Illinois, Wisconsin, and Minnesota. In fact he was so identified with Minnesota that official accounts of that state's development always include his name; and this although he was a citizen of Wisconsin.

His connection with the development of Minnesota began before he had settled in La Crosse. In 1856 he, with some others, incorporated the Minneapolis Water Power Company.

This led on to the erection of his first flour mill in 1866, the largest mill on the falls and having eleven run of stones. It was managed by the firm of Christian, Tomlinson & Company, the owners being Washburn and George H. Christian. It was known as "B Mill." The firm name afterwards became Washburn and Hazard, Washburn being the principal owner. Then it changed into the hands of Washburn, Crosby & Company in 1877, the membership being C. C. Washburn, John Crosby, and William Drew Washburn. It was in "B Mill" that the first experiments were made in "new process" flour manufacture and there that the first purifier was installed. The mill was six stories high and was known as the "Big Mill." It was remodeled on the roller system in 1880. It then turned out 650 barrels of flour per day.

The second Washburn mill, "Mill A," was built in 1873–4. This was seven stories high and had forty run of stones. It was a "new process" mill producing from 1200 to 1500 barrels per day. It was the greatest mill in the country and accordingly famed. By the explosion and fire of May 2, 1878, it was absolutely demolished. The day after this catastrophe the ground for the third mill, "C," was surveyed and the mill built by 1879. The site of the "Diamond Mill," which had also been destroyed, was bought and Washburn "A Mill" erected on it. This, then, was the largest mill in the world. The new "C Mill" contained about twenty pairs of mill stones. It was changed afterwards to a roller mill with a capacity of 1650 barrels per day. Here in 1878–9 Washburn started his experimental roller mill. Then in 1880–81 the greatest of the mills was built on the site of the old mill "A." This started with a capacity of 3500 barrels per day, and soon exceeded that amount. The daily capacity of the three mills when General Washburn died was 6500 barrels per day, requiring 30,000 bushels of wheat daily, with elevators holding 308,000 bushels, with 231 pairs of rolls in operation and thirty-five run of feeders,—the principal owner of them all being C. C. Washburn. They were operated by Washburn, Crosby & Company, the firm comprising Cadwallader Washburn, John Crosby, Wm. H. Dunwoody, and Charles J. Martin.

When the fire occurred in the flour mills an interesting question arose over the liability of the insurance companies to pay the premiums. If the destruction was from an explosion alone they could escape; if from fire they were liable. There was no doubt that there had been both but Washburn insisted that the chief cause of the destruction was fire. He protected his interests with his wonted energy and free-spoken denunciation of those who opposed him. To Elihu, August 2, 1878, from Cincinnati he wrote:

"Have had another interview with the scoundrels. They won't decide what they will do, and I have got to wait another day. I am afraid that I can do nothing and shall have to resort to violent measures . . . The scoundrels want to creep out."

From Minneapolis, November 13, 1878:

"I have not shown the White feather yet, and don't want to. Have paid all bills so far."

It was after the fire of 1878, indeed in consequence of it, that the milling industry was revolutionized by Cadwallader Washburn. The story of how he invoked the aid of William de la Barre and employed him is simple and can best be told by Mr. de la Barre himself as he detailed it in a letter recently (July, 1917) sent to Mrs. A. Warren Kelsey, Mr. Washburn's daughter:

. . .

I came to Minneapolis early in June 1878, about one month after the great Mill explosion of May 2nd, 1878, which destroyed the big Washburn "A" Mill and four other flour mills, one grain elevator, and damaged the Washburn "B" Mill.

I came there from Philadelphia where I had been employed for ten years as a draughtsman and engineer of the Pascal Iron Works of Morris Tasker & Company, Fifth and Tasker Streets.

During the Centennial Exposition at Philadelphia in 1876, I became acquainted with the German mill builder Gustave Behrns who exhibited, in the exposition, a small model of a device intended to prevent flour dust explosions on millstones, which device Mr. Behrns endeavored to introduce in this country but without success. He became discouraged and returned to Europe. At the close of the Exposition the model illustrating this millstone ventilation got into possession of Brehmer Brothers, engineers and machinists in Philadelphia, together with the agency of this invention for the United States.

About two weeks after the mill explosion, Governor Washburn telegraphed Brehmer Brothers that they should send someone conversant with the Behrns invention to Minneapolis and to explain and demonstrate the usefulness of the invention and they engaged me to make the trip for them. In this way I came to meet your father in June, 1878, who from the first took great interest in the device and I soon enjoyed his unqualified confidence after demonstrating that it would do all I claimed for it. This millstone ventila:ing he adopted for all of his mills and thus helped me to have the other millers do likewise.

In the fall of 1879 he engaged my services as his engineer and technical superintendent of mills and I remained in that position until 1891. In 1880 I was sent to Europe to study the Hungarian Process of milling, after having made the plans for the building into which the new process was to be installed. After an absence of five months I returned and made the designs for the new Mill "A."

The first Roller Mill approaching anywhere near the Hungarian or Gradual Reduction Process of making flour was built in one corner of the Washburn "C" Mill, originally called the "B" Mill extension, early in 1880. It was an experimental mill of small capacity. Governor Washburn, while in Europe in 1879, had arranged with Oscar Oexle of Augsburg, Bavaria, to make plans for such a mill and the machinery for it was mostly imported from Europe. The grinding rolls were of porcelain and they, as well as other appliances, did not prove satisfactory for American conditions so that this experimental mill was remodelled after a short time and chilled iron rolls, imported from Budapest, Hungary, were installed, and these were more satisfactory. These rolls were the first corrugated chilled iron rolls in this country. . . .

PHILANTHROPIC PURSUITS

It is impossible to follow Washburn's career far without seeing that there ran through it a strain of benevolence and appreciation for the higher things of life. He had pity for the Southerners even when he was fighting to make their condition most pitiful, and he always carried in his mind a desire to ameliorate the lot of the fatherless and the unfortunate. We see how carefully he guarded the educational interests of the state. The great State University, now one of the foremost educational institutions in the country, and the Historical Society, which has no superior among historical societies, owe him a debt of gratitude. His interest in the Historical Society was as old as the society itself. When it was organized in 1854 his partner, Cyrus. Woodman, was one of the vice presidents; two years later Washburn began giving books to its library. In 1873 he arranged to give $100 annually to the library binding fund. In 1875 he became vice president of the society and in 1878 was made president, which office he held until his death.

When he was abroad, struggling against the diseases which killed him a few months later, he wrote to Lyman C. Draper, secretary of the society, approving of the projects then forming to obtain a new building. "Though I am told by my physicians," he wrote, "that I must stop writing, and even thinking, I will bid them defiance so far as to say to you that I approve of every word you say. The State is justly proud of the Historical Society, and to you, especially, and to your associate, Mr. Durrie, is due the honor of its being what it is."

His connection with the State University began actively when he was governor. He had always approved of the institution and kept himself informed of its progress. He did everything he could to advance its interests. Cyrus Woodman was on the first board of regents chosen in 1848. The two friends kept up their mutual interests.

The honorary degree of Doctor of Laws was conferred upon Washburn in 1872. In 1877 he determined to show his interest in the University in a substantial manner. He, therefore, erected an observatory and equipped it with every type of apparatus necessary to make it complete. It is told in this connection, that he had made an engagement with one of the regents of the University to meet him at nine o'clock on the morning of May 3, 1878, to mark off the ground where the observatory should stand. On the night of the 2nd occurred the explosion and fire in the Minneapolis mills which destroyed Cadwallader Washburn's greatest work. With this knowledge, when the regent repaired to the appointed place, he little expected to find Washburn, but the latter promptly appeared and showing no signs of excitement or depression. To the condolences of the regent he replied that the loss was heavy in property, but that he regarded as of small consequence. He was distressed, however, over the loss of life and resultant suffering among the employees. Then he and the regent staked off the ground upon which the observatory was to be built. That done he left for Minneapolis to meet the problem of rebuilding the mills which had been destroyed. The observatory was completed in 1878 and stands on a beautiful hill in the college grounds. Over the door of the rotunda the regents placed a tablet with these words: "Erected and finished, A. D. 1878, by the munificence of Cadwallader C. Washburn, and by him presented to the University of Wisconsin—A tribute to general science. In recognition of this gift, this tablet is inserted by the regents of the University."

By act of the legislature in 1879 Washburn was made an honorary member of the board of regents of the University "for and during his good pleasure." It was his pleasure to be a regent for the rest of his life. The observatory not being large enough to satisfy all needs was enlarged by Mr. Washburn in 1879. It still stands as one of the best equipped observatories in the country and one of the important institutions devoted to astronomical science. Having put up the observatory, he took a continuous interest in its career. The reports both of a business and scientific nature were submitted to him and even during the days of his last illness he saw the proof sheets of the first volume of the *Observations*. At that time the head of the observatory was Professor Edward S. Holden, an admirer and friend of Washburn's, who when he died, gave perhaps the fairest estimate of him. "His soul was such as Chaucer has described—sober, pitiful, wise, true as steel itself."

The observatory was the largest benefaction Washburn made during his life, but he had it in mind before his death to establish the orphanage at Minneapolis in honor of his mother. As usually happens in such cases, he died before he had carried out his intention.

LAST DAYS

Cadwallader Washburn had gone from Maine with a foundation of good health. His digestion was not exacting, his lungs were sound, all his organs normal. His physical strength was good. When the final breakup of his system came it was his first serious illness. Probably it was hastened by the driving energy of his life. He had never known inaction or leisure until the stricken body refused to work. He was always working, always planning, always moving, never giving the noble machine a moment to cool.

Early in January, 1881, he suffered a paralytic stroke and ever afterwards was an invalid. He had not the least idea of giving up his life, however, and never, up to the very end, ceased to believe that he would get well.

In the summer of 1881 he went abroad to consult the best physicians of Europe and try the curative powers of European springs. He wrote with such difficulty that his correspondence was conducted by an amanuensis, usually in this case, his daughter. From Carlsbad, Angers Hotel, July 11, 1881, to Elihu he wrote:

> "I suppose the recovery of Garfield is assured or it is to be hoped so as his death would have lead to terrible complications . . . but then what do I care? I am no longer 'forced' and am relieved from the necessity of getting myself glass eyes and like a scurvy politician seeing the things that are not."

391

AGAIN TO ELIHU

Carlsbad, July 16, 1881

"I am glad that matters seem prosperous to you in Minneapolis. I don't hear much from there and they evidently look upon me as a perfect cypher. I will astonish them some day. . . . I do not think that doctors can do me any good but that time and rest can alone restore me. Seegin speaks more lightly of my ailment than any of the doctors and they all disagree, which makes me hopeful . . . The best doctors I have had are Anderson and McArthur of La Crosse."

He wanted to get back to La Crosse. He was lonely. The Doctor Seegin said his organs were normal; but that his brain had been overworked. It was imperative that he should give himself a long rest. He ought to live away from business for a full year in a good climate and out in the open air.

He began planning a winter in Florida or Cuba, yet he wrote from Wildbad August 13, 1881, to Elihu:

"I am very anxious to get home and I have sundry great enterprises that I want to take hold of as soon as my health is restored."

Sen Montreaux, September 6, 1881

I do not think that I am essentially better than when I left the Hot Springs. I have little appetite and little strength. All the doctors join in saying that I must not go home at present, which I think is about the only truth they have told me. I shall probably spend the winter in Southern Europe.

But he might go to Algiers. He wrote long careless letters, full of boy's reminiscences and assumed abuse of his brothers under which he hid the deep affection he felt for them.

At Paris October 13, 1881, there was a consultation of doctors who diagnosed his disease as renal cirrhosis with consecutive percardiatrophia which meant disease of the kidneys and the heart, a diagnosis which proved to be correct for he died of those disabilities six months later. He left Europe the end of October on the *Elbe*.

To Elihu B. Washburne

October 16, 1881
"I am glad to go home and think I made a mistake in coming here. If I had stuck by the Prairie doctors I think I would have been all right or if I had spent the summers at Norlands. As it is I am as badly off as Hall Hersey who was 'thoroughly discouraged.'"

He wanted to try Dr. Weir Mitchell's treatment and in November was in Philadelphia living at the St. George Hotel. While there he summoned his old friend Cyrus Woodman, who found him in good spirits although in poor health. It was at this time that he made his will, which Woodman drew up under his direction and which he signed on December 31. His brother, William Drew, who was in Congress came over to Philadelphia to see him. Israel had met him in New York Bay when he returned from Europe.

Early in the spring he went to Eureka Springs, Arkansas, to try the wonderful medicinal springs of the place. His health seemed to improve,—or his hopes were aroused,— and he believed he would be back in La Crosse in May, there to pass the summer and return to Eureka in the autumn. He believed the Eureka waters had a wonderful effect and that if he had drunk them sooner they would have saved him many years of suffering. He saw signs of improvement in his paralysis even. He was intensely anxious that Elihu should try the springs for his health. His last letter to Elihu was dated April 9.

His death was gradual. Israel came to see him. William Drew and Elihu were there, also his daughters and their husbands and his sister, Mrs. Buffum and her husband. He was attended constantly by his faithful valet, William L. Freman.

A great paralysis set in on Saturday, May 12, 1882, early in the morning, and they thought him dying. Then he sank into a comatose state. He died at 5:30 o'clock in the afternoon of Tuesday, May 15. He was sixty-four years old, and was the first of Israel Washburn's sons to die.

There was a funeral service in the hotel, the Perry House, at Eureka Springs and the body was carried to La Crosse where there was a public funeral.

The governor of the state issued a proclamation eulogizing Washburn and appointed a committee to meet the body at the state line and accompany it to La Crosse. The railway gave a special train to transport the committee with Washburn's body from Chicago, and gave also free travel to the funeral from all the towns of the state and from Minneapolis. As the funeral train passed through the state there were demonstrations of respect at every station. At the funeral nearly every town in the state was represented. By order of the governor all public business was suspended. In Minneapolis the great mills did not move, and business in La Crosse was generally suspended.

The body arrived from Chicago at seven o'clock in the evening of Wednesday, May 16, and was taken to the Court House under military guard. The next day, May 17, it lay in state and an enormous crowd gathered about the Court House. Many of the people had come from Milwaukee, Chicago, and Minneapolis. The funeral services were conducted in the Court House by the Rev. J. C. Tuttle, the Universalist minister from Minneapolis. Then there was a military funeral with full honors. The governor, judges and other officials entered the procession to Oakwood cemetery.

A great deal of interest centered in Washburn's will. His property was worth between two and three millions of dollars. It was found that after making special provision for his relatives, he left $375,000 for the orphan asylum at Minneapolis, and $50,000 for a public library at La Crosse. He had already given to the University of Wisconsin the $50,000 observatory and his beautiful Edgewood to the sisters of charity for their school. The Washburn Orphan Asylum he provided should be for orphans and half orphans and should be open to any child under fourteen years of age, to remain for one year, not to remain after he or she reached the age of fifteen and a half years.

ADDENDUM

It was originally intended to include in this volume sketches of the seven sons of Israel Washburn. The material for the lives of Algernon Sidney Washburn, Charles Ames Washburn and Samuel Benjamin Washburn was actually in hand while the sketch of William Drew Washburn had been finished.

Owing to the outbreak of the world war, work on the book was put aside and the Ms. pertaining to William Drew Washburn disappeared. It has been deemed advisable to publish this volume in its present form.

William Drew Washburn was a great force in opening up the Northwest. Minneapolis, his home, was the center of his activities. He was interested in lumber, flouring mills, and was the builder of several railroads. He served in the House of Representatives for three terms and for six years in the United States Senate.

Should a second edition of the book be published it is now planned to incorporate in it, if possible, the biographies of the four brothers omitted from the first printing.